Advance Praise for *Trumping Obama*

"The negative impact Barack Obama's presidency had on America's economy, energy production, race relations, and foreign policy can still be felt nationwide. Upon taking office, President Trump had the huge task of cleaning up the mess Obama left behind. Matt Margolis shows us, in impressive detail, how President Trump has succeeded with that task. *Trumping Obama* is a must read for everyone who cares about making America *America* again."

—Jeff Reynolds, author of *Behind the Curtain*

"What exactly is left of Barack Obama's legacy a few short years after his disastrous presidency? The answer, thanks to President Trump is: next to nothing. Matt Margolis chronicles how President Trump has systematically undone the failed Obama experiment. From ending the tyrannical Obamacare individual mandate to pulling out of the globalist power grab that was the Paris Climate Treaty, to returning America's judiciary branch to those who believe in the Constitution—Margolis dazzlingly details a plethora of examples of how Trump hit the reset button and set America back on the path to prosperity and security. *Trumping Obama* is not only an important tome for conservatives, but also for liberals and Never Trumpers. Tell 'em to read it and weep!"

—Peter D'Abrosca, Investigative Reporter and author of *Enemies: The Press vs. The American People*

Also by Matt Margolis

The Worst President in History: The Legacy of Barack Obama
The Scandalous Presidency of Barack Obama

TRUMPING OBAMA

HOW PRESIDENT TRUMP SAVED US FROM BARACK OBAMA'S LEGACY

MATT MARGOLIS

Post Hill PRESS

A BOMBARDIER BOOKS BOOK
An Imprint of Post Hill Press
ISBN: 978-1-64293-137-2
ISBN (eBook): 978-1-64293-138-9

Trumping Obama:
How President Trump Saved Us From Barack Obama's Legacy
© 2019 by Matt Margolis
All Rights Reserved

Cover Illustration by John Cox

Post Hill Press, LLC
New York • Nashville
posthillpress.com

Published in the United States of America

CONTENTS

America is divided, goes the common phrase of the day. Democrats are so convinced President Donald Trump is an easy mark to beat for re-election in 2020 that the list of would-be nominees is long enough to fill a small airliner.

Not so fast.

In *Trumping Obama,* Matt Margolis, author of *The Worst President in History: The Legacy of Barack Obama,* makes plain in detail just why President Trump has been such an effective chief executive—and exactly why the Trump base sticks with him. Running through one Trump policy triumph after another, Margolis illustrates how Donald Trump has set about trumping Obama—which is to say undoing if not shredding completely the entire eight years of the Obama presidential legacy.

The story is helped by the Margolis confession that in 2016 he was hardly a Trump enthusiast, and as with so many, was sadly convinced that all the relentless headlines about the inevitability of a Hillary Clinton victory were accurate. They weren't—in more ways than one.

What Matt Margolis contributes in the following pages is considerable. "Thanks to President Donald Trump," he writes, "the Obama era—once seen as transformative and consequential—will now be a mere footnote in history." Margolis then proceeds to detail exactly how this has been done.

From re-implementing President Ronald Reagan's Mexico City policy that "requires foreign non-governmental organizations (NGOs)…to agree, as a condition of their receipt of [U.S.] federal funds" that they would "neither perform nor actively promote abortion as a method of family planning in other nations" to other domestic policy items like reversing the Obama gun grab and open border policies, repealing the craziness of so-called "net neutrality," dismantling ObamaCare, overturning racial quota policies, rolling back the financial regulatory jungle that was Dodd-Frank regulation, and oh so much more domestically. Margolis has the historical goods.

Needless to say, the specifics of Trump's military and foreign policy are examined here as well. From the pullout from the Trans-Pacific Partnership to reversing the Obama policy towards the Cuban Castro family dictatorship and, particularly irritating to the Left, withdrawing the US from the appallingly dangerous "Iran deal" and finally defeating ISIS, the Obama "legacy" has headed for the historical exits. Or as Ronald Reagan might say, "the ash heap of history."

But perhaps no reversal of Obama policy has gotten under the skin of the Obama loyalists and the Left in general more than the Trump decision to pull the United States out of The Paris Climate Agreement. Margolis correctly describes the Paris accord as "the pièce de résistance of his (Obama's) environmental legacy." And indeed it was. Frantic yelps went out from leftist environmentalists that in undoing this particular Obama legacy, Trump, but of course, "would destroy the planet and that the United States no longer cared about the environment." To no avail.

Trumping Obama further explores a policy by policy analysis of just how—and importantly, why—the Obama legacy deserved dismantling.

As the 2020 election season arrives, *Trumping Obama* is the essential handbook for Trump supporters (and Trump opponents!) that will provide a serious reminder of what exactly is at stake—and just why so many millions of Americans voted for Trump in the first place.

Jeffrey Lord is a former CNN contributor, columnist, and author of Swamp Wars.

INTRODUCTION

In the fall of 2012, despite polls suggesting otherwise, I was convinced America would not re-elect Barack Obama. Mitt Romney was not my ideal candidate, but he was what America needed: a politician with private sector business experience who could get our economy moving again. I took Romney's defeat very hard. In 2016, I determined not to let my personal political biases cloud my judgment. I wouldn't write off polls and assume they were skewed like many of us assumed back in 2012. I spent the entire 2016 presidential campaign season preparing myself for the Hillary victory that virtually everyone considered a sure thing.

The last few months were brutal for me and for most of America's so-called deplorables. Since the aggregates of national and state polling at the time showed Mrs. Clinton cruising to victory, most of Trump's supporters believed his defeat was inevitable. A CNN/ORC poll at the end of October showed that nearly seven out of ten voters thought Hillary was on the path to victory.[1] Eight years of Obama had been devastating for the country. Would we survive another four to eight with Hillary at the helm?

The outlook seemed bleak. I didn't even like watching the news on television or listening to talk radio in my car. Instead, I'd lose myself in novels just to escape the gloomy future toward which America hurtled. Perhaps I wouldn't have been so glum if I liked the alternative, but I didn't. I was not happy when Donald Trump announced his campaign. Sure, he was a successful businessman (as Romney was) but his style irked me. I didn't see him as a true conservative. I thought it was a just an ego-boosting publicity stunt and winning wasn't a priority. I was not on the Trump train.

In fact, for Halloween, mere days before the election, a liberal friend of mine at work suggested I dress up as Donald Trump and she'd come as Hillary Clinton.

"You mean you're gonna dress up in an orange jumpsuit?" I asked.

She didn't get it, but she convinced me to go along with her plan anyway. So, I bought a Trump wig, wore a suit and a red tie, and walked into the office looking like Donald Trump. My friend couldn't find a Hillary wig and abandoned the plan.

So, I spent the whole day dressed up as Trump, without a Hillary to complete the effect. I was pretty bitter about it. Not just because my friend had not come in dressed as Hillary, meaning I was the only one in costume in the entire office, but because I was still strongly against Trump and did not plan to vote for him.

I live in New York State, so who I voted for didn't matter—Hillary would win the state easily. I planned to write in Ted Cruz or skip that ballot question entirely. I couldn't vote for Evan McMullin.

It wasn't until the Sunday before the election that I finally got on the Trump Train when, for the second time, former Federal Bureau of Investigation (FBI) Director James Comey announced that Hillary would not face charges for her mishandling of classified information with her unsecured, private email server. If she got into the White House, she'd have Comey's support as she continued her corrupt and criminal behavior from the Oval Office. She'd make Obama look like a Boy Scout. Not that I didn't already know how filthy the Clinton machine was, but Comey's announcement was the last straw. I still thought Trump had zero chance of winning, so election day left me with a pit in my stomach the size of the national debt.

But then, something strange happened. As that night progressed, Trump's odds of winning kept getting better and better. Eyes were on Florida as Trump outperformed expectations in key areas where Hispanic turnout was expected to keep the Sunshine State blue. My wife and I watched the proceedings on CNN and the panel of supposed experts tap danced and practically pleaded with the voters as the votes were tallied. Four years earlier, Karl Rove criticized the premature declaration of Obama's win in Ohio (and thus the presidency), but now we were witnessing the opposite scenario. CNN's liberal pundits were visibly distraught as Florida, Ohio, Pennsylvania, Iowa, Wisconsin, and Michigan began to look good for Trump. As they called each state, they stared at the map and scrambled to find outlandish alternate pathways for Clinton. At 9 p.m. eastern time, Hillary's handlers told her crowd of supporters to go home—she couldn't even bring herself to face her own party. The atmosphere on CNN was like a funeral.

It was hilarious.

Trump had done it. He saved us from a Hillary Clinton presidency against all odds. For that, I'll always be grateful to him. He still wasn't my preferred candidate, and there were plenty of reasons to question his alleged conservative credentials. He had run on a platform of dismantling the legacy of Barack Obama, and I sincerely hoped he would keep his promises. Many predicted that, once in office, Trump's moderate and liberal tendencies would eclipse the conservative agenda he promised. And, had that happened, I wouldn't be writing this book. The Obama years were a disaster for the United States, but Obama's govern-by-executive-pen approach meant that his legacy could be reversed. If Trump wanted to, he could undo Obama's unconstitutional executive orders, and, with the full support of a Republican-controlled House and Senate, he might roll back Obama's few legislative victories.

And, believe it or not, he has. Thanks to President Donald Trump, the Obama era—once seen as transformative and consequential—will now be a mere footnote in history. Just five months into the Trump presidency, Peter Baker, the chief White House correspondent for the *New York Times,* wrote, "rarely has a new president appeared so determined not just to steer the country in a different direction but to actively dismantle what was established before his arrival."[2]

Former vice president Joe Biden was none too happy about Trump's success erasing Obama's legacy. During an interview with CNN's Chris Cuomo, he called Trump's tenure a disaster and lamented, "All he seems to be trying to do is undo everything that President Obama has done." Perhaps to reassure himself, if not all of Obama's loyal followers, he added, "but, he's not able to do that, by the way."[3] Andrew Sullivan, writing in *New York Magazine* in May 2018, disagreed. He argued Trump had been "remarkably successful" in reversing Obama's achievements. "In 17 months, he has effectively erased Barack Obama's two-term legacy."[4]

That Trump has succeeded in doing this is no small thing. The executive director of *The Weekly Standard,* Fred Barnes, called Trump's success historic. "Presidents often vow to wipe out big chunks of their predecessor's legacies. President Eisenhower was going to take on the New Deal. Ronald Reagan targeted the Great Society. Both backed down. Trump, working with congressional Republicans, hasn't. He's eager to deflate Obama's standing and inflate his own."[5] Despite the doubts of Never Trump conservatives and the mainstream media, Obama's legacy is in utter ruins; his executive pen was really a pencil and Trump was the eraser.

I should acknowledge that this book is not a comprehensive collection of all of Trump's achievements. Trump has achieved many positive things that aren't just reversals of Obama-era policies. His decision to move the US Embassy in Israel to Jerusalem was the reversal of a longstanding policy supported by both Democrat and Republican administrations, for example. But, as the author of two other books about Barack Obama, one about his record and one devoted to his scandals, I felt it was important to focus this book only on how Trump saved us from Obama's legacy. Why? Because had Hillary Clinton won in November 2016, Obama's odious agenda would have become impossible to undo by any future Republican president. The 2016 election was our last hope to save this country from an enduring age of leftist, overreaching government. Trump may not have been the candidate you wanted, but he's defied the odds and won. Even if you don't like his style or his Twitter habit, this book will show you he was the president we needed.

CHAPTER 1

GENERAL DOMESTIC POLICY

On October 30, 2008, candidate Barack Obama told a crowd of his supporters, "We are five days away from fundamentally transforming the United States of America." Obama made good on his promise in myriad ways. His changes to domestic policy all increased the government's role in our daily lives and altered the culture. The Obama years saw a dramatic shift in American norms, where what was once unfathomable became federal policy in the name of "social justice."

Obama saw abortion rights as a sacred right to be enshrined, protected, and federally funded. Once self-evident truths—like men are men and women are women—were now disputed by the federal government. As the joke goes, "John F. Kennedy put men on the moon. Barack Obama put men in the women's room." It would be funnier if it weren't true. Religious liberty lost its hallowed place in the halls of government during the Obama years. If you were a religious florist, a baker, or a photographer who offered those services for weddings, the Obama administration compelled you to provide those services for a same-sex wedding, regardless of your beliefs.

Paul Kengor, professor of political science and executive director of The Center for Vision & Values at Grove City College, put it best. "That is a fundamental transformation of a culture and a nation that did not exist prior to Barack Obama's ascent."[6] In the Obama era, those who didn't subscribe to the radical reinterpretations of gender and marriage were, Kengor noted, "portrayed as the outliers, as abnormal, as extremists, as 'haters.'" He added, "If you dissent from this new vociferous breed of human-nature redefiners, they sue you, they jail you, they smear you, they boycott you, they harass you, they ruin you—and they do so (with no sense of their hypocrisy) in the name of 'tolerance' and 'diversity.'"[7] While the battle for the culture never ends, Trump has taken it out of the hands of bureaucrats and politicians and put it back in the hands of the American people. They'll decide how they wish to live—not the president or an oppressive government wrapping itself in a rainbow-colored flag.

Reinstating the Mexico City Policy

Many on the right weren't convinced that Trump would govern as a conservative—let alone a social conservative. Though he campaigned as a pro-life Republican who promised to defund Planned Parenthood and appoint pro-life justices to the Supreme Court, his past comments suggested he wasn't committed to such policies. He praised Planned Parenthood, saying, "They do great things for women."[8] Pro-life advocacy groups waited to see whether he would keep his promises or govern like a New York liberal.

He gave the first clue of how he'd lead on the social issues a few days after he took the oath of office. First implemented by Ronald Reagan in 1984, the Mexico City policy requires foreign non-governmental organizations (NGOs) "to agree, as a condition of their receipt of [U.S.] federal funds" that they would "neither perform nor actively promote abortion as a method of family planning in other nations."[9] The policy remained in effect until it was rescinded by Bill Clinton, after which George W. Bush reinstated the policy in 2001. Barack Obama rescinded the policy again when he took office.

Despite some doubt, President Trump reinstated the policy on January 23, 2017. "The President, it's no secret, has made it very clear that he's a pro-life president," said Trump's then-spokesman Sean Spicer during his first daily briefing. "He wants to stand up for all Americans, including the unborn, and I think the reinstatement of this policy is not just something that echoes that value, but respects taxpayer funding as well."[10]

Restoring Race-Neutral Guidelines for College Admissions

In 2011 and 2016, the Obama administration issued guidelines to encourage colleges and universities to use race as a factor in admissions. While race-based admissions claim to be about reversing discrimination and promoting diversity, they also have unintended negative consequences. For example, the Students of Fair Admissions sued Harvard University in 2014 on behalf of Asian American students who faced an unfair higher standard to gain access to the Ivy League giant. Despite having higher academic and extracurricular scores than any other racial group, Harvard admissions officers gave Asian American applicants the lowest "personal" score ranking of any racial group. According to 2013 analysis by Harvard's Office of Institutional Research, if race weren't a factor in the admissions process, Asian Americans would make up a higher percentage of admitted classes each year.[11] In 2017, Trump's Justice Department launched an investigation into Harvard's race-based discrimination. "The Department of Justice is committed to protecting all Americans from all forms of illegal race-based discrimination," said Justice Department spokeswoman Sarah Isgur Flores.[12]

The Trump administration revoked these guidelines, reinstating Bush-era race-neutral standards, arguing that Obama exceeded Supreme Court precedent and encouraged racial bias in admissions.[13] Democrats predictably attacked the move as racist. "It is yet another clear Trump administration attack on communities of color and the principle that every student deserves a high-quality education that allows them to thrive," said Nancy Pelosi. Rep. Cedric L. Richmond (D-LA), the chairman of the Congressional Black Caucus, also condemned the race-neutral admission guidance. "I continue to be disappointed that the president of this great country demonstrably cares so little for its non-white residents and their interests."[14] Many others played the race card and their statements are equally ridiculous.

Black conservatives, however, praised Trump's actions. Dr. Carol M. Swain, a former professor at Vanderbilt University and Princeton University, and a member of the Project 21 black leadership network, praised the action. "I've always felt that acceptance to higher education should be merit-based and means-tested. I believe President Trump is wise to rescind the aggressive Obama-era affirmative action directive for the use of race in student admissions," she said. According to Dr. Swain, the Obama-era policy placed students "in situations where they are doomed to fail, become embittered by rising debt and frustrated with the mismatch between abilities and expectations."[15] Horace Cooper, the co-chairman of Project 21, agreed. "In the 21st century, we shouldn't be making race a basis for who gets into school and who doesn't," he said. "The Obama Administration pressured schools to do just that. Now President Trump is moving us away from that approach back to the color-blind vision of Dr. Martin Luther King."[16]

Reversing Obama's Eleventh-Hour Gun Grab

In the years following the 2012 Sandy Hook Elementary School shooting, the Obama administration began pushing for stricter gun control measures. In 2015, that push grew to include a ban on gun purchases for Social Security beneficiaries if they needed a representative to manage their pensions or disability payments. The government would integrate Social Security Administration data into the National Instant Criminal Background Check System (NICS). This ban was called "the largest gun grab in American history" by the NRA and an "egregious case of bureaucratic overreach."[17] The Social Security

Administration finalized the rules a few short weeks before Obama left office.[18]

The policy was short-lived as President Trump signed a bill, on February 28, 2017, reversing the regulation. Naturally, the media aggressively pushed the narrative that Trump and the GOP had repealed background checks and were allowing the mentally ill to have guns. This was completely false. For starters, NICS is still in place. Charles C. W. Cooke, the editor of *National Review*, explained that the Obama rule "would have allowed bureaucrats within one of our federal agencies to bar American citizens from exercising a con stitutional right—and on the highly questionable grounds that to be incapable of managing one's finances is, by definition, to be a 'mental defective.'"[19] Even the American Civil Liberties Union (ACLU) opposed the Obama gun grab, saying, "There is no data to support a connection between the need for a representative payee to manage one's Social Security disability benefits and a propensity toward gun violence."[20] Paul Appelbaum, a leading expert on legal and ethical issues in medicine and psychiatry, said the Obama rule was "fundamentally not a rational policy" and that people targeted by the rule "are not a particularly high-risk group for violent behavior."[21] Gun violence researcher Jeffrey Swanson said the NRA's position was in the right. "This is one of these times where the progressive politics du jour and the science – and, I think, the legal analysis – diverge."[22]

Allowing States to Deny Planned Parenthood Funding

Abortion isn't just a sacred cow for the radical left—it's big business for their allies. Planned Parenthood is America's largest abortion provider,[23] and they received millions in taxpayer dollars, ostensibly to subsidize female reproductive health care. In turn, Planned Parenthood donated heavily to the Democratic Party.[24]

Months before Obama left office, his administration proposed regulations to prevent states awarded federal family-planning funds under Title X from withholding those funds from clinics that provide abortions. Even though the regulation never mentioned

Planned Parenthood, he obviously wrote it with them in mind. At the time, Obama assumed Hillary Clinton would be his successor, but America had other plans. When Trump was elected, the Obama administration rushed to finalize the regulations, which they did in mid-December 2016. The new rules took effect two days before Trump's inauguration.[25]

Trump promised to defund Planned Parenthood on the campaign trail and, as a first step, he signed House Joint Resolution 43, effectively rescinding the Obama regulation on April 13, 2017. Marjorie Dannenfelser, the president of the Susan B. Anthony List, a pro-life women's group, called the move "a promise kept" by Trump. "This puts an end to the outgoing gift that Obama gave the Trump administration which was to disallow states from being in charge of its [sic] own family planning funds."[26] It isn't a full defunding yet, but, thanks to Trump, states still have the freedom to deny Title X funding to clinics that provide abortions, including Planned Parenthood.

Pro-Worker, Not Pro-Union

Barack Obama's relationship with unions goes back many years. In his book, *The Audacity of Hope,* Obama wrote, "'I owe those unions. When their leaders call, I do my best to call them back right away. I don't consider this corrupting in any way.'"[27] The influence of big labor on American politics is undeniable. They collect billions in union dues a year, and spend a nice chunk of that backing politicians who support them—like Barack Obama and other leftist candidates. Their support has earned them influence. As president Obama owed a lot to his union supporters, he supported pro-union causes like card check, and opposed anti-union causes like right-to-work laws. When the issue of compulsory union dues came before the Supreme Court in 2016, Obama's Justice Department sided with the unions.

The Trump administration reversed that position, arguing that compulsory union dues violated workers' free speech rights.[28] The Supreme Court ruled 5–4 in favor of the Trump administration's position—a major blow to public-sector unions. A ruling two years earlier on a similar case resulted in a 4–4 split because of the empty seat left by Justice Scalia, so Justice Neil Gorsuch was seen as the deciding vote.[29] The Trump administration also axed an Obama-era exemption to a federal law preventing states from "skimming" Medicaid subsidies paid to independent in-home care workers. The 2014 exemption created by the Obama administration allowed unions in eleven blue states to collect $200 million annually from health workers without them even being aware of it.[30]

Now, let's talk about the National Labor Relations Board (NLRB). With a Trump-picked majority on the NLRB, Obama-era pro-union rulings were quickly reversed, restoring many pre-Obama precedents friendlier to workers than to partisan unions.[31] Trump vowed to be an advocate for American workers, and he has successfully managed to dramatically shift labor laws in favor of hard-working Americans instead of powerful partisan labor union bosses.

Reversing Obama's Reinterpretation of Title VII

In 2014, the Obama administration reinterpreted Title VII of the Civil Rights Act of 1964, which makes it unlawful for employers, including federal, state, and local governments, from discriminating against employees on the basis of sex, race, color, nationality, or religion. "'I have determined that the best reading of Title VII's prohibition of sex discrimination is that it encompasses discrimination based on gender identity, including transgender status,'" wrote Attorney General Eric Holder in a memo to Justice Department employees.[32]

Liberals have a very nebulous and broad interpretation of what constitutes "discrimination." As Ryan T. Anderson, Ph.D., of the Heritage Foundation explains, "According to liberals advocating such policies, 'discrimination' on the basis of 'sexual orientation' can be something as reasonable as an adoption agency preferring married moms and dads for orphans. And 'discrimination' on the basis of 'gender identity' can be something as simple as having a bathroom policy based on biological sex, not gender identity."[33] The Obama administration had no constitutional authority to do this; they rewrote existing legislation by changing the meaning of the word "sex"—a bio-logical reality—to "gender identity." Congress couldn't possibly have intended this when they passed the Civil Rights Act. Transgenderism wasn't even a part of the public discourse in 1964.

When the City Council of Charlotte, North Carolina expanded their non-discrimination ordinance to include sexual orientation and gender identity, and allowed individuals to choose restrooms corre-sponding to their gender identity instead of their biological sex, the state Legislature responded by passing House Bill 2 (H.B. 2) which prevented local governments from allowing transgender people (or anyone else, for that matter) from using bathrooms that don't corre-spond with their biological sex. Then-Governor Pat McCrory signed the bill. Obama's Attorney General Loretta Lynch accused McCrory of violating Title VII and Title IX of the Civil Rights Act and threat-ened to withhold millions in federal funding unless state officials con-firmed that "'the State will not comply with or implement'" the law.[34]

The Trump administration reversed the Obama administration's unconstitutional reinterpretation of Title VII in October 2017. Attorney General Jeff Sessions explained, in a memo to federal pros-ecutors, that when Congress passed the law, the word "sex" meant "biologically male or female," and the Obama/Holder policy exceeded its authority in expanding the law without the consent of Congress. Sessions elaborated that the change in policy should not "be con-strued to condone mistreatment on the basis of gender identity, or to express a policy view on whether Congress should amend Title VII or provide different or additional protections." He added, "The Justice Department must and will continue to affirm the dignity of all peo-ple, including transgender individuals." While Democrats and LGBT activists cried foul, the blame really rests with the Obama administra-tion. "The Department of Justice cannot expand the law beyond what Congress has provided," explained DOJ spokesman Devin O'Malley. "Unfortunately, the last administration abandoned that fundamental principle, which necessitated today's action."[35]

Reversing Obama's Transgender Bathroom Rules in Schools

In 2016, the Obama administration issued guidance to public schools declaring that the Departments of Justice and Education would "treat a student's gender identity as the student's sex for purposes of enforcing Title IX."[36] Title IX is a law passed in 1972 prohibiting sex-based discrimination in education. Under this guidance, the Obama administration directed schools to allow students "to participate in sex-segregated activities and access sex-segregated facilities consistent with their gender identity"[37] or else they'd be in noncompliance with Title IX and lose federal funding. So, Obama told schools that students could use the bathrooms, locker rooms, dorm rooms, even hotel rooms for field trips of their choice. A biologically male student could simply claim he "identified" as a female and the school would have to oblige or risk losing their federal funding. The brazen disrespect Obama and his allies showed for the dignity and privacy of women and young girls who objected to sharing bathrooms and changing facilities with biological males is galling.

Eleven states sued the Obama administration over its transgender bathroom policy. The lawsuit asked the Federal District Court in Wichita Falls, Texas to block the federal government from "implementing, applying or enforcing the new rules, regulations and guidance interpretations," and accused the Obama administration of conspiring to "turn workplaces and educational settings across the country into laboratories for a massive social experiment, flouting the democratic process, and running roughshod over common-sense policies protecting children and basic privacy rights."[38] US District Judge Reed O'Connor agreed that the Obama administration exceeded its authority by redefining sex as "gender identity" and, in August 2016, temporarily blocked the policy from going into effect, leaving the status quo intact until the lawsuit worked its way through the courts.[39] The Obama administration appealed this decision and a Hillary Clinton administration would have continued to fight for it, but the Trump administration revoked the Obama transgender policy about a month after Trump took office, arguing that states and school districts—not the federal government—should make such policy decisions.[40]

Reversing Obama's Campus Sexual Assault Policy

Obama exceeded his authority to expand Title IX in other ways as well. In 2011, his Department of Education issued a "Dear Colleague" letter which compelled colleges and universities to investigate any incidents of sexual harassment or sexual assault, whether they occurred on or off campus, and drastically lowered the standard of evidence in order to increase the likelihood of finding the accused guilty. Schools had to comply or risk losing funding under Title IX—all at the expense of due process for the accused. "Essentially the procedure there works under the assumption that the accused is guilty and needs to use the hearing to prove his innocence," K. C. Johnson, author of *Until Proven Innocent: Political Correctness and the Shameful Injustice of the Duke Lacrosse Rape Case* explained to Fox News. "But he isn't given the tools to do that. He doesn't have discovery, he can't get the relevant evidence he needs, he doesn't have an attorney representing him [and has] limited right of cross-examination. So there's virtually no way, once an accusation is made and gets into the system […] that the accused can be exonerated." In some cases, students were found to have been falsely accused after getting kicked off campus. For those students, one lie ruined their lives. Despite hundreds of lawsuits by male students who said they were falsely accused and denied due process, the Obama administration never wavered. They continued to pressure schools to hold kangaroo courts to address campus sexual assaults. Harvard Law professor Janet Halley, in a 2015 essay in *Harvard Law Review*, was critical of the "pressure on schools to hold students responsible for serious harm even when—precisely when—there can be no certainty about who is to blame for it. Such calls are core to every witch hunt." Christina Hoff Sommers, the author of *The War Against Boys,* agreed schools often complied with these rules out of the fear of losing federal funding. "University and college officials were terrified of running afoul of the new version of Title IX mandated by the Department of Education in 2011. […] Due process is being treated as a barrier to justice—rather than its essence."

That was until the Trump administration stepped in. In September 2017, the Obama-era guidance on campus sexual assaults was rescinded. "Schools must continue to confront these horrific crimes and behaviors head-on," explained Education Secretary Betsy DeVos. "There will be no more sweeping them under the rug. But the process also must be fair and impartial, giving everyone more confidence in its outcomes."

A year later, the Trump administration released a draft of new federal guidance on campus sexual assault and harassment, designed to achieve a balance between the rights of both the accuser and the accused. The proposed rule requires schools "to respond meaningfully to every known report of sexual harassment and to investigate every formal complaint." Colleges and universities are ordered to "apply basic due process protections for students, including a presumption of innocence throughout the grievance process; written notice of allegations and an equal opportunity to review all evidence collected; and the right to cross-examination, subject to 'rape shield' protections."

"Every survivor of sexual violence must be taken seriously, and every student accused of sexual misconduct must know that guilt is not predetermined," Secretary DeVos added. "We can, and must, condemn sexual violence and punish those who perpetrate it, while ensuring a fair grievance process. Those are not mutually exclusive ideas. They are the very essence of how Americans understand justice to function."

Due process may have been an antiquated notion during the Obama years, but under Trump, the Constitution still matters.

Reversing Obama's Transgender Prison Rules

In the United Kingdom, a convicted rapist and pedophile raped a woman and sexually assaulted four others within a day of being incarcerated in an all-female prison. How did this happen? Why would anyone be stupid enough to place a convicted rapist in a female prison?

The felon claimed to be a transgender female. Despite not undergoing gender reassignment surgery, state officials placed this man in a cage with easy targets.[41]

This was the absurdity Obama wanted for America. Obama introduced rules that took effect two days before Trump took office, which dictated the gender identities of "transgender" inmates would determine where they'd live and what facilities they could use. The justification for this policy was to help prevent transgender prisoners from being harassed, assaulted or abused. The threat that women might get raped by male prisoners "identifying" as female was of no concern to Obama.

Four women in a Texas detention center were concerned, however, and sued the federal government, arguing that the Obama-era policy created "a situation that incessantly violates the privacy of female inmates; endangers the physical and mental health of the female Plaintiffs and others, including prison staff; [and] increases the potential for rape."[42] In May 2018, the Trump administration rolled back the Obama-era guidelines. The revised guidelines "will use biological sex as the initial determination," and officials would consider gender identity only if "there has been significant progress towards transition as demonstrated by medical and mental health history."[43]

Reversing Obama's Rule Allowing Transgender People in the Military

Even the military couldn't avoid Obama's radical social engineering. In his view, "social justice" was more important than combat readiness. Two concrete examples of this bias stand out: women in combat and transgender people in the service. In January 2013, Defense Secretary Leon Panetta announced plans to integrate women into more combat roles in the military, a reversal of a 1994 ban on women in combat.[44] As a result, the military would reevaluate their physical standards. "If we do decide that a particular standard is so high that a woman couldn't make it, the burden is now on the service to come back and explain to the secretary, why is it that high? Does it really have to be that high?" said Army Gen. Martin Dempsey, chairman of the Joint Chiefs of Staff.[45]

After nearly three years of study, Obama's Defense Secretary Ash Carter announced, in December 2015, that all combat jobs would be open to women. "They'll be allowed to drive tanks, fire mortars, and lead infantry soldiers into combat. They'll be able to serve as Army Rangers and Green Berets, Navy SEALs, Marine Corps infantry, Air Force parajumpers, and everything else that previously was open only to men." Carter said, claiming that women would still have to "qualify and meet the standards."[46] But women *couldn't* meet the standards…and the Obama administration knew this. In 2014, half of female Marines in boot camp reportedly couldn't do three pull-ups; that minimum was reduced from prior standards and women still couldn't reach it. That requirement was subsequently delayed.[47]

The Marine Corps attempted to see if female officers could complete its Infantry Officer Course. Only four made it through the first day, and none graduated. According to Robert Maginnis, a retired Army officer, "The pressure is on the services from the White House's politically correct crowd vis-à-vis Obama's Pentagon appointees, who will force the services to accept degraded standards."[48] According to the Marine Corps' research, "women often couldn't carry as much weight or shoot as well as the men. Allowing women to compete for ground combat jobs […] would make the Marine Corps a less-efficient fighting machine."[49]

Nevertheless, the ban on women in combat was formally lifted by the Pentagon in March 2016, opening up more than two hundred thousand military jobs previously only open to men. With military readiness not a primary concern of his, Obama defended his decision as a civil rights issue, comparing the move to desegregation.[50] Trump has yet to formally reverse Obama's policy of forming coed combat units and opening all combat roles to women.

As for the policy on transgender people, Ash Carter announced plans for the military to end the ban on transgender people serving in the military in June 2016, ordering a new policy to be drafted within six months. Once again, military readiness was considered less important than political correctness. "This is yet another example of President Obama using America's military to fight culture wars instead of to fight real wars against the enemies of our nation," said Family Research Council President and Marine Corps veteran Tony Perkins.[51]

When asked about Obama's transgender policy for the military, Trump said, "We're going to get away from political correctness." He added he would leave decisions about such issues to "the generals, the admirals, the people on top."[52] Obama's policy was to take effect on July 1, 2017, but Trump's Defense Secretary Jim Mattis gave military chiefs another six months to determine the impact of transgender soldiers on military readiness and lethality.[53] Allowing transgender persons into the armed forces also came with a hefty bill. One study found it would cost the Pentagon $1.3 billion over ten years to cover the costs of transgender surgeries. This could even be a conservative estimate, since taxpayer funding would serve as an incentive for transgender people to enter the service so their surgeries might be covered.[54] Near the end of July 2017, Trump announced a full ban on transgender people in the military, which was then blocked by a federal judge in October 2017.[55]

The Pentagon released its review of Obama's transgender military policy in February 2018. They found, "there are substantial risks associated with allowing the accession and retention of individuals with a history or diagnosis of gender dysphoria and require, or have already undertaken, a course of treatment to change their gender." Exempting transgender individuals from military mental, physical, and sex-based standards "could undermine readiness, disrupt unit cohesion, and impose an unreasonable burden on the military that is not conducive to military effectiveness and lethality." The study also faulted the Obama administration's policy, which was largely based on a RAND National Defense Research Institute study which relied on "limited and heavily caveated data to support its conclusions, glossed over the impacts of healthcare costs, readiness, and unit cohesion, and erroneously relied on the selective experiences of foreign militaries with different operational requirements" than the United States military. The study recommended transgender persons without a history or diagnosis of gender dysphoria should serve in their biological sex, while transgender persons requiring or who have undergone sex reassignment surgery should be disqualified from service.[56]

The following month, Donald Trump issued another, more focused memorandum, based on the Pentagon's recommendations.[57] Thomas Spoehr of the Center for National Defense said the Pentagon's transgender policy was "no different from its treatment of hundreds of other medically disqualifying conditions such as bipolar disorder, asthma, or diabetes." Because individuals suffering from gender dysphoria have been found to "experience significant distress and impairment in social, occupational, or other important areas of functioning," allowing them to serve in the military puts them and others at high risk. Spoehr also noted that "the Pentagon went to great length to carve out an ability for transgender individuals to serve in the military if they don't suffer from gender dysphoria. This was a logical and sound conclusion that helps the military fill its ranks."[58] LGBT activists succeeded in blocking the new guidelines, gaining injunctions from four federal judges pending various discrimination lawsuits.[59] In January 2019, the Supreme Court allowed the ban to stay in place pending ongoing litigation. However, the constitutionality of the ban will eventually end up back at the US Supreme Court. Considering the makeup of the court at the time of this writing, I'm confident Trump's policy will be upheld.

Restoring Religious Liberty

Under Barack Obama, religious liberty, a bedrock right guaranteed by the first amendment to the Constitution, was constantly under attack. "Obama views traditional religion as a temporary opiate for the poor, confused, and jobless—a drug that will dissipate as the federal government assumes more God-like powers, and his new secularist beliefs and policies gain adherents," wrote Phyllis Schlafly and George Neumayr in their book *No Higher Power: Obama's War on Religious Freedom.*[60] I already covered Obama's abortion and contraceptive mandates, but his attacks on churches and faith-based non-profits went far beyond the seamy underbelly of Obamacare. He cut funding for faith-based groups, he unilaterally decided the 1996 Defense of Marriage Act (DOMA) was unconstitutional, he threatened the tax-exempt status of religious institutions that oppose same-sex marriage, and his justice department went after family-owned businesses for refusing to serve gay couples seeking to get married owing to their religious convictions. I could go on, but the point should already be clear: Obama was an enemy of religious liberty.

Under Donald Trump, religious groups found an ally. In October 2017, Attorney General Jeff Sessions "issued twenty principles of religious liberty to guide the Administration's litigation strategy and protect religious freedom." In January 2018, the Justice Department updated the US Attorneys' Manual, "raising the profile of religious liberty cases and directing the designation of a Religious Liberty Point of Contact for all U.S. Attorney's offices." The Department of Health and Human Services also announced policy changes geared toward defending religious freedom for health care providers. The new rules created a new Conscience and Religious Freedom Division and mandated more vigorous enforcement of existing statutory conscience protections.[61] The ACLU predictably opposed the order, but it's been decades since they've stood for civil liberties that didn't conform to a left-wing worldview.[62]

Trump issued two other executive orders expanding religious freedoms of all Americans. The first came in May 2017, establishing religious exemptions from the contraception mandate in Obamacare for religious groups. The second, a year later, rolled back Obama-era rules he found offensive that prevented faith-based groups and charities with social beliefs from providing services to the public.[63] The latter executive order also established the White House Faith and Opportunity Initiative, which would focus on protecting religious freedom and ensure that "the faith-based and community organizations that form the bedrock of our society have strong advocates in the White House and throughout the federal government."[64]

According to the Family Research Council, Trump's executive order allowed religious groups and charities to provide health care and social services to nearly 14 million people and at least forty-four schools with 148,000 students to continue operating. "Thanks to President Trump, over the last year we have witnessed nothing less than a revival of legal protections for religious freedom in America," said Family Research Council president Tony Perkins.[65]

Reversing Obama's Military Surplus Rule

The "1033 Program" which allowed the Department of Defense to transfer surplus military equipment to civilian law enforcement agencies, was created as part of the National Defense Authorization Act of 1996. It was passed by Congress and signed into law by President Clinton.

Then, in August 2014, Michael Brown assaulted a police officer and paid for it with his life. Riots ensued and Barack Obama signed an executive order establishing the Law Enforcement Equipment Working Group, which would review the program. "We've seen how militarized gear can sometimes give people a feeling like there's an occupying force as opposed to a force that's part of the community that's protecting and serving them," Obama said when he signed the executive order. "It can alienate and intimidate local residents and send the wrong message." That group ultimately issued a report recommending that the military be prohibited from transferring certain equipment, while also imposing stricter rules on others.[66]

Aside from the issue that Obama had used an executive action to roll back an act of Congress, this action also ignored the fact that situations escalating due to overreactions to heavily protected law enforcement are rare. John Malcolm, the vice president for the Institute for Constitutional Government, said, "It is also true that there are occasions where law enforcement authorities need such equipment in order to protect the public—for instance, during terrorist attacks, search-and-rescue operations, or in the wake of natural disasters." Malcolm cited Hurricane Harvey, the terrorist attacks at the Pulse nightclub in Orlando, and San Bernardino as examples.[67] The American Economic Association commissioned a study called *Police Officer on the Frontline or a Soldier: The Effect of Police Militarization on Crime* which determined the 1033 Program is a cost-effective deterrent on crime.[68]

President Trump signed an executive order reversing the Obama-era restriction in August 2017. "These restrictions that had been imposed went too far," Sessions said at the Fraternal Order of Police national convention in Nashville. "We will not put superficial concerns above public safety. We will do our best to get you what you need."

While there may be legitimate concerns, equipment obtained through the 1033 Program saved lives and has been instrumental in emergency and disaster response efforts. Images of police officers in military gear may have left a bad impression with the American public after the riots in Ferguson, but the benefits of the program weren't given enough consideration before Obama once again exceeded his constitutional limits and saddled the American people with bad policy.

Reversing Obama's Racial Quota Discipline Policies

On July 26, 2012, Barack Obama issued an executive order titled "White House Initiative on Educational Excellence for African Americans," which linked the high dropout rate of African-American students to allegedly discriminatory enforcement of school discipline.[69] He followed up with a guidance letter in January 2014 from the Departments of Justice and Education instructing schools to adopt racial quotas for enforcing discipline. If schools failed to comply with the order, the Obama administration would consider them in violation of Title VI of the Civil Rights Act of 1964, which would cost them their federal funding.[70]

Hans A. von Spakovsky and Roger Clegg of the Heritage Foundation made a compelling case that this guidance violated both the Congressional Review Act and the Administrative Procedure Act. "The Education Department lacks authority to use the 'disparate impact' standard in enforcing Title VI of the 1964 Civil Rights Act, which prohibits discrimination in programs or activities that receive federal funds. [...] Title VI bans only 'disparate treatment.' In any event, the letter's hyper-aggressive approach violates other Supreme

Court and lower federal-court decisions, including a ban on racial quotas in school discipline."[71]

Unfortunately, the issues with this policy weren't simply legal. The real-world consequences of the Obama guidance resulted in schools being unable to protect students who were victims of bullying, sexual harassment, or violence. One family in the Baltimore County Public School system in Maryland sent their kids to private schools after their public school failed to protect them. Their nine-year-old son endured bullying for months "to the point of being suicidal," but the school did nothing. Their twelve-year-old daughter was repeatedly sexually harassed, but the school did nothing. Their eighteen-year-old son was threatened after reporting a student with a knife in class, but the school did nothing. All this because of a misguided attempt at social engineering.[72]

School districts nationwide have experienced surges in violent behavior since changing their discipline policies under Obama's new directive. "Large shares of teachers now say they feel unsafe, as more and more students physically attack faculty and staff, according to school-climate and teacher surveys from dozens of districts, including Buffalo, Syracuse, Philadelphia and Denver."[73]

In December 2015, a sixteen-year-old black student beat and choked a science teacher in St. Paul, Minnesota. The student called him a "f–king white cracker," put him in a stranglehold, and beat his head into a concrete wall and the pavement, causing a concussion and brain damage. The victim of this assault believes school violence has gone out of control because of the Obama policy. "The district is not suspending students for fighting, theft, drugs and alcohol in an effort to show less students of color are suspended." Principals got bonuses as high as $2,500 for low suspension rates.[74] In Buffalo, New York, an elementary school teacher was thrown to the ground and kicked in the head by a student who said, "we can't be suspended."[75]

In March 2018, Trump announced the creation of a school safety commission to be led by Education Secretary Betsy DeVos. A survey by the commission found that just 27 percent of the public supports the racial discipline quotas and DeVos has heard arguments from both sides of the issue,[76] but, as of this writing, the policy stands, though it is expected that the commission will repeal it soon.[77]

Ensuring Election Integrity

The Obama administration actively fought attempts by several states to enact voter ID laws and ensure the integrity of our elections. Obama believed that voter fraud was nearly non-existent and attempts to improve the integrity of elections were racist. He once opined, "It traces directly back to Jim Crow and the legacy of slavery, and it became sort of acceptable to restrict the franchise.... This whole notion of election-voting fraud, this is something that has constantly been disproved. This is fake news."[78]

It's not, of course. The Heritage Foundation has a massive, searchable database of provable voter fraud that resulted in criminal convictions.[79] But, Obama, like many on the left, couldn't care less. Any attempts to prevent voter fraud are met with accusations of trying to suppress minority votes. Obama even promised to continue to fight after leaving office. He also brazenly made the false claim that no advanced democracies have voter ID laws. As John Fund at *National Review* explained, "All industrialized democracies—and most that are not—require voters to prove their identity before voting."[80] Britain doesn't have national voter ID, but areas prone to corruption require a passport or other official documentation. Both Mexico and Canada have voter ID. According to Fund, the lack of voter ID in the United States is actually surprising to most other countries. "In 2012, I attended a conference in Washington, D.C. of election officials from more than 60 countries," Fund wrote. "They convened there to observe the U.S. presidential election. Most were astonished that so many U.S. states don't require voter ID."[81]

The Obama administration blocked a voter ID law in Texas in 2012 over alleged concerns that it harmed Hispanic voters.[82] But, unlike Obama, President Trump is a proponent of voter ID laws and restoring the integrity of our elections. In February 2017, the Justice

Department reversed the government's position on the Texas voter ID law, allowing the state legislature to address concerns with the law.[83]

Obama opposed several other efforts to maintain the integrity of elections. In 2016, Ohio Secretary of State Jon Husted sought to purge inactive voters from the state's voter rolls, like many other states do, and was challenged in court. Those who hadn't voted since 2008, and failed to respond to notices regarding their registration, would be removed from the voter rolls. The Obama administration sided against Husted, but the Trump administration reversed the government's position in August 2017,[84] and the US Supreme Court sided with Husted in June 2018.[85]

While various states and municipalities have been making it easier for illegal immigrants to vote, Trump has continued to advocate for commonsense laws to protect our elections. "In some states, Democrats are even trying to give illegal immigrants the right to vote," Trump said, at a rally in Florida, in July 2018. "We believe that only American citizens should vote in American elections. Which is why the time has come for voter ID."[86]

CHAPTER 2

DEREGULATION AND DOMESTIC POLICY

When Obama took office, his mission was to change America and, with Democrat majorities in both Houses of Congress, he squandered trillions of dollars on failed legislative "achievements" like Obamacare, the stimulus of 2009, and the auto industry bailout. He also pushed through enormous regulatory reforms that made it far more expensive to do business in America, such as the consumer protection package known as Dodd-Frank.

But, once Republicans took back the House in 2010 and the Senate in 2014, Obama's interest in the usual constitutional methods of governing waned. Even after two years of a rubber stamp Congress, Obama was so dissatisfied with America that, if Congress wasn't willing to go along with his agenda anymore, he grossly extended the power of the administrative state through executive orders and backdoor regulations. "We're not just going to be waiting for legislation in order to make sure that we're providing Americans the kind of help they need," Obama said during his first Cabinet meeting of 2014. "I've got a pen and I've got a phone." Obama's dictatorial style of governing came at a steep price. In fact, Obama imposed more regulations than any other president in history.[87] The American Action Forum found he'd issued 145 "midnight" regulations just before leaving office; those alone cost $21 billion.[88]

President Trump established himself as a change agent the minute he stepped in, however. In the first days of his presidency, he issued a regulatory freeze and directed agencies to ax two regulations for every new one created and offset all new regulatory costs.[89] Six months into his presidency, the Trump administration "had withdrawn or removed from active consideration more than 800 proposed regulations that were never finalized during the Obama administration."[90] In fact, Trump's first six months were the least regulatory since Ronald Reagan's first six months in office.[91] The American Action Forum tallied the score in May 2018 and found that Trump doubled his deregulation goal.[92]

But Trump isn't content to rule by the pen alone. After a titanic fight in both chambers of Congress, Trump and Republicans on Capitol Hill passed the most sweeping tax reform since the Reagan tax cuts in 1986.[93] The cuts reduced corporate taxes from 35 percent to 21 percent, reduced the top individual tax rate from 39.6percent to 37 percent, doubled the standard deduction for individuals and families, and slashed personal income taxes for the middle class.[94] He also reversed some of Obama's legislative victories, killing or structurally gutting harmful bills passed by Democrats. Since it would take forever to discuss every achievement, this chapter will only cover the most significant Trump victories over Obama's big government regulatory policies.

Ending Michelle Obama's School Lunch Program

The school lunch program promoted by Michelle Obama and implemented by the Obama administration may have had the intent of combating childhood obesity, but it became another big government disaster. When kids across the country began posting unflattering pictures of the meals they were being served on Twitter, it became clear that all was not well with the Smarter Lunchrooms initiative. *The Washington Post* reported on November 24, 2014 that the tweets, which all included a #ThanksMichelleObama hashtag, "were being sent out at a rate of 40 per minute late last week, but started to gain momentum some 10 days back and are still continuing to be posted as of this morning." The hashtag had been used at least as far back as 2012.[95]

Perhaps the intentions were good, but kids weren't interested in bland lunches with foods only a privileged health nut would enjoy, and multiple studies bore this out. Even though school districts could opt out of the program, they would lose federal subsidies if they did. According to the School Nutrition Association, "Overly prescriptive regulations have resulted in unintended consequences, including reduced student lunch participation, higher costs, and food waste. Federal nutrition standards should be modified to help school menu planners manage these challenges and prepare nutritious meals that appeal to diverse student tastes."[96]

In response to the problems with the program, the Trump administration relaxed those school lunch standards in May 2017 in favor of letting local leaders decide what their kids should eat. "I applaud former First Lady Michelle Obama for addressing those obesity problems in the past," said Trump's Agriculture Secretary Sonny Perdue. "This is not reducing the nutritional standards whatsoever."[97] Giving local school districts more control over how the plan and deliver school lunches allows them to adjust more readily to changing food prices, regional tastes, the dietary needs of their students, and an ever-changing scientific consensus. It's a good thing, too, because many of the expert opinions backing Michelle Obama's program have come under fire. In September 2018, the *Journal of the American Medical Association* (*JAMA*) retracted six nutrition studies by food scientist Brian Wansink after a grad student tried to reproduce his results and they didn't hold up. The Department of Agriculture relied heavily on Wansink's advice when crafting Michelle Obama's Smarter Lunchrooms program, and most of it was bogus.[98]

Dodd-Frank Rollback

In response to the 2008 financial crisis, Congress passed the Dodd-Frank Wall Street Reform and Consumer Protection Act (with only three Republican votes in the Senate and zero in the House) and Obama signed it into law in 2010. As the Heritage Foundation explained, Dodd-Frank was "based on a mistaken belief that the 2007–2009 financial crisis stemmed from unregulated financial markets." But there has been "no substantial reduction in U.S. financial regulations" in over a hundred years.[99]

The intent of the Dodd-Frank Act was to protect consumers and stabilize financial markets. But, at two thousand three hundred pages, the legislation was really a behemoth of complex regulations that protected big banks over smaller community banks, hurt businesses, and stifled job growth.[100] The bill "spawned 400 separate rulemakings across the financial sector, and was the most extensive financial regulatory bill since the 1930s."[101] Despite Dodd-Frank, Obama's economic recovery was the worst since the Great Depression. "This is principally attributable to the heavy load of new regulation imposed by the Dodd-Frank Act, which has affected—among other firms—small community banks that are important sources of credit for small businesses." Because of Dodd-Frank, small businesses struggled to grow, while big businesses eventually recovered.[102]

Under Dodd-Frank, America lost about one community bank or credit union per day. The bill also caused a sharp decline in banks offering free checking, down from 75 percent before the law took effect to only 39 percent five years later.[103] Bank fees also increased, which significantly hurt lower- and middle-class Americans.

Did Dodd-Frank make America's financial system more secure, as was its mission? Nope. In a July 2015 letter to the *Wall Street Journal,* Congressman Jeb Hensarling, chairman of the House Financial Services Committee, explained: "Many of the threats to financial stability identified in the latest report of Dodd-Frank's Financial Stability Oversight Council are primarily the result of the law itself, along with other government policies."[104]

On the campaign trail, Donald Trump promised that he would "dismantle" Dodd-Frank. "Dodd-Frank has made it impossible for bankers to function. It makes it very hard for bankers to loan money for people to create jobs, for people with businesses to create jobs. And that has to stop."[105] He came through on that promise. In February 2017, Trump signed an executive order designed to sabotage Dodd-Frank.[106] Two months later, he signed two more executive orders with the same goal in mind.[107] On May 24, 2018, he signed a rollback of Dodd-Frank. The bill passed with bipartisan support in Congress as a result of his systematic attacks on the failed policy.

Ending Net Neutrality

In November 2014, Obama publicly endorsed net neutrality, painting it as an important protection of free speech. Obama's Federal Communications Commission (FCC) chairman Tom Wheeler echoed this idea, saying that "like the president, I believe that the Internet must remain an open platform for free expression, innovation, and economic growth." The internet existed and thrived for years before net neutrality, but Obama saw it as an opportunity to further regulate American businesses.[108] In 2015, the Federal Communications Commission voted 3–2 to regulate internet service providers (ISPs) under Title II of the Telecommunications Act of 1934. Title II was an act designed to give the government the authority to regulate telephone and telegraph wires nearly fifty years before the internet was born.

There are plenty of reasons net neutrality is bad policy. Ian Tuttle, the former Thomas L. Rhodes Journalism Fellow at the National Review Institute, called net neutrality "a solution looking for a problem." Anti-competitive behavior by ISPs was so rare that, when the FCC originally attempted a weaker version of net neutrality in 2010, "it could cite just four examples of anticompetitive behavior, all relatively minor."[109] Net neutrality rules would hamper innovation by giving the FCC enormous power to dictate various aspects of the internet with no means to appeal these decisions. It would also empower the FCC to levy taxes against ISPs, making it harder for smaller ISPs to thrive, reducing competition and increasing costs for consumers.[110] One 2014 study estimated a loss of $45.4 billion in new ISP investments over the next five years from net neutrality regulations.[111] Government regulation tends to decrease competition, not encourage it. The internet thrived on free market capitalism, not government regulation. Competition should be encouraged to benefit the consumers.

Thankfully, net neutrality was put on death watch when President Trump appointed FCC commissioner Ajit Pai, an opponent of net neutrality, as FCC chairman, and in December 2017, the FCC voted 3-2 to approve the Restoring Internet Freedom Order, reversing net neutrality.[112] Its proponents were furious, predicting disastrous Orwellian consequences. One man was so angry over the repeal of net neutrality he threatened to kill Mr. Pai's family. "I will find your children and I will kill them," the man wrote in an email to Pai's personal and government email accounts. The FBI traced emails and arrested the man for threatening a family member of a federal official.[113] Yet, since the repeal of net neutrality, the internet apocalypse predicted by its proponents hasn't happened.

The repeal faces legal challenges as of this writing. In August 2018, twenty-two states and the District of Columbia issued a brief for the D.C. Court of Appeals urging the court to vacate and reverse the roll-back of net neutrality.[114] California passed its own version of the federal bill and the Trump administration is suing the state on the grounds that it lacks the right to override the FCC.[115] But, as of this writing, the internet remains free and open...thanks to President Trump.

Reversing Obama's Federal Overtime Rule

In March 2014, Barack Obama unilaterally changed regulations in the Fair Labor Standards Act of 1938 via an executive order, making millions of "executive and professional" employees eligible for overtime pay. Congress never debated this or held a vote despite business groups warning that this change would greatly increase the costs of doing business. Twenty-one states sued the Obama administration in September 2016, arguing that the new rules violated states' rights and would "place a heavy burden on state budgets." The US Chamber of Commerce and other business groups also filed a separate lawsuit to challenge the rule change, which they said would likely force businesses to lay off workers and cut budgets to save costs.[116]

This abuse of power was so egregious that US District Court Judge Amos Mazzant III issued an injunction blocking the implementation of the rule a week before it would've taken effect, siding with business interests. Obama's Labor Department announced they were considering all of their legal options,[117] but with the Trump administration soon to be taking over, there wasn't much they could do. A week after Judge Mazzant officially struck down the overtime rule, on September 5, 2017, Trump's Justice Department announced it would not appeal the judge's ruling.[118] Business groups applauded the decision. "This will allow the U.S. Department of Labor (DOL) time to consider input from the business community to enact workable changes to these regulations," said Angelo Amador, executive director of the National Restaurant Association's Restaurant Law Center.[119]

Reversing Obama's Pay Gap Rule

Although wage disparity based on sex has been outlawed since 1963, liberals have used misleading statistics to "prove" that the gender pay gap still exists. As president, Barack Obama was more than willing to perpetuate the mythical gender pay gap. The first bill he signed as president was the Lilly Ledbetter Fair Pay Act. During his 2013 and 2014 State of the Union addresses, he cited the bogus statistic that women "make seventy-seven cents for every dollar a man earns." *The Washington Post* fact-checker Glenn Kessler called Obama out for this misleading claim, noting that using a broad calculation of annual wages to measure average pay ignored many important variables.[120] Despite making equal pay one of Obama's pet causes, a *Washington Post* analysis in the summer of 2014 found a 13 percent gender pay gap in the Obama White House. The White House response to this accusation was to point out that the aggregate statistic may show a gap, but "Men and women in equivalent roles earn equivalent salaries," which brilliantly refutes the national discrepancy as well.[121] In fact, a 2009 Department of Labor study found that "differences in education, experience, choice of industry and occupation, career interruptions, and hours worked explain all but 5 cents of the so-called wage gap."[122] The Heritage Foundation argues that "Immeasurable components of compensation—such as flexible work schedules—likely account for the remaining gap."[123]

Yet, Obama felt it was the government's role to fix a fictional problem by creating a real one. In January 2016, on the seventh anniversary of the signing of the Lilly Ledbetter Fair Pay Act, Obama announced new government regulations to close the nonexistent gender pay gap which would require companies with over one hundred employees "to provide the federal government annual data for how much they pay employees based on gender, race and ethnicity."[124]

Business groups led by the US Chamber of Commerce pleaded with the Trump administration to rescind the Obama-era rules. Randy Johnson, a senior vice president of the Chamber of Commerce, called the rules a gross abuse of regulatory power. "If ever there was a regulation that imposed an incredible amount of burden with no utility [...] it's this one," he explained. "It was pushed through under the prior administration because it met a political goal. But as far as the substance and merits, there just isn't any that would justify it being kept on the books."[125] According to Romina Boccia, a leading fiscal and economic expert at the Heritage Foundation, the Obama rules "would have dimmed the job and wage prospects of all workers, and especially of those workers the policy sought to help in the first place."[126]

Employers who are weary of costly discrimination lawsuits against them react most effectively to such a rule by adopting more rigid pay structures.

To the detriment of workers, the best way to protect against unfounded discrimination claims based on incomplete data is to have one-size-fits-all pay structures that fit neatly into the boxes on government reporting forms.

The problem is that this reduces the availability of flexible work arrangements, which are especially important to working parents. It also leads to less performance-based pay, like bonuses, which encourage and reward excellence.

Boxes on government forms simply can't capture sufficient data to explain differences in wages and promotions based on employee behavior and preferences. The result is less flexibility and more rigidity in the workplace.[127]

On August 31, 2017, President Trump blocked the Obama rule with an executive order of his own.[128] American businesses and families will thank him for years to come.

Weakening the Consumer Financial Protection Bureau

Created under the Dodd-Frank Act, the Consumer Financial Protection Bureau (CFPB) became a powerful and unaccountable federal agency that—like the legislation that created it—did more harm than good.[129] Competitive Enterprise Institute fellow Iain Murray even argued that the CFPB is actually harmful to consumers. The authors of Dodd-Frank wanted the CFPB to be protected from political influence, but the result was an agency with extraordinary power that was "insulated from accountability to the president, Congress, and the courts." The CFPB is not funded by Congress, but directly from the Federal Reserve, and purely at the discretion of its director. The CFPB director is appointed by the president for a five-year term, but can't be fired without cause. The courts are also "required to give extra deference to the CFPB's decisions in some cases." These provisions, Murray says, "violate constitutional norms of checks and balances on executive power and have led the CFPB to abuse its power, including by trying to regulate in areas where its statutory authority is expressly limited."[130]

In November 2017, Trump called the CFPB "a total disaster" run by Obama loyalists[131] as he took on the ambitious task of weakening the CFPB in the hopes of ultimately dismantling it. Trump appointed Mick Mulvaney, the director of the White House Office of Management and Budget and a known critic of the CFPB, as the board's acting director.[132] Mulvaney chose not to request more financial support from the Federal Reserve for the second quarter of 2018, instead opting to spend down their reserve funds—reducing the CFPB's funding and their ability to operate.[133] Mulvaney has also pushed for congressional oversight for the CFPB by giving Congress control over the CFPB budget (instead of the Federal Reserve) and the authority to approve CFPB rules and regulations before they go into effect.[134] In June 2018, Mulvaney fired all twenty-five members of the CFPB advisory board.[135] Ironically, the same impenetrable wall of bureaucratic protectionism that empowered the CFPB to become an abusive juggernaut for the left also insulated Mulvaney from the liberal pushback and allowed him enormous freedom to cripple the board. Score a big win for Trump.

CHAPTER 3

IMMIGRATION

Donald Trump and Barack Obama had very different visions for the United States' immigration policy. Barack Obama didn't understand the purpose of the borders, resulting in a collection of confused, mostly open policies that left America less safe. Donald Trump, however, has aggressively sought to secure our border and enforce our immigration laws.

According to a 2016 report by the Federation for American Immigration Reform (FAIR), the Obama administration gradually and systematically undermined immigration enforcement without the consent of Congress. "The administration hoped that while the American people were focused on unemployment, crashing real estate values, banking scandals, health care reform, foreign policy crises, and countless other issues, they would not notice what was actually taking place."[136] Obama's actions were "designed to achieve a single purpose: to render enforcement of U.S. immigration laws ineffective."[137]

Obama didn't just undermine our immigration enforcement; he also opened the floodgates for refugees to enter the United States in the wake of the Syrian refugee crisis. It caused significant problems in Europe. Sweden took in more refugees per capita than any other European nation, and a surge in violent crime and sexual assaults followed.[138] Germany had their own rape crisis although political correctness has resulted in authorities downplaying the connection.[139] Obama ignored the risks. Donald Trump didn't. "You look at what's happening in Europe, you look at what's happening in other places, we can't allow that to happen to the United States," President Trump declared. "Not on my watch."

Several ISIS militants involved in the November 2015 terror attacks in Paris entered Europe via Greece, posing as Syrian refugees.[140] Those attacks left 130 people across the city dead, and many others injured. "The vast majority of Syrian refugees are legitimate victims of terror and persecution," explained Marc Thiessen, American Enterprise Institute fellow and former senior policy adviser to the Senate Foreign Relations Committee chairman. "But it only takes a handful of ISIS infiltrators hiding among them to bring the carnage we saw in Paris to our streets."[141] In fact, an ISIS commander even gloated: "We have sent many operatives to Europe with the refugees." He also warned, "Some of our brothers have fulfilled their mission, but others are still waiting to be activated."[142] As of March 2017, the FBI had over 300 people who came to the United States as refugees on their watch list "for potential terrorism-related activities."

Besides the national security risks, there is a huge financial cost of accepting large numbers of refugees. According to a 2018 analysis by FAIR based on "recent admissions figures, data on federal and state public assistance programs, and information from the Office of Refugee Resettlement," the average cost to American taxpayers was nearly $80,000 per refugee over their first five years after resettlement in the United States. Most refugees come to America "without financial resources and possessing few marketable job skills. And the American taxpayer is being asked to feed, clothe and shelter them, in addition to funding job training programs." Refugees have access to public assistance programs, including Temporary Assistance for Needy Families (TANF), Medicaid, food stamps, public housing, Supplemental Security Income (SSI), Social Security Disability Insurance, and several other programs.[143] And that's just after they make it to the United States. "Additionally, the U.S. incurs significant expenses before refugees even get here: vetting applicants for refugee status, processing immigration applications and transporting approved applicants to the United States." Those seeking asylum can cost more because they are already in the country when they apply for protection and are entitled by law "to a hearing on their asylum claim before U.S. Citizenship and Immigration Services, an additional hearing before the U.S. Immigration Court if the government intends to deny their claim, and an appeal to the Board of Immigration Appeals."[144]

When Donald Trump took the oath of office, we gained a commander-in-chief willing to take the steps necessary to protect the interests and security of Americans first. America remains a beacon of hope for the world, but we need a reasonable commonsense approach to dealing with the immigration crisis.

Reversing Obama's Open Borders Policy

Under Obama, a surge of illegal immigration occurred, and his administration made it a lot tougher to deport illegal immigrants.[145] In 2016, he effectively reinstated "catch-and-release" by ordering Border Patrol agents not to even bother arresting illegal immigrants.[146] Trump's first executive order addressing illegal immigration, "Border Security and Immigration Enforcement Improvements," directed the Department of Homeland Security to secure the southern border by planning the design and construction of a border wall; end the "catch-and-release" policy; detain those suspected of violating Federal or state law; expedite processing of claims of eligibility to remain in the United States; deport those whose claims are rejected; enhance the coordination of Federal and State law enforcement when dealing with illegal immigrants; and hire 5,000 new border patrol agents.[147] This executive order was a significant shift from Obama's immigration enforcement policy.

Despite Trump's executive order, Hector Garza, the vice president of the National Border Patrol Council, appeared on Fox News in April 2018 to report that "Obama holdovers within the agency are implementing those same policies that were in effect under the Obama administration." According to Garza, "Catch and release is alive and well."[148] A few days later, Trump signed a memorandum ordering federal agencies to end "catch and release" and requested regular updates on their progress from the Departments of State, Defense, Homeland Security, and Health and Human Services.

The memo also directed a crackdown on abuse of the asylum system. And there is clear evidence that illegal immigrants took advantage of the system under Obama. On his watch, the percentage of migrants claiming asylum jumped from 1 percent to over 10 percent. "Smugglers themselves are gaming the system, pure and simple. They take advantage of the loopholes in our laws," said Trump's Homeland Security Secretary Kirstjen Nielsen. "They know that we cannot prosecute as we need to to stop their behavior."[149]

The most well-known aspect of Trump's border security policy is his plan to build a wall at the border, and his executive order called for the southern border of the United States to be secured "through the immediate construction of a physical wall on the southern border, monitored and supported by adequate personnel so as to prevent illegal immigration, drug and human trafficking, and acts of terrorism."[150] In October 2017, eight border wall prototypes were unveiled.[151] Military special forces tested the prototypes over a three-week period to identify the strengths and weaknesses of each design.[152] Construction of the border wall began in September 2018 in El Paso, Texas.[153] For the first time in decades, a presidential administration is physically marking our borders, a fact that should make future immigration policy disputes less difficult. As many conservatives have said, secure the border first, improve legal immigration second.

Reversing the Downward Trend in Deportations

Trump's next executive order addressing illegal immigration, called "Enhancing Public Safety in the Interior of the United States," ramped up enforcement of immigration laws nationwide, by directing the hiring of 10,000 new immigration officers; cutting off funding to sanctuary cities from the Homeland Security and Justice Departments; expediting deportations of illegal immigrants, prioritizing those who have committed crimes; supporting victims of crimes committed by illegal aliens; reviewing existing immigration policies; and other actions.[154]

In testimony before the House Judiciary Committee on March 27, 2017, Jessica Vaughan explained that under Obama, "ICE's deportation caseload shifted from mostly aliens who were arrested in the interior to mostly aliens who were arrested by the Border Patrol and turned over to ICE for deportation." According to Vaughan, this change in caseload "enabled the Obama administration to claim 'record' deportations while simultaneously masking the steep decline in interior enforcement."[155]

According to the CATO Institute, a libertarian think tank hostile to border enforcement, deportations from the interior of the United States declined every year of the Obama administration, with a significant downward trend "beginning in 2011 and continuing through the end of fiscal year 2016." From 2009 to 2016, interior deportations dropped over 70 percent. Things changed when Trump took office. Interior immigration enforcement during Trump's first year in office showed "a reversal of the declining interior immigration enforcement efforts under the Obama administration" with 81,603 illegal immigrants being deported from the interior of the United States, up from 65,332 in 2016.

Despite the reversal, the Trump administration hasn't "reached peak enforcement performance yet." There is a worsening backlog of immigration court cases pending review, implying that many more are on the road to deportation than currently indicated in the data. This backlog is closely related to a surge in arrests related to immigration issues in 2017. ICE also revived the Secure Communities protocols under Trump, which enables the Department of Homeland Security and the FBI to share data and resources with the goal of catching and arresting more illegal aliens within the interior of the United States. All these factors suggest a continued rise in deportations in the coming years.[156]

Reduction of Refugees

Back in 2015, House Homeland Security Committee Chairman Rep. Michael McCaul (R-TX) warned that the United States lacked the ability to vet Syrian refugees fully and that he believed ISIS would "exploit the refugee crisis to infiltrate the west."[157] James Clapper, Obama's Director of National Intelligence, also called the terrorist infiltration of refugee flows "a huge concern of ours."[158] In April 2016, officials at the European Border and Coast Guard Agency admitted that ISIS was doing exactly that to infiltrate Europe.[159] Obama's CIA director John Brennan also told Congress, in June 2016, that ISIS was likely trying to smuggle fighters into the United States among refugees.[160] Despite the undeniable risks and the repeated warnings, Obama announced he would increase the number of refugees the United States would admit in fiscal year 2017 to 110,000 in September 2016. This number reflected his desire to admit *more* Syrian refugees.[161]

Obama may not have been concerned about the risks, but President Trump was. He signed an executive order freezing immigration from seven countries that are terrorism hotspots and suspending acceptance of refugees from those countries pending a ninety-day review of screening procedures. His order also capped the number of refugees that the United States would accept at 50,000, slashing Obama's goal by more than half.[162] He would later lower his refugee cap to 45,000 for FY2018, the lowest cap since the passage of the Refugee Act in 1980.[163]

In December 2017, the Trump administration pulled out of the United Nations Global Compact for Migration. Obama and various other world leaders adopted the compact in September 2016 to address the refugee crisis and coordinate a global solution to manage the problem. The US mission to the United Nations said many provisions in the declaration were "inconsistent with U.S. immigration policy and the Trump Administration's immigration principles."[164] According to a statement by then-Secretary of State Rex Tillerson, the compact undermined "the sovereign right of the United States to enforce our immigration laws and secure our borders."[165]

During his campaign, Trump promised to restrict immigration from "dangerous countries" plagued by radical Islamic terrorism. "We want to make sure we're only admitting those into our country who support our values and love—and I mean love—our people," Trump said at a campaign rally in Toledo, Ohio on September 21, 2016.[166] He did what he promised to do, but activist judges tried to stop him. Liberal activists challenged Trump's travel ban and succeeded in getting it blocked in federal court. He followed up with two more versions of the travel ban. Both of them also got blocked by federal judges. However, the Supreme Court allowed the travel ban to take effect in December 2017, before ultimately ruling the ban was constitutional in June 2018.[167] Despite the ban being in limbo for seventeen months, the number of refugees admitted into the United States in his first year of office came in at roughly 30,000, the lowest since 2002. Chief Justice John G. Roberts Jr. wrote that the travel ban "is expressly premised on legitimate purposes: preventing entry of nationals who cannot be adequately vetted and inducing other nations to improve their practices."[168]

Deny the threat of terrorists gaining access into the United States, as Obama has, and you deny a mountain of evidence to the contrary. For example, in August 2018, an Iraqi refugee with ties to Al-Qaeda and ISIS was arrested in California; he was wanted in his home country for an ISIS-connected slaying of a police officer. The terrorist, Omar Ameen, came to the United States in 2014 as a refugee. According to court documents:

> *Ameen concealed his true identity as a member of (Al-Qaeda in Iraq) and ISIS to immigrate to the United States. He lied about his background and the circumstances of his departure from Iraq in order to evade detection, seeking to blend into the flow of legitimate refugees fleeing the conflict zone.*[169]

Despite the reduction in refugees, the United States still resettles more refugees than any other country.[170] We haven't abandoned those seeking freedom around the world whose best hope of a better life lies within our borders. We're simply taking a commonsense approach to protecting American citizens from enemies we *know* want to abuse the refugee crisis to penetrate our borders and wage war on American soil.

Ending DACA

Barack Obama routinely acknowledged the constitutional limitations on his power to alter immigration law unilaterally during his early years in office. In March 2011, he told Univision, "With respect to the notion that I can just suspend deportations through executive order, that's just not the case." During a July 2011 speech to La Raza, Obama said, "I know some people want me to bypass Congress and change the laws on my own. [...] That's not how our system works. That's not how our democracy functions. That's not how our Constitution is written." During a September 2011 Hispanic Roundtable at the White House, Obama said, "I just have to continue to say this notion that somehow I can just change the laws unilaterally is just not true."[171]

When the DREAM failed to gain traction in the Senate, Obama forgot about what the Constitution said he couldn't do. On June 15, 2012, Obama announced the Deferred Action for Childhood Arrivals (DACA) program. The program, created without the consent of Congress via executive action, granted a temporary amnesty to over a million illegal immigrants who came into the United States as children—echoing the goals of the DREAM Act. Those eligible under DACA, colloquially called "Dreamers" by Democrats, gained temporary immunity from deportation and could get work permits for a two-year period. After the two-year period, they could apply for a renewal.[172] At the time of Obama's executive action, the Pew Research Center estimated over 1.7 million illegal immigrants might benefit from DACA.[173]

In September 2017, the Trump administration formally announced they would stop processing new applications for the DACA program. "I am here today to announce that the program known as DACA that was effectuated under the Obama administration is being rescinded," explained Jeff Sessions. DACA protected over 800,000 illegal immigrants during its first five years.[174] President Trump said in a statement, "The temporary implementation of DACA by the Obama Administration, after Congress repeatedly rejected this amnesty-first approach, also helped spur a humanitarian crisis – the massive surge of unaccompanied minors from Central America including, in some cases, young people who would become members of violent gangs throughout our country, such as MS-13."[175] Despite ending DACA, Trump called on Congress to "advance responsible immigration reform that puts American jobs and American security first."[176] Immediately, advocates of illegal immigration went to the courts to save DACA. A group of sixteen state attorneys general, all Democrats, sued in Federal District Court in Brooklyn.[177] On January 9, 2018, US District Judge William Alsup, a Clinton appointee, temporarily blocked Trump's ending of DACA while a lawsuit was still pending.[178]

Trump reiterated his call for Congress to act in his 2018 State of the Union address. "I am extending an open hand to work with members of both parties—Democrats and Republicans—to protect our citizens of every background, color, religion, and creed. My duty, and the sacred duty of every elected official in this chamber, is to defend Americans—to protect their safety, their families, their communities, and their right to the American Dream," he said. "Because Americans are dreamers too."[179]

On February 13, 2018, US District Judge Nicholas Garaufis, another Clinton appointee, issued an injunction to order the Trump administration to keep DACA. The Justice Department vowed to keep fighting to end DACA, which Justice Department spokesman Devin O'Malley described as "an unlawful circumvention of Congress."[180]

In April 2018, another federal judge in the District of Columbia ruled that the Trump administration should not only restore DACA but also accept new applications. The decision was stayed for ninety days, but in August the judge upheld the order, alleging that the Trump administration failed to justify eliminating it.[181] On August 31, 2018, a federal judge in Texas declared that DACA is likely unconstitutional, but did not issue an injunction because Texas and nine other states waited too long to bring their case to the courts. "If the nation truly wants a DACA program, it is up to Congress to say so," wrote Federal District Judge Andrew Hanen in his decision.[182] With the various court cases and contradictory rulings, it is likely that the Supreme Court will ultimately decide the fate of DACA.

Ending DAPA

Two years after creating DACA via executive action, Obama took another stab at executive amnesty, creating a new program called Deferred Action for Parents of Americans and Lawful Permanent Residents (DAPA). This new program aimed to protect more than 4 million illegal immigrants not previously covered by DACA from deportation, deeming them "lawfully present" in the United States, by virtue of his exercise of prosecutorial discretion.[183]

Twenty-six states sued the Obama administration over the program. "DAPA would deem over four million unlawfully present aliens as 'lawfully present' and eligible for work authorization," explained the attorney general and solicitor general of Texas. "And 'lawful presence' is an immigration classification established by Congress that is necessary for valuable benefits, such as Medicare and Social Security."[184] DAPA was blocked in federal court in 2015 before it took effect.[185] That block was left in place by a split decision by the US Supreme Court in June 2016. The order was rescinded by the Trump Administration on June 15, 2017.[186] The same logic underpinning DAPA has also been used by advocates for relaxed immigration laws to justify chain migration—the process by which a single successful immigration lottery winner can bring many other family members with them to reside legally in the United States. As was the case with DAPA, Trump opposes this line of thinking and has vowed to end chain migration. We can only hope he succeeds.

Reversing Obama's Policy Allowing
Abortions for Illegal Immigrant Minors

The Trump administration reversed another Obama-era policy by refusing to allow pregnant illegal immigrant minors access to abortions while in federal custody. According to documents obtained by *Politico* in October 2017, the Health and Human Services Department "has instead forced minors to visit crisis pregnancy centers, religiously affiliated groups that counsel women against having abortions." Under the Obama administration, when an illegal immigrant minor requested federal funding for an abortion, those requests were reviewed. The ACLU sued the Trump administration on behalf of an unaccompanied illegal immigrant minor in federal custody. Despite the seventeen-year-old "Jane Doe" receiving permission from a judge to have the abortion, even without parental consent, HHS officials at the Office of Refugee Resettlement "refused to transport her to her abortion appointment, instead taking her to a crisis pregnancy center, and calling her mother in her home country to tell her about the pregnancy."[187] HHS officials argued that they were within their rights to prevent unaccompanied illegal immigrant minors in their custody from getting abortions. "There is no constitutional right for a pregnant minor to illegally cross the U.S. border and get an elective abortion while in federal custody," they said in a statement. "Federal law is very clear on giving the director of the Office of Refugee Resettlement the legal responsibility to decide what is in the best interests of a minor in the unaccompanied alien children program and, in this case, her unborn baby. We cannot cede our responsibility to care for minors and their babies by releasing them to ideological advocacy groups."[188]

In March 2017, an Obama-appointed federal district judge ordered the federal government to not block illegal immigrant teens from receiving abortions. The ACLU cheered the move. "With today's rulings, we are one step closer to ending this extreme policy once and for all and securing justice for all of these young women," said Brigitte Amiri, deputy director of the ACLU Reproductive Freedom Project.[189] Their celebration would be short-lived. On June

4, 2018, the Supreme Court struck down the lower court ruling on the grounds that the dispute was moot since the girl had an abortion before the case reached the high court, thus eliminating the precedent established by the lower court. As of this writing, litigation continues in the lower courts, and the Trump administration promised to continue fighting for their position. "The Supreme Court has repeatedly made clear that the federal government is not required to facilitate abortions for minors and may choose policies favoring life over abortion," said Justice Department spokeswoman Kerri Kupec. "We look forward to continuing to press the government's interest in the sanctity of life."[190]

CHAPTER 4

MILITARY AND FOREIGN POLICY

Where do I begin when dissecting Barack Obama's terrible record on foreign policy? There just aren't enough bad things that can be said about it. In 2009, Obama went on what conservatives called the "Global Apology Tour." He spent his days abroad telling the leaders of other nations throughout the world that he would govern America's foreign policy differently; we would no longer be the world's police. Obama renounced America's claim to moral authority on the world stage and signaled his weakness to every tin pot dictator. And these weren't idle words; Obama didn't see America as a beacon of hope for the world. He took the postmodern position that America was an immoral country and not an exceptional one.

Obama praised the Castro regime in Cuba, saying that America could learn from their record health care, education, and human rights.[191] He even praised Fidel Castro in a statement following the brutal dictator's death.[192] Only in Obama's bizarre worldview could America have anything good to learn from Cuba.

Without a coherent vision of America as a leading nation defending human rights and democracy around the world, Obama spent eight years insulting world leaders, alienating our allies, kowtowing to our enemies, and weakening our military, and the rest of the world took notice. He reluctantly killed Osama bin Laden, but Al-Qaeda grew massively as he took his victory lap. The vacuum created by his premature withdrawal from Iraq caused the rise of ISIS, whom he treated as such a non-entity that he referred to them as, "the JV team."[193] When he did try to project strength in his responses to threats to America and its allies, he didn't follow through, emboldening America's enemies.[194]

But all that changed when Trump took office.

Pulling Out of the Trans-Pacific Partnership

The Trans-Pacific Partnership (TPP) is an interesting case. The trade agreement among the United States and Australia, Brunei, Canada, Chile, Japan, Malaysia, Mexico, New Zealand, Peru, Singapore, and Vietnam was signed on February 4, 2016. Obama never sought ratification for the treaty as required by the Constitution. The issue of TPP divided both the Republican and Democratic parties. Donald Trump opposed it. Mike Pence supported it. Barack Obama obviously supported it, but Hillary Clinton, despite helping negotiate TPP as Obama's Secretary of State, opposed it, while her running mate Tim Kaine supported it.[195] It's anyone's guess whether Hillary would have pulled out of it had she won the election. But President Trump, following through on his campaign promise, signed an executive order three days after his inauguration formally withdrawing the United States from the Trans-Pacific Partnership.[196]

The reason Trump could do this was the lack of involvement of the Senate in the ratification of TPP. That alone was enough reason to pull out. While many on the right support freer trade, TPP was not a model of transparent free trade. The negotiations were held in secret, and the resulting document was a regulatory behemoth. "Rather than a simple agreement to lower tariffs for mutual benefit, it morphed into a massive international regulatory regime over 5,000 pages long," explained Iain Murray, of the Competitive Enterprise Institute.[197]

"There are aspects of the released text that suggest very strongly that the benefits of approving TPP as is are not worth the costs," wrote Kevin Williamson in *National Review* in 2015. Williamson pointed out a major issue is the incorporation of the then-yet-to-be-completed Paris Climate Treaty. "It is one thing for a trade deal to incorporate changes to environmental practices—regulatory differences are an inhibitor of truly liberal trade—but there is a world of difference between incorporating specific environmental policies and incorporating environmental policies to be named later,"[198] especially another treaty Obama knew he'd sign without Senate approval.

Williamson argued, at the time, that smaller bilateral free trade agreements were a preferable approach. Trump agreed and said—despite his withdrawal from TPP—if a better deal was offered, he would consider it. "I don't want to go back into TPP, but if they offered us a deal I can't refuse, on behalf of the United States, I would do it. But I like bilateral better. I think it's better for our country, I think it's better for our workers and I much would prefer a bilateral deal."[199] On that front, Trump has undoubtedly succeeded. As of this writing, he's already renegotiated NAFTA into the new USMCA with Canada and Mexico, and achieved new trade deals with South Korea, Japan, and the European Union.

Cutting UN Funding

The election of Donald Trump signaled a major shift in policy towards the United Nations. Barack Obama embraced the United Nations and showered it with American tax dollars while, on the campaign trail, Donald Trump was a fierce critic. "The United Nations is not a friend of democracy. It's not a friend to freedom," Trump said while speaking at the American Israel Public Affairs Committee (AIPAC) conference in March 2016. "It's not a friend even to the United States of America, where as all know, it has its home. And it surely isn't a friend to Israel."[200] Even after he won the 2016 election, he dismissed the UN as "just a club for people to get together, talk and have a good time."[201]

Donald Trump criticized the UN for its ineffectualness despite its lavish funding—funding that disproportionately came from the American taxpayers. "The United States is one out of 193 countries in the United Nations, and yet we pay 22 percent of the entire budget and more. In fact, we pay far more than anybody realizes," he said when addressing the United Nations General Assembly for the first time on September 19, 2017. "The United States bears an unfair cost burden, but, to be fair, if it could actually accomplish all of its stated goals, especially the goal of peace, this investment would easily be well worth it."[202] According to analysis from Brett Schaefer of the Heritage Foundation, "The U.N. system for calculating member nations' 'fair share' payment toward its regular and peacekeeping budgets has increasingly shifted the burden away from the vast majority of the 193 members and onto a relative handful of high-income nations, especially the U.S." Some nations pay next to nothing. In 2015, the United States was assessed "more than 176 other member states *combined* for the regular budget and more than 185 countries combined for the peacekeeping budget."[203]

In his last year in office, Obama's administration gave the United Nations and its various suborganizations at least $9.2 billion. Fox News reported that total is based on a State Department document that "summarizes U.S. government spending for international organizations, and is about 20 per cent higher than the $7.7 billion figure given out by State for 2010, before the Obama Administration abruptly quit providing any overall tally for its U.N. support."[204] In his last days in office, Obama "ran through over $700 million in a spending binge designed to fund U.N.-related priorities that lacked support in the Republican-controlled Congress" and, of course, the incoming Trump administration. This included $500 million to the United Nations Green Climate Fund; $221 million to the Palestinian Authority; and extra peacekeeping funds that weren't approved by Congress.[205]

President Trump was not so "generous" with your tax dollars. In December 2017, Trump's UN Ambassador Nikki Haley announced a

$285 million cut to the UN operating budget. "The inefficiency and overspending of the United Nations are well known. We will no longer let the generosity of the American people be taken advantage of or remain unchecked," Haley said. "This historic reduction in spending – in addition to many other moves toward a more efficient and accountable U.N. – is a big step in the right direction."[206] The announcement came just days after the UN voted to condemn the United States for moving its Israeli embassy to Jerusalem.

Reversing Obama's Cuba Policy

The Castro regime in Cuba is a brutal, oppressive dictatorship, guilty of human rights abuses and the mass murder of its political opponents. But it's a socialist country, so many on the political left in America harbor fantasies that Cuba is misunderstood and achieves far more for social justice than America with its evil capitalism. Obama proved he believed in this Utopian delusion by announcing, in December 2014, that he was opening up diplomatic relations with Cuba and establishing a new embassy in Havana.[207] This followed eighteen months of secret talks that resulted in a prisoner swap of an American government contractor held prisoner in Cuba for three convicted Cuban criminals.

His announcement was met with bipartisan condemnation. Senator Bob Menendez, then-chairman of the Senate Foreign Relations Committee, said Obama's actions "vindicated the brutal behavior of the Cuban government." Menendez, who was born to Cuban immigrants, added that the prisoner swap set "an extremely dangerous" precedent. "It invites dictatorial and rogue regimes to use Americans serving overseas as bargaining chips." Senator Marco Rubio, also the son of Cuban immigrants, called Obama's plan to open diplomatic relations disgraceful. "The White House has conceded everything," and called Obama the "worst negotiator" to occupy the White House.[208] In restoring diplomatic relations with Cuba, the Castro regime, and not the oppressed Cuban people, stood to benefit.

Yet Obama pushed on. In May 2015, Obama took Cuba off the State Department's list of State Sponsors of Terrorism—despite three decades of Cuba's direct support to terrorist organizations, including the Revolutionary Armed Forces of Colombia (FARC). This action allowed Cuba to receive foreign aid and conduct trade with the US and its allies. Worse yet, Obama's unilateral action was actually in violation of U.S.C. 50 section 2405(j)(4)(A), which establishes the conditions under which a country can be removed from the list. Cuba did not meet those requirements, according to Ana Quintana, a senior policy analyst at the Heritage Foundation.[209] While Obama couldn't unilaterally lift the Cuban trade embargo—Congress was very much opposed to it—he was able to ease sanctions and allow more travel and commerce with Cuba.

As a presidential candidate, Donald Trump criticized Obama's attempts to normalize relations with Cuba, calling it a very weak agreement. "We get nothing. The people of Cuba get nothing, and I would do whatever is necessary to get a good agreement."[210] He acted quickly after the election, and in June 2017, President Trump announced he was reversing Obama's "one-sided deal" with Cuba. "We will very strongly restrict American dollars and intelligence services that are the core of the Castro regime. They will be restricted. We will enforce the ban on tourism. We will enforce the embargo. We will take concrete steps to ensure that investments flow directly to the people so they can open private businesses and begin to build their country's great, great future, a country of great potential," Trump said in a speech in Miami. "The previous administration's easing of restrictions on travel and trade does not help the Cuban people. They only enrich the Cuban regime." Trump added, "The outcome of last administration's executive action has been only more repression and a move to crush the peaceful democratic movement."[211]

The US Embassy in Havana remains open, but it's now occupied by a skeleton crew following the unexplained "health attacks" of two dozen State Department employees working in the embassy in 2017. Those stationed at the embassy experienced hearing loss, brain damage, and other health issues. In response to the Cuban government's failure to protect American diplomats in the embassy, fifteen Cuban diplomats (about two-thirds of the diplomatic delegation) were also expelled back to Cuba. "Cuba is not upholding its commitments of the Vienna convention, of protecting diplomats," said a source close to the State department.[212] The Cuban government was not formally accused of perpetrating the attack, but the Trump administration clearly believes they were involved.

As a result of the attack, the Trump administration also banned US citizens from doing business with various entities linked to Cuba's military, intelligence, and security agencies with the goal of spurring economic activity amongst private entities. "We have strengthened our Cuba policies to channel economic activity away from the Cuban military and to encourage the government to move toward greater political and economic freedom for the Cuban people," said Treasury Secretary Steven Mnuchin.[213] The United States also renewed its defense of the Cuban trade embargo at the UN, which annually votes to condemn the embargo. In 2016, the United States abstained for the first time, but under Trump the United States voted "no." "The Trump administration policy gives greater emphasis to advancing human rights and democracy in Cuba, while maintaining engagement that advances U.S. interests," said State Department spokeswoman Heather Nauert.[214]

Pulling Out of the Iran Deal

Obama believed the security of the Middle East was best shepherded by Iran, as hard as that is to believe. From the beginning of his presidency, he made every attempt to appease the Mullahs. When Iranian students protested following Iran's June 2009 sham elections, igniting the short-lived "Green Revolution," Obama wouldn't say that the election was stolen nor lend his support to the people fighting for their freedom. Although Obama supported similar uprisings in Egypt and the Ukraine, he ordered the CIA to stand down and offer the protesters no aid. As Eli Lake, writing for *Bloomberg,* explained, "Obama from the beginning of his presidency tried to turn the country's ruling clerics from foes to friends. It was an obsession."

Obama personally assured Ayatollah Ali Khamenei that the United States wasn't trying to overthrow him and halted programs documenting Iranian human rights abuses. Iran's ally in Syria, Bashar al-Assad, ran afoul of international law by using chemical weapons on innocent Syrian citizens in 2013 and Obama stood by and did nothing. Iran itself repeatedly engaged in blatant acts of aggression against the United States including: sending warships to patrol along US maritime borders, capturing a US stealth drone in 2011 (which they refused to return), and attacking another American drone in 2012. Obama had no answer.

Why? Obama dreamed of a nuclear deal with Iran—one that would at least appear to curb Iran's nuclear weapons ambitions and justify his Nobel Peace Prize awarded for talking a big game about nuclear disarmament. Supporting freedom fighters in Iran, intervening in Syria against Bashar al-Assad, responding to Iran's aggressive posture, or documenting Iran's grotesque human rights abuses would have ended their nuclear negotiations.[215] To save his precious Iran Nuclear Deal, Obama not only turned his back on the people of Iran who craved democracy—he demonstrated incredible weakness and damaged the credibility of the United States.

Obama did get his nuclear deal with Iran. Called the Joint Comprehensive Plan of Action (JCPOA), the deal essentially guaranteed a path for nuclearization for Iran. Sanctions were lifted, their nuclear sites remained open, and research and development continued. American concessions were many, but Iranian concessions were virtually nonexistent.[216] Despite the agreement, Iran's aggression toward the United States continued, all with Obama's tacit approval. The Iranian military repeatedly harassed US Navy ships and even captured ten US Navy sailors after mechanical problems caused them to drift into Iranian waters in January 2016. The Iranians publicly humiliated members of our armed forces and Obama's Secretary of State John Kerry *thanked* Iran for releasing them. The Iranian Republican Guard Corps even claimed the United States formally apologized for the incident.[217]

And let's not forget the infamous $400 million ransom payment Obama made later that year to procure the release of five American hostages, breaking America's commitment to never negotiate with hostage-takers. The Obama administration claimed the money, paid to Iran in foreign currency, was unrelated to the release of the hostages. But the payment came on the very same night the hostages, including a *Washington Post* reporter, were released. The State Department eventually conceded that the $400 million cash payment was held until the prisoners were airborne.[218]

Iran also repeatedly violated the terms of the nuclear deal and UN resolutions. Within four months of the start date, Iran had already test-fired long-range ballistic missiles three separate times, in violation of the terms of the deal, and the White House did nothing. "We're still trying to get to the bottom of what exactly transpired," administration officials claimed. Obama was not willing to concede that Iran was violating the deal, claiming, "Iran so far has followed the letter of the agreement." The best he could do to admit to his failure was to criticize Iranian leaders for undermining the "spirit" of the deal.[219] The State Department even dismissed Iranian chants of "Death to America" as heated political rhetoric.[220]

Donald Trump was not so naïve about Iran. On the campaign trail, he blasted Obama over the nuclear deal, "Never, ever, ever in my life have I seen any transaction so incompetently negotiated as our deal with Iran. And I mean never," he said at an anti-Iran Deal rally on the Capitol lawn in September 2015. "We are led by very, very stupid people."[221] When Iran was caught violating the agreement, Trump viciously mocked Obama. "I hear Obama is very unhappy with Iran because he feels they haven't lived up to the 'spirit' of the agreement. What the hell did he think was going to happen? He is like a baby. He's like a baby," he said at a campaign rally in Eau Claire, Wisconsin. "They defaulted on day one. How we have this man as a president is so embarrassing. Anybody in their right mind would have known what he is getting into."[222] Trump was also highly critical of the ransom payment. Obama "put every American traveling overseas, including our military personnel, at greater risk of being kidnapped," Trump said. "He denied it was for the hostages, but it was. He said we don't pay ransom, but he did. He lied about the hostages—openly and blatantly."[223]

With Trump in charge, the deal was in jeopardy, since presidents can't unilaterally enter into international treaties and Obama never got Senate approval (or even tried to get it). He didn't immediately withdraw from the deal, but he took a much tougher stance against the world's number one state sponsor of terrorism. He imposed new sanctions against Iran following another missile test in February 2017,[224] and piled on again five months later.[225] Both times, he certified Iran was in compliance with the nuclear deal but, in October 2017, Trump refused to certify Iran's compliance. He pressured Congress to step in with even tougher sanctions and to strengthen the deal.[226] With no progress in Congress, in May 2018, Trump withdrew from the Iran nuclear deal, and started reinstating sanctions. "At the heart of the Iran deal was a giant fiction that a murderous regime desired only a peaceful nuclear energy program," Trump said. "The fact is this was a horrible, one-sided deal that should have never, ever been made. It didn't bring calm, it didn't bring peace, and it never will." He also noted that, since the conclusion of negotiations, Iran's military budget grew by 40 percent, but their economy didn't improve. "After the sanctions were lifted, the dictatorship used its new funds to build nuclear-capable missiles, support terrorism, and cause havoc throughout the Middle East and beyond."[227] By November 2018, all sanctions lifted by the Iran Deal were reinstated.[228]

Trump added, "America will not be held hostage to nuclear blackmail. We will not allow American cities to be threatened with destruction. And we will not allow a regime that chants 'Death to America' to gain access to the most deadly weapons on Earth." That his predecessor was willing to send billions to the Iranian regime without assurances that their nuclear ambitions were at an end is baffling. He made a bad situation worse. President Trump had a message for "the long-suffering people of Iran" who didn't benefit one bit from the huge influx of money Obama gave to Iran's leaders: "The people of America stand with you." He also signaled willingness to negotiate a new deal. "They are going to want to make a new and lasting deal, one that benefits all of Iran and the Iranian people. When they do, I am ready, willing, and able."[229]

Ending Obama's Military Micromanagement

Barack Obama has a rare distinction amongst US presidents: three of his former Defense Secretaries came out as critics of his military strategies and foreign policy.

The *Washington Times* reported in January 2016:

> *In his memoir, Robert Gates wrote that Mr. Obama did not always live up to budget agreements with him and suspected the top brass of conspiracies against the commander in chief. Mr. Obama once retorted to the command by saying "that's an order"—a pronouncement that "shocked" Mr. Gates as unprecedented.*
>
> *"That order was unnecessary and insulting, proof positive of the depth of the Obama White House's distrust of the nation's military leadership," he wrote.*
>
> *Mr. Gates' successor, Leon Panetta, wrote that the president "misses opportunities" to act, such as in the Syrian civil war. He roundly criticized Mr. Obama's swap of five hardened Taliban leaders for one Army soldier, Sgt. Bowe Bergdahl.*
>
> *Now comes Mr. Panetta's successor, former Republican Sen. Chuck Hagel, who did not wait for his memoir after the president pushed him aside. [...] Mr. Hagel was particularly critical of Mr. Obama's decision to draw a "red line" that Bashar Assad should not cross. But once the Syrian president breached the line by unleashing chemical weapons, Mr. Obama ordered a stand-down of forces set to bomb military targets in exchange for Mr. Assad giving up that arsenal.*

"There's no question in my mind that it hurt the credibility of the president's word when this occurred," Mr. Hagel told the Foreign Policy website. *"A president's word is a big thing, and when the president says things, that's a big deal."*[230]

According to Hagel, Obama "permitted a process in which White House staffers went around the chain of command and telephoned four-star combatant commanders to make policy, while micromanaging day-to-day operations at the Pentagon."[231]

"I think three [defense secretaries] in a row should give the president pause and good reason to re-evaluate the administration's decision-making processes in detail," said Retired Army Lt. Gen. James Dubik, a scholar at the Institute for the Study of War and a professor in national security at Georgetown University. "In effect, what they are saying is that the current decision-making methodologies being used to wage our wars are neither sufficiently effective nor efficient. These are three experienced leaders, and their critique should be taken seriously. No process will be perfect, and none will satisfy everyone. But when three [defense secretaries] identify problems, I'd say that's a 'trend' worth acting upon."[232]

Hagel was also chastised by the White House for trying to label ISIS a new kind of powerful terrorist army—a clear indication that Obama didn't take the ISIS threat seriously. Hagel said he was accused of "trying to hype something, overstate something and make something more than it was." Bob Gates had similar concerns, which he expressed in his memoir. "The controlling nature of the Obama White House and the staff took micromanagement and operational meddling to a new level."[233] Gates and Panetta had previously criticized Obama's micromanagement of the military. "It was micromanagement that drove me crazy," Gates said at the Reagan National Defense Forum. He described a situation where White House staffers routinely called four-star generals on matters of strategy and tactics and attempted to contact the Joint Special Operations Command (JSOC). According to Gates, the micromanagement was purely political. "I think when a

President wants highly centralized control at the White House, that's not bureaucratic, that's political," he said. Panetta had similar criticisms, and rebuked Obama's decision to rule out the use of ground troops to combat ISIS. "Never tell your enemy what the hell you're going to do," Panetta said.[234]

President Trump quickly reversed Obama's politicized military micromanagement, "shifting more authority over military operations to the Pentagon," according to White House officials.

The New York Times reported on this shift two months into Trump's presidency:

> *The change is at the heart of a re-engineering of the [White House] National Security Council's role under its new leader, Lt. Gen. H. R. McMaster, and reflects Mr. Trump's belief that the N.S.C. should focus less on military operations and tactics and more on strategic issues. A guiding precept for the president and his team is that the balance of power in the world has shifted against American interests, and that General McMaster should focus on developing foreign and economic policy options in concert with the Pentagon, State Department and other agencies to respond to that challenge.*[235]

As a result, the military has taken a more aggressive approach to dealing with threats. Within a few short months, Trump approved troop surges in Iraq and Syria, and "stepped up" raids against ISIS.[236] Trump "appears to be going back to a model of greater delegation of authority," said Michèle A. Flournoy, the Pentagon's top policy official under Barack Obama. "The benefit is that it allows the military campaign to go forward without undue pauses, interruptions or delays. That enables it to create more momentum and to be more responsive to changes on the battlefield."[237]

Keeping the Guantánamo Bay Terrorist Prison Open

Obama promised to close the Guantánamo Bay detention camp during his first presidential campaign. In 2007, he declared, "As President, I will close Guantánamo," calling it a "sad chapter in American history." Two days after his inauguration, he signed an executive order to close the prison within a year.[238] That didn't happen, of course, due to strong bipartisan opposition in Congress. Obama had no plan for released detainees, and attempts to relocate prisoners to domestic prisons were rejected.[239] Without assurances that homeland security would be maintained after the transfer, Congress refused to fund any move of terrorists from Guantánamo Bay to the United States.

Obama worked around Congress by freeing Gitmo detainees or transferring them to foreign countries. Upon his departure as Secretary of Defense, Chuck Hagel told CNN that he was pressured by the White House to increase the pace of releasing detainees.[240] Obama was so determined to close Guantánamo that his administration lied about how many former detainees returned to terrorism after being let go. In 2016, he claimed the terrorists' recidivism rate was only 5 percent,[241] but retired CIA officer Gary Berntsen called such low numbers absurd. "Many of these people that we captured would tell us right to our faces: We're going to be released and kill you and your families when we get out," Berntsen said. "That's their attitude. Because they don't believe the United States is going to act harshly against them. They see the light at the end of the tunnel, they want to continue the fight against us. And the administration's release of these guys is insane."[242] According to the government's official count of Guantánamo recidivism, nearly a third of former detainees returned to the fight against the United States. Obama's claims that jihadists use Guantánamo as a recruiting tool have also been debunked by national security experts.[243]

For pushing so rashly to close Guantánamo, Obama has the blood of Americans on his hands. For example, former Guantánamo detainees were involved in the 2012 attack on the US consulate in Benghazi, which resulted in the deaths of four Americans, including US Ambassador Chris Stevens.[244] During a House Foreign Affairs Committee hearing in March 2016, Defense Department special envoy for Guantánamo closure Paul Lewis said, "unfortunately, there have been Americans that have died because of Gitmo detainees." He nevertheless defended Obama's policy when pressed, stating, "We don't want anyone to die because we transfer detainees. However, it is the best judgment and the considered judgment of this administration and the previous that the risk of keeping Gitmo open is outweighed, that we should close Gitmo."[245]

Despite the obvious national security concerns and resistance from Congress, the population of Guantánamo went from 242 when Obama took office to forty-one when he left. Nineteen inmates were transferred between Election Day 2016 and Inauguration Day 2017 alone.[246] While Obama officially abandoned plans to close the prison, he hoped to reduce the number of inmates to a level so low that it was impractical to keep it open.

Trump had other ideas. In January 2018, he signed an executive order to keep Guantánamo open and commission a review of the detention policy. "In the past, we have foolishly released hundreds of dangerous terrorists, only to meet them again on the battlefield – including the Isis leader, al-Baghdadi," Trump said. "Terrorists who do things like place bombs in civilian hospitals are evil. When possible, we have no choice but to annihilate them. When necessary, we must be able to detain and question them. But we must be clear: terrorists are not merely criminals. They are unlawful enemy combatants. And, when captured overseas, they should be treated like the terrorists they are."

Reversing Obama's Afghanistan Withdrawal

An eternity back in my faded memory, Barack Obama won the Nobel Peace Prize for absolutely no reason. He ended up being the first president to serve two full terms at war. He was a fierce critic of the War in Iraq, but his hasty withdrawal led to the rise of ISIS. Cities previously liberated by former President George W. Bush fell back into the hands of terrorists within a year of Obama's reelection, and ISIS reigned bloody death on the whole world.[247] I've covered all of that.

But Afghanistan was different. Obama was committed to fighting that war and, upon taking office, he increased troop levels to their highest ever—nearly triple the highest boot count under George W. Bush.[248] But victory was never his ultimate goal. Obama's first Secretary of Defense Bob Gates wrote in his memoir that Obama "doesn't trust his commander, can't stand Karzai, doesn't believe in his own strategy and doesn't consider the war to be his. For him, it's all about getting out."[249] Obama's failure to properly manage the war had disastrous results. New and restrictive rules of engagement led to dramatic increases in fatalities.[250] In 2011, he began a rapid reduction in troop levels and things got much worse. "Afghanistan today is much more violent than when Obama came into office," wrote Elise Jordan, former director for communications in the National Security Council, in *The Daily Beast* in 2014. "Fewer Americans may be dying. But many more Afghan civilians are being killed, according to UN statistics. More guns, more warlords, more militias—that's Obama's probable legacy. It's what happens when you can't deal with reality and commit one way or the other in wartime—you lose."[251] What Obama had called "the right war" became his Vietnam.

Despite the declining conditions in Afghanistan, Obama pressed on with withdrawal. Obama's goal was likely a full withdrawal from Afghanistan by the time he left office, but military leaders advised him not to repeat his mistakes in Iraq. He settled for smaller reductions in troops, with a force of 8,400 remaining when Trump took charge.[252] It was not a full withdrawal, but with the threat of Al-Qaeda, the Taliban, and ISIS looming, military leadership and Congress warned him that just wasn't enough manpower.[253]

Donald Trump came into office wanting to withdraw from Afghanistan, but he, unlike, Obama, trusts his generals and is open to new ideas. In a speech, in August 2017, Trump announced he would not withdraw troops from Afghanistan and a new strategy for victory would be put in place. "My original instinct was to pull out—and, historically, I like following my instincts. But all my life I've heard that decisions are much different when you sit behind the desk in the Oval Office," Trump said. "The consequences of a rapid exit are both predictable and unacceptable. […] A hasty withdrawal would create a vacuum that terrorists, including ISIS and al Qaeda [sic], would instantly fill, just as happened before September 11th."[254] Trump continued:

> *And, as we know, in 2011, America hastily and mistakenly withdrew from Iraq. As a result, our hard-won gains slipped back into the hands of terrorist enemies. Our soldiers watched as cities they had fought for, and bled to liberate, and won, were occupied by a terrorist group called ISIS. The vacuum we created by leaving too soon gave safe haven for ISIS to spread, to grow, recruit, and launch attacks. We cannot repeat in Afghanistan the mistake our leaders made in Iraq.*[255]

Trump's reversal of Obama's Afghanistan strategy was met with significant praise. "President Trump inherited a mess in Afghanistan, so give him credit for heeding his generals and committing to more troops and a new strategy,"[256] wrote the *Wall Street Journal*. Zalmay Khalilzad, the former ambassador to Afghanistan and Iraq, wrote in the *New York Times*, "President Trump deserves high marks for his new Afghanistan strategy. It is bold, reasoned, and offers the prospect of success against the violent Islamist groups of the region."[257] General John Allen, Former Commander of Coalition Forces in Afghanistan, and Michael O'Hanlon of the left-leaning Brookings Institution, also praised Trump. "In these trying circumstances, with no great policy options available to him, we would especially commend Mr. Trump for making a difficult and very presidential decision about future American policy."[258]

In August 2018, a year after Trump's new strategy was announced, Army General John Nicholson, the outgoing Commander of US forces in Afghanistan, declared, despite some setbacks, "the strategy is working."[259]

Reversing Obama's Anti-Israel Policies

To say that Barack Obama was not a friend to Israel is an understatement. He called on Israel to return to its 1967 borders, which they consider indefensible. He refused to acknowledge Jerusalem as Israel's capital. He repeatedly refused to meet with Prime Minister Benjamin Netanyahu, while often meeting with leaders of other Middle Eastern nations, including representatives of Hamas. He also spied on Netanyahu and sent campaign operatives to Israel in 2015 in an attempt to influence Israeli elections with hopes of ousting him. He exposed top secret information about Israel's nuclear program. He attempted to ban American flights to Israel. He refused to veto an anti-Israel UN resolution stating all territory taken by Israel in 1967 was occupied territory and no settlements should be built there, thus allowing it to pass.[260] Whenever Israel clashed with anyone in the region, including with enemies of America, Obama was a reliable supporter of anyone but Israel.

Trump fiercely criticized Obama's policies towards Israel on the campaign trail. "Israel, our great friend and the one true democracy in the Middle East, has been snubbed and criticized by an administration that lacks moral clarity," Trump said. "President Obama has not been a friend to Israel. He's treated Iran with tender love and care and has made it a great power. All at the expense of Israel, our allies in the region and, very importantly, the United States itself."[261]

Trump promised to be a "true friend to Israel," and it was clear very early on that Israel could once again rely on the United States as an ally with Trump in office. Prior to leaving office, Obama secretly sent $221 million to the Palestinian Authority—not even notifying Congress about the payout until the morning of Trump's inauguration, just hours before Trump took the oath of office. The Trump administration quickly froze the payment.[262] In March 2018, Trump signed The Taylor Force Act as part of the Consolidated Appropriations Act of 2018, cutting all US payments to the Palestinian Authority over its payments to terrorists and their families.[263]

Israel vocally criticized Obama and his European partners after they publicized the terms of the infamous Iran Nuclear Deal. Prime Minister Netanyahu warned the deal "doesn't block Iran's path to the bomb; it paves Iran's path to the bomb."[264] Netanyahu's concerns were validated when, in April 2017, Iran "paraded a missile with the sign 'Death to Israel' attached to it during a huge military parade showcasing deadly weapons."[265] A year later, Netanyahu also revealed that Israel had evidence Iran was cheating on the deal, and was secretly producing nuclear weapons.[266] President Trump, however, withdrew from the nuclear deal and re-imposed sanctions.

Every major candidate for the Presidency promises to recognize Jerusalem as the capital of Israel, but none have had the stones to follow through on their promise. In fact, the Democratic Party experienced a public relations nightmare when its leaders temporarily removed Jerusalem's true status—along with any mention of God—from the official platform. Though Obama took credit for strong-arming the committee and getting those provisions back onto the platform, he approved those same changes before the negative attention. And, as we all know, the Obama administration refused to acknowledge Jerusalem as Israel's capital. According to a State Department spokesman, Jerusalem was "an issue that should be resolved in final status negotiations between Israelis and Palestinians."[267]

But Donald Trump showed no ambiguity on that issue. On December 16, 2017, he formally recognized Jerusalem as Israel's capital and made good on his promise to move the US Embassy there from Tel Aviv. "Today we finally acknowledge the obvious: that Jerusalem is Israel's capital," he said. "This is nothing more or less than a recognition of reality. It is also the right thing to do. It's something that has to be done." Trump also noted that previous presidents had made the same campaign promise but failed to deliver.[268] In President Trump, Israel found the ally that Barack Obama didn't want to be.

Stronger on Human Rights and Tougher on Trafficking

Barack Obama proved himself to be far more concerned with his legacy than with the real impact of his policies—even at the expense of basic human rights and dignity. Due to Obama's lax enforcement of immigration laws, there was a surge of young children being sent across the border. This overwhelmed US officials who, in turn, relaxed policies designed to protect children. As a result, illegal immigrant minors ended up being placed "with sponsors who subjected them to sexual abuse, labor trafficking, or severe abuse and neglect," the Associated Press revealed.[269] The Senate subsequently concluded the Obama administration "failed to protect thousands of Central American children who have flooded across the U.S. border since 2011, leaving them vulnerable to traffickers and to abuses at the hands of government-approved caretakers," *The Washington Post* reported in January 2016.[270]

> *The Office of Refugee Resettlement, an agency of the Department of Health and Human Services, failed to do proper background checks of adults who claimed the children, allowed sponsors to take custody of multiple unrelated children, and regularly placed children in homes without visiting the locations, according to a 56-page investigative report released Thursday.*
>
> *And once the children left federally funded shelters, the report said, the agency permitted their adult sponsors to prevent caseworkers from providing them post-release services.*[271]

The report concluded that the Obama administration's "policies and procedures were inadequate to protect the children in the agency's care."[272]

While Barack Obama may have been lax in combating human trafficking to protect his legacy, fighting human trafficking has become a cornerstone of Donald Trump's agenda. In the earliest days of his presidency, he promised to use the "full force and weight" of his administration to combat the human trafficking epidemic.[273] And there's evidence to prove he has. Liz Crokin, a journalist and advocate for sex crime victims, reported just one month after Trump took office, that there was "a staggering 1,500-plus arrests" of sex traffickers, compared to "less than 400 sex trafficking-related arrests in 2014 according to the FBI." Sex trafficking rings in Tennessee, California, Illinois, Texas, Michigan, Virginia, and Florida met their ends in Trump's first year on the job.[274] The media is curiously silent on this issue. In December 2017, Trump signed an executive order freezing the assets of human traffickers.[275] In April 2018, he also signed bipartisan legislation to crack down on online sex traffickers—though he lamented how difficult it was for the bill to reach his desk. "This was a tough one. It shouldn't have been tough. I guess people have reasons [to oppose the legislation], but I personally don't understand those reasons."[276]

Obama's poor record with human trafficking extended beyond America's borders—especially when it got in the way of his agenda. Despite signing the 2012 Magnitsky Act, a bipartisan bill sanctioning human rights abusers in Russia, Obama refused to enforce the law when he had the opportunity.[277] Donald Trump, however, has. In 2016, the Magnitsky Act was expanded to apply globally and, in December 2017, the Trump administration "imposed financial and travel restrictions on 52 government-linked people from Uzbekistan, Russia, Ukraine, and elsewhere," under the newly-comprehensive law.[278]

While Obama negotiated the Trans-Pacific Partnership trade deal, he decided that his policy objectives were more important than human rights yet again. According to a Reuters report, in 2015, Obama political appointees pressured those writing an annual State Department report on human trafficking worldwide to soften their language. They inflated assessments of fourteen "strategically important countries,"[279] including Cuba and Malaysia. Several months after this sham report, Obama normalized relations with Cuba.

This report also gave Obama cover to continue working with Malaysia during the Trans-Pacific Partnership trade deal negotiations. Prior to the report, twenty-eight suspected human trafficking camps were discovered in Malaysia along with 139 mass graves of human trafficking victims.[280] Congress had imposed trade restrictions with countries with horrible records in combating human trafficking and those limits would have precluded Malaysia from participating in TPP. Obama had the human rights report changed to ensure his precious trade deal would move forward.[281] Rep. Lloyd Doggett, a Texas Democrat, was critical of Malaysia's upgraded status. "This report is another indication that the Trans-Pacific Partnership is not being used to bring about meaningful change on critical issues." Other Democrats expressed concerns that upgrading Malaysia's status conflicted with Obama administration promises that TPP would include stronger labor and human rights protections. Bradley Myles, the CEO of Polaris, a nonprofit group working to combat and prevent modern-day slavery and human trafficking, said, "Upgrades like this seriously weaken the U.S. government's credibility as it works to combat human trafficking around the world."[282] Trump, of course, pulled the US out of TPP and re-imposed sanctions on Cuba, citing human rights violations in the latter case.

Soon after Barack Obama took office, he reversed a Bush administration decision not to join the UN Human Rights Council because the body permitted human rights abusers to join it. The predecessor to the Human Rights Council, the Human Rights Commission, had lost credibility for the same reason. Trump took a tough stance on human rights abuses at the United Nations. In September 2017, Trump, during his first speech to the UN General Assembly, attacked the UN Human Rights Council for including human rights abusers. "It is a massive source of embarrassment for the United Nations that some governments with egregious human rights records sit on the U.N. Human Rights Council," he said. Some of those countries are US allies.[283] In June 2018, Trump formally withdrew the United States from the UN Human Rights Council due to its human rights hypocrisy and bias against both Israel and the United States.[284] No president will ever be perfect on human rights issues, but Trump has built a record of accomplishment in this area unmatched by any recent chief executive—a far cry from the hypocrisy of a certain recent people's champion.

Defeating ISIS

Obama didn't just fail when faced with the threat of ISIS; he ignored them entirely. He was completely blindsided by their international reign of terror—even blaming the intelligence community for underestimating the threat. Yet, for over a year before those comments, Obama received well-documented presidential daily briefings (PDBs) on that very subject, but failed to act on them. One former Pentagon official accused Obama of either not reading his PDBs or lying.[285] Somehow, the same White House that micromanaged the military into a chaotic mess failed to act against ISIS.

Although Hillary Clinton and Obama were eager to topple the Libyan government, Obama nixed a plan to remove Syrian President Bashar al-Assad from power in 2012 to stay cozy with Iran. General David Petraeus, Defense Secretary Leon Panetta, and others within Obama's administration believed ousting Assad could have prevented the rise of ISIS.[286] CNN found, by February 2018, ISIS had "conducted or inspired more than 140 terrorist attacks in 29 countries other than Iraq and Syria," killing more than 2,000 people and injuring thousands more.[287] In 2015, in the midst of this carnage, Obama declared that ISIS was contained—the day before the deadly attacks in Paris by ISIS fighters that killed more than 120 people.[288]

Donald Trump ended Obama's failed policy of plugging his ears and humming as loudly as possible. "We're gonna beat ISIS very, very quickly folks. It's gonna be fast," he said at a campaign rally in 2016.[289] And so he has. Robin Simcox, an expert on terrorism and national security, says the facts on the ground "have changed dramatically." He added, "ISIS lost control of Mosul, the second-largest city in Iraq, in July 2017. Three months later, ISIS' capital—the Syrian city of Raqqa—fell. Many fighters retreated to Deir ez-Zor in the country's east. In November 2017, that too fell. The 'Caliphate' that Abu Bakr al-Baghdadi announced with such fanfare in the summer of 2014 was in tatters."[290] Trump fully liberated Iraq from ISIS control within his first year in office.[291]

How did this happen? Within days of his inauguration, President Trump signed an executive order requesting the Pentagon review their ISIS strategy. According to then Defense Secretary Jim Mattis, two significant changes in strategy resulted from Trump's review of their findings. "First, he delegated authority to the right level to aggressively and in a timely manner move against enemy vulnerabilities," Mattis explained. "Secondly, he directed a tactical shift from shoving ISIS out of safe locations in an attrition fight to surrounding the enemy in their strongholds so we can annihilate ISIS. The intent is to prevent the return home of escaped foreign fighters."[292] Trump's team also revised the overly restrictive rules of engagement implemented under Barack Obama.[293]

Even *New York Times* columnist (and Trump critic) Ross Douthat conceded that Trump deserves credit for turning the tide in the war on ISIS. "[I]f you had told me in late 2016 that almost a year into the Trump era the caliphate would be all-but-beaten without something far worse happening in the Middle East, I would have been surprised and gratified. So very provisionally, credit belongs where it's due—to our soldiers and diplomats, yes, but to our president as well."[294] In a few short years, Obama allowed ISIS to grow large enough to declare itself a caliphate and to threaten the entire world; Trump all but solved the problem in a single year. It doesn't get much better than that.

CHAPTER 5

ENERGY AND ENVIRONMENT

No one can forget that incredible moment when, after Obama defeated Hillary Clinton in the Democratic primaries, he declared that future generations would look back on the moment and tell their children that, amongst other things, "this was the moment when the rise of the oceans began to slow and our planet began to heal."[295] I'm not sure which is the scarier prospect—that Obama was cynical enough to believe his followers would believe such obvious hyperbole, or that he might believe himself capable of single-handedly saving the world.

Obama would like you to believe he was an advocate for the environment in a time of great need. Aside from spending tons of taxpayer dollars on "green energy" and trying to create a "green economy" where demand for it was nonexistent, his real environmental legacy was a corrupt Environmental Protection Agency (EPA). The organization blossomed under Obama, crafting a nightmarish regulatory labyrinth more effective at growing government than improving the environment or stopping anthropogenic climate change.

On Trump's watch, many Obama-era environmental regulations met their end. But that doesn't mean Trump doesn't believe in being a good steward of the environment. "We want clean, beautiful water.

We want crystal clear air. We want our air to be the best," Trump explained in his August 2, 2018 rally in Wilkes-Barre, Pennsylvania. The day before this rally, his administration decided after a year of review to keep and defend an Obama-era regulation on smog, "which set the allowable ozone level in ambient air at 70 parts per billion, down from 75."[296] Trump's enemies are wrong when they argue that he cares nothing for the environment, or just axes Obama-era regulations because they are Obama-era regulations. For example, Trump's EPA has done a better job than Obama's at cleaning up hazardous waste sites. *The Daily Signal* compiled an analysis of administrative efforts to clean up contaminated sites and found that, by the end of July 2018, Trump's EPA "cleaned up more polluted or contaminated sites in less time and at a faster pace than the Obama administration did in all of 2015 and 2016."[297] Perhaps the EPA was too busy dealing with its repeated scandals under Obama to give its full attention to protecting the environment.

Rolling Back Obama's National Monument Declaration Abuse

Many presidents have abused the Antiquities Act of 1906, but none more than Barack Obama, who designated more national monuments than any other president. According to the Antiquities Act, monuments should be "confined to the smallest area compatible with proper care and management of the objects to be protected."[298] But, Obama added over 550 million acres of monument real estate, tripling the amount of land and water under strict federal control.[299] Creating national monuments under the Antiquities Act doesn't require congressional approval, and these monuments are often opposed by the people in the states where they're established. "It's these people who suffer most directly from the new limits placed on economic and recreational activities," explains Dr. H. Sterling Burnett of the non-partisan Heartland Institute. In August 2016, Obama quadrupled the size of Papahanaumokuakea Marine National Monument in the waters around Hawaii, making the protected region nearly double the size of Texas and closing 60 percent of

Hawaii's waters to commercial fishing.[300] According to Burnett, these monument declarations weren't about protecting lands threatened with destruction, but were instead about "building his legacy with far-Left environmental zealots. Millions of people are suffering so that Obama's vanity can be satisfied."[301]

In April 2017, President Trump did something about these abuses and signed an executive order to review monument declarations dating back to President Clinton.[302] The move was primarily in response to several controversial eleventh-hour designations—including the creation of the Bears Ears Monument in Utah and the Gold Butte Monument in Nevada—forged over intense opposition from some local Native American tribes.[303] Those two monuments created 1.64 million acres of newly protected government land.

In September 2017, Interior Secretary Ryan Zinke recommended modifying ten monument sites. In December, Trump announced his intention to scale back two monuments in Utah. The Bears Ears National Monument would be reduced by 85 percent, and the Grand Staircase-Escalante National Monument by 39 percent, bringing two million acres back under local control. "These abuses of the Antiquities Act give enormous power to faraway bureaucrats at the expense of the people who actually live here, work here, and make this place their home," said Trump in Salt Lake City while announcing the reduction of the monuments.[304]

Reversing Obama's Position That Climate Change Is a National Security Threat

Though it would be difficult to say which was the most absurd notion floated by Obama's green coalition, the position that climate change was a national security risk has to be among the top three. In October 2014, the Pentagon released a report "asserting decisively that climate change poses an immediate threat to national security, with increased risks from terrorism, infectious disease, global poverty and food shortages," according to the *New York Times*. During his 2015 State of the Union, Obama referenced this policy, saying, "The Pentagon says that climate change poses immediate risks to our national security. We should act like it."[305]

Whether you believe long-term shifts in the climate are caused by man's contribution to atmospheric carbon dioxide or by natural factors, it's not a national security issue. "National security problems aren't caused by climate, changing or not. They're caused by what people do," says Dr. Theodore R. Bromund, a senior research fellow in the Heritage Foundation's Margaret Thatcher Center for Freedom. "And people don't do things because it's getting hotter, or colder. They do things because of what they believe. The problem is never weather: it's always ideology."[306]

Bromund also noted the weak language used to justify the policy. Despite a lack of any direct connection, climate change could or may cause various conflicts, according to the Pentagon report. Obama even suggested that climate change could cause a refugee crisis, which begs the question: how exactly?[307] While overseas, Obama's second Secretary of State John Kerry said climate change is "the greatest challenge of our generation," and the world's "largest weapon of mass destruction," though even he eventually conceded that terrorism was a bigger threat.[308] Still, the climate change radicalism continued.

In March 2016, Obama's Deputy Secretary of Defense Robert Work signed a directive putting climate change "front and center" in military strategic planning. According to the directive, "All DoD operations worldwide must be able to adapt current and future operations to address the impacts of climate change in order to maintain an effective and efficient U.S. military."[309] That September, Obama doubled down on his climate fever by issuing a presidential memorandum ordering twenty defense and intelligence agencies to "ensure that climate change-related impacts are fully considered in the development of national security doctrine, policies, and plans."[310]

As commander-in-chief, Obama's foreign policy record was already shameful, but this was a whole new level of absurd. He dropped the ball on Iraq, Afghanistan, Syria, and Libya. He gave billions to Iran. He was blindsided by the rise of ISIS. But those are all temporary conditions. His lasting defense legacy was a military that cared more about preventing temperature rises of fractions of a degree over a century than protecting Americans from actual national security threats. Obama even told the *Atlantic*—and I swear I am not making this up—"ISIS is not an existential threat to the United States. Climate change is a potential existential threat to the entire world if we don't do something about it."[311] Never mind that ISIS has carried out or inspired more than a hundred attacks worldwide, including inside the United States.[312]

President Trump was never so disillusioned and, when his administration released its National Security Strategy, he removed climate change from the list of national security threats. "The United States will remain a global leader in reducing traditional pollution, as well as greenhouse gases, while growing its economy. This achievement, which can serve as a model to other countries, flows from innovation, technology breakthroughs, and energy efficiency gains—not from onerous regulation." The environment is still a concern, but it's not the job of our military or intelligence agencies to use their resources to address environmental issues.

Reversing Obama's Eleventh-Hour Oil and Gas Drilling Restrictions

As a proponent of a "green economy," Obama spent billions to prop up his allies in the green energy business. For Obama, being an ally of "green energy" meant being an enemy of the oil industry—the lifeblood of the American economy. His investing in "green jobs" didn't exactly go well (remember Solyndra?), but that didn't stop Obama from clamping down on big oil to help his friends and donors in the green energy sector. In his 2010 budget, Obama expected a sharp reduction in offshore oil drilling revenues from the previous year. He had big plans to suffocate the oil industry, and he got the political cover he needed for this after the Deepwater Horizon oil spill. In the wake of the disaster, he issued a moratorium on new offshore drilling. Industry leaders challenged the moratorium in court and won, but the Obama administration found other ways to keep a lid on drilling. They denied and delayed federal drilling permits and blocked oil exploration in the Arctic, sending gas prices to nearly four dollars per gallon for three years and stifling economic growth. It took oil and natural gas production on state and private land to relieve Americans from soaring gas and energy prices and begin the slow recovery of the economy. Incredibly, Obama claimed credit for the improvement.[313]

As a parting gift to Americans who struggled because of his environmental policies, a month before he left office, Obama issued an eleventh-hour ban on oil and gas drilling on "hundreds of millions of acres of federally owned land in the Arctic and Atlantic Ocean." His allies in the media asserted this action, taken after the election of Donald Trump, would be indefinite, immune to reversal by a subsequent administration. "There is no authority for subsequent presidents to un-withdraw," said a White House aide. "I can't speak to what a future Congress will do."[314]

President Trump did exactly what the Obama White House claimed he couldn't. In April 2017, President Trump signed an executive order reversing Obama's ban. "Our country is blessed with incredible natural resources, including abundant offshore oil and natural gas reserves," Trump said at the signing of the America-First Offshore Energy Strategy Executive Order. "But the federal government has kept 94 percent of these offshore areas closed for exploration and production. And when they say closed, they mean closed. This deprives our country of potentially thousands and thousands of jobs and billions of dollars in wealth. I pledged to take action, and today I am keeping that promise."[315] The Department of the Interior estimates the Outer Continental Shelf "contains approximately 90 billion barrels of technically recoverable oil and 327 trillion cubic feet of technically recoverable natural gas," and the United States controlled areas of the Gulf of Mexico have "an estimated 48.46 billion barrels of technically recoverable oil and 219.46 trillion cubic feet of technically recoverable natural gas."[316]

Environmental activists were livid but, according to James Taylor, the president of the Spark of Freedom Foundation, their opposition to Trump's executive order "is misguided" because "there is no current feasible substitute for oil in transportation fuel, and it is better to have U.S.-produced oil as an option to compete against foreign oil." And there are other reasons. "More importantly, natural gas is an affordable, low-emissions power source for electricity, responsible for ongoing declines in U.S. carbon-dioxide emissions. True environmentalists should support more, rather than less, natural gas production."[317]

Ending Obama's War on Coal

"If someone wants to build a new coal-fired power plant they can, but it will bankrupt them because they will be charged a huge sum for all the greenhouse gas that's being emitted," Barack Obama promised while running for president in 2008. "Under my plan…electricity rates would necessarily skyrocket." There was nothing ambiguous about it. Obama promised that if elected, he would wage a war on coal. In 2010, despite having Democratic majorities in the House and Senate, Obama failed to pass cap-and-trade legislation.[318] Not one to let checks and balances get in his way, Obama enacted cap-and-trade via regulation at the Environmental Protection Agency.

The *coup de grâce* of Obama's efforts to regulate coal out of business was his Clean Power Plan. Originally proposed in 2014, these new EPA regulations set a goal of cutting carbon emissions by 30 percent by 2030 by declaring carbon dioxide a pollutant subject to the Clean Air Act. At the time when Obama's EPA proposed the Clean Power Plan, West Virginia had already lost 3,000 coal mining jobs. The US Chamber of Commerce predicted an average of "224,000 fewer jobs every year leading up to 2030" under the new regulations.[319] A study by NERA Economic Consulting found the Clean Power Plan would devastate the energy economy while having a miniscule positive impact on the environment. It would reduce carbon dioxide levels in the atmosphere by under 0.5 percent, and global average temperature by 0.02 degrees. Despite the virtually nonexistent environmental improvement, the plan would cost consumers and businesses $41 billion a year, and electricity prices would skyrocket.[320]

Obama's team unveiled the final rules in August 2015 and published them in the *Federal Register* in October. But legal challenges to the regulations by two dozen state attorneys general resulted in a stay by the US Supreme Court in February 2016, pending those lower court challenges.[321] The Obama administration continued to fight for the Clean Power Plan in court. He would continue waging his war on coal to the end.

Meanwhile, on the campaign trail, Donald Trump vowed to end Obama's war on coal, and he made good on that promise once elected. With Trump's urging, Congress repealed the Obama-era Stream Protection Rule, which Dr. Burnett of The Heartland Institute explained was unwarranted and threatened over one-third of American coal-mining jobs. "The Interior Department's own reports show the rule was unnecessary, since coal mines have virtually no offsite impacts and lands are being restored successfully under existing federal and state regulations." Via executive orders, President Trump also ended a moratorium on new coal leases on federal land and declared federal agencies "should no longer consider speculative climate change impacts when implementing federal contracts, issuing permits, or formulating planned uses of federal lands."[322] The order also directed a review of the Clean Power Plan. "My administration is putting an end to the war on coal. We're going to have clean coal—really clean coal," Trump said. "With today's executive action, I am taking historic steps to lift the restrictions on American energy, to reverse government intrusion, and to cancel job-killing regulations."[323]

The results were indisputable. Within six months, coal production increased 14 percent, and exports to Europe and Asia increased 70 percent and 50 percent, respectively.[324] In October 2017, the EPA announced that the Clean Power Plan would be repealed. "The war on coal is over," said Trump's then-EPA administrator Scott Pruitt.[325]

The Trump administration instead proposed a new rule, called the Affordable Clean Energy (ACE) rule, which allowed states to craft their own emissions reduction plans, rather than a universal approach from the federal government. The EPA projected the ACE rule would achieve emissions cuts greater than the targets set by the Clean Power

Plan—all while protecting consumers from harmful energy price increases.[326] The left advocates for a top-down approach to achieving a sustainable energy future, but they'll soon discover that today's sources of energy can be replaced without declaring war on every American who consumes electricity if we unshackle our corporations and give them the freedom to innovate. Trump ended the war on coal and, in so doing, he may have taken one of the most important steps toward a cleaner, brighter tomorrow that any president has ever taken.

Reversing Obama's Job-Killing Fracking Rule

One might think, given the left's antipathy for coal, that they would embrace cleaner energy alternatives, not shun them. Hydraulic fracturing, or fracking, is a process of cutting into subterranean rock formations with pressurized liquid, allowing for the extraction of oil and natural gas. It is highly controversial due to alleged environmental concerns like groundwater contamination and increased tectonic activity near large-scale drilling sites. But many studies show fracking is fundamentally safe. In 2012, Obama's then–Secretary of the Interior Ken Salazar told Congress there's "a lot of hysteria" regarding fracking, but said fracking "can be done safely and has been done safely hundreds of thousands of times."[327] In 2013, Obama's Secretary of Energy Ernest Moniz said, "To my knowledge, I still have not seen any evidence of fracking per se contaminating groundwater."[328]

For over twenty years, the EPA has been studying the environmental impact of fracking, and has found "no evidence" of "any contamination or endangerment of underground sources of drinking water."[329] Even Obama's own EPA studied the environmental impact of fracking and concluded, in their 2015 draft report, that there was no evidence that fracking had "led to widespread, systemic impacts on drinking water resources in the United States." Enraged environmental activists forced the EPA to soften their conclusion in their final report by including absurd hypothetical scenarios where fracking could contaminate water. They warned against the "injection of hydraulic fracturing fluids directly into groundwater resources," and other scenarios that would never happen.[330]

The Department of Energy released a 2013 study that determined fracking didn't pollute groundwater.[331] There have been numerous non-government studies too, all of which have reached the same conclusions. A Yale study released in 2013 found that: "Fracking safely produces energy that powers the American economy, creates jobs, and saves consumers money."[332] A 2015 study by the Harvard Business School and the Boston Consulting Group reached similar conclusions.[333] For years, every expert team looking at the technology found fracking to be environmentally safe and a boon to the economy. Thanks to fracking, energy production in the United States boomed, with natural gas extraction increasing 8 million cubic feet between 2005 and 2014, and US carbon emissions hitting a twenty-year low.[334]

Despite mountains of evidence supporting fracking as a viable path to a cleaner, more prosperous world, Obama listened to his lobbyists and green energy money bundlers. He imposed needless strict regulations against the practice. The new regulations required disclosure of chemicals used, restrictions on many common extraction practices, and approval from the Bureau of Land Management before fracking on federal land. The Department of the Interior imposed these regulations without any debate in Congress.

Oil and gas industry groups and several states immediately sued over the regulations, calling them "arbitrary and unnecessary burdens" and redundant to existing state regulations.[335] In June 2016, a federal judge temporarily blocked the new fracking rules, citing the Interior Department's lack of authority from Congress to impose them.[336] Due to another court challenge, the rules never took effect by the time the Trump Administration repealed them in December 2017. Barry Russell, the president and CEO of the Independent Petroleum Association of America (IPAA), applauded the Trump administration's action, and said the Obama–era rule "was overly restrictive and did not make hydraulic fracturing any safer than current state laws." By rescinding the rule, the Trump administration saved the companies operating on federal lands "hundreds of millions of dollars in compliance costs" without compromising safety. Kathleen Sgamma, the president of the Western Energy Alliance, said politics drove the Obama fracking rule, not environmental concerns. "It was clear from the start that the federal rule was redundant with state regulation and politically motivated, as the prior administration could not point to one incident or regulatory gap that justified the rule."[337] The only thing Obama could point to was the "green energy" companies that donated heavily to his campaign.[338]

Reversing Obama's Policy on Accidental Bird Deaths

Imagine for a moment that a bird flew into the window of your house and died. If that bird was a protected species, rules implemented by the Obama administration made you criminally liable for that accidental death. Similarly, if you owned a cat that killed a protected bird species, or if a protected bird collided with your car, the Obama administration wanted you to be criminally responsible and prosecuted under the 1918 Migratory Bird Treaty Act.[339]

Punishment for an accidental death could be six months in prison or fines as high as $15,000. The law was written only to curtail intentional killing until the Obama administration unilaterally reinterpreted it when they issued a legal opinion shortly before Obama left office in January 2017.[340] Was this really about protecting birds? Nope. In fact, this was really about punishing oil and natural gas companies while protecting Obama's favored industries, like wind energy. "During the Obama administration, seven oil and natural gas companies were prosecuted for killing 28 birds at the same time that wind energy companies were allowed to kill thousands of birds, including bald and golden eagles," said Kathleen Sgamma, president of the Western Energy Alliance.[341] In fact, in December 2016, the Obama administration finalized new regulations quadrupling the number of Bald Eagles wind farms could accidentally kill without prosecution.[342] Bald Eagles are protected by the Bald and Golden Eagle Protection Act and the Migratory Bird Treaty Act,[343] but it's only a crime to kill them accidentally if you're in the wrong line of work.

The Obama administration also turned a blind eye to bird deaths caused by solar power plants. According to the Institute for Energy Research, a solar farm in Nevada incinerated "[triple] the number of bats allowed under an agreement by Obama Administration regulators and massive solar facilities are incinerating up to an estimated 28,000 birds per year using sophisticated solar technology."[344]

The administration was already giving preferential treatment to his pet industries at the expense of ordinary Americans. The Associated Press reported the Obama administration prosecuted over 200 cases involving accidental bird deaths from 2009 through 2013, but never prosecuted or fined wind and solar plants. Oil and gas companies were a different story.[345] Obama's eleventh-hour action codified his preferential treatment of wind and solar and predatory treatment of oil and gas companies—all while leaving the possibility that individuals would have their lives ruined by a clumsy feathered friend on the highway.

But it didn't happen, thanks to the Trump administration. The regulations were temporarily suspended in February 2017, pending a review. Ten months later, the administration lifted the rule. The Obama regime's broad, radical interpretation of the Migratory Bird Treaty Act "makes every American a potential criminal, from those who merely drive cars or own buildings with windows, to those who operate windmills or oil facilities," read the one-page decision.[346] This shouldn't be a surprise, though; Obama made a career out of tormenting everyday people in the interest of "fairness."

Reversing Obama's Car Fuel Standards

Obama's environmental agenda was so important to him and his donors that he refused to go through Congress to achieve it. Despite having majorities in both the House and Senate, in May 2010, Obama ordered the federal government to develop new strict fuel-efficiency standards for cars and trucks. Obama called the action an "essential" part of his energy strategy. He said there were still steps Congress should take, but "I'm going to take every sensible, responsible action that I can take using my authority as president."[347] In April 2012,

Obama's new Corporate Average Fuel Economy (CAFE) standards were finalized, mandating an increase in fuel economy "to the equivalent of 54.5 mpg for cars and light-duty trucks by Model Year 2025." According to the Obama White House, "When combined with previous standards set by this Administration, this move will nearly double the fuel efficiency of those vehicles compared to new vehicles currently on our roads. In total, the Administration's national program to improve fuel economy and reduce greenhouse gas emissions will save consumers more than $1.7 trillion at the gas pump and reduce U.S. oil consumption by 12 billion barrels."[348]

Though he gave CAFE a rosy spin, the new Obama fuel-efficiency standards were not only unrealistic but incredibly costly—and not just in financial terms. According to energy and environmental expert Larry Bell, there wasn't "any realistic way car-makers can meet this requirement without radically transforming their product lines, most particularly by slashing vehicle weight and going to more expensive all-electric or plug-in hybrid electric drive technologies." Even the most efficient hybrid cars at the time didn't meet (CAFE) standards.[349]

What happens when you reduce the weight of a car? Bell explained:

> *A 2003 NHTSA study estimated that every 100 pounds of weight taken off a car weighing more than 3,000 pounds increases the accident death rate slightly less than 5%, and the rate increases as vehicles become lighter than that. Two years earlier a National Academy of Sciences study estimated that CAFÉ standards at that time were responsible for as many as 2,600 highway deaths in a single year. A 1999 study conducted by USA Today applying federal government Fatality Analysis Reporting System Data attributed deaths of 7,700 people for each additional mpg mandated to meet CAFE regulations.[350]*

And what about SUVs, vans, and pickups? They'd mostly get replaced, rather than updated with more fuel-efficient models. "The likely replacement options will be limited to much smaller battery electric vehicles (BEV) and plug-in hybrid electric vehicles (PHEV). A study by the Center for Automotive Research (CAR) provides estimates of actual fuel savings vs. costs for PHEVs, and they don't look particularly terrific."[351]

So, what is the financial scenario under these new standards? Will these Obama-approved vehicles save us money? They certainly won't at the time of purchase. The Heritage Foundation found the Obama fuel-economy mandates would increase "new-car prices $6,800 more than the pre-2009 baseline trend," or $7,200 by 2025.[352] But what about at the pump? Obama said you'd save money at the pump…that should make up for the up-front cost, right? Nope.

First, Bell noted that, under real-world conditions, you won't get the mandated 54.5 mpg fuel efficiency, but rather 44.8 mpg "unless you intend to do all of your driving in an EPA laboratory where such numbers are calculated."[353]

> *Then, based on 44.8 mpg, let's assume that any final savings are benchmarked to average fuel costs of $3.50 per gallon, the vehicle is driven 12,000 miles per year, and the owner keeps it for 5 years. On that basis, the CAFE standard would net the purchaser a $2,858 loss. At $6.00 per gallon there would be an estimated $873 gain.*[354]

Who wants to pay $6 a gallon for gas to make Obama's fuel efficiency standards economical for consumers? No one. So, what's the answer? According to the Obama administration, the answer is tax credits and rebates. In other words, taxpayers would help cover the added costs of these fuel-efficient cars. To date, tax credits and rebates haven't made electric and hybrid cars more attractive to buyers. So, Obama's new standards would likely turn into "Cash for Clunkers 2.0." In case you forgot, the original Cash for Clunkers ended up costing taxpayers $24,000 per car.[355]

Nevertheless, Obama's EPA bypassed the formal rulemaking process and affirmed the new standards before leaving office, over the objections of automakers. According to the *New York Times*, they "had asked for more time to contest the government's target for fuel economy in 2025." They thought activating the standards would "most likely make it more difficult for a Trump administration to dial it back."[356]

Ah, how they underestimated Trump.

In spring 2018, Trump's EPA drafted plans to roll back the Obama fuel economy standards. Rather than attempting to reset fuel-efficiency standards to levels comparable to before CAFE was written, Trump's EPA proposed revised standards. Called the Safer Affordable Fuel-Efficient (SAFE) Vehicles Rule, existing CAFE standards would be maintained through 2020, and increase to 43 mpg through 2026.[357] The proposed rules changes went public in August 2018.

According to the Environmental Protection Agency (EPA) and National Highway Traffic Safety Administration (NHTSA), the rollback of the Obama standards would reduce vehicle crash fatalities by up to 1,000 annually, reduce average ownership costs of new vehicles by $2,340, and save $500 billion for the US economy. What about the change in carbon emissions? The difference between the Trump standards and the Obama standards: "CO2 concentrations would increase from 789.11 parts per million to 789.76 ppm, a minuscule change measured in the 'ten-thousandths' of one percent range." The resulting change in global temperature: a whopping 3/1,000ths of a degree Celsius in eighty-two years. Meaning the Trump standards would make "no practical difference to weather patterns, sea levels, polar bear populations, or any other environmental condition people actually care about," compared to the Obama standards.[358]

So, given that Obama's fuel standards would have made you pay a lot more money to make you less safe on the road, with virtually no environmental benefit, reversing it should have made everyone— even environmentalists—happy. After all, it's hard to enjoy the few ten-thousandths of 1 percent cleaner air and the three-thousandths of a degree Celsius in cooler temperatures when you're broke or dead.

Despite outcry from environmentalists, no environmental scientists advocating for maintaining the Obama standards argued that the estimated change in carbon emissions and global temperature between the two standards was incorrect.[359]

Approving the Keystone and Dakota Pipelines

For most of his presidency, Obama delayed deciding on the nearly 1,200-mile-long Keystone XL pipeline. While environmentalists that donated heavily to his campaign lined up against it, his big labor unions supported it. The potential for job creation was a benefit too good to ignore—especially when much of his presidency was plagued by high unemployment and high gas prices. Obama played a political waiting game, postponing his decision for seven years, until finally, in November 2015, he made the choice most people expected. He rejected the proposed Keystone XL pipeline.[360] The following September, the Obama administration also temporarily blocked the 1,100-mile-long Dakota Access pipeline.[361]

The benefits of both pipelines were significant. According to the Global Energy Institute, the $7 billion Keystone pipeline expansion would have doubled the capacity of the existing Keystone system, and it would "be able to transport approximately 1.1 million barrels of crude oil daily, non-stop, from Alberta, Canada to market hubs in the Midwest and Texas." This would significantly strengthen the United States' energy security and add about 20,000 well-paying manufacturing and construction jobs generating $6.5 billion in income for American workers during construction. Tax revenue for local governments would also balloon and the project would "generate additional private sector investment of around $20 billion on food, lodging, fuel, vehicles, equipment, construction supplies and services."[362] The Dakota Access pipeline had similar economic benefits while providing energy security and stability.

What about the environmental risks? Analysis of data from the Department of Transportation by the Manhattan Institute also found that "in addition to enjoying a substantial cost advantage, transporting [oil and natural gas] by pipeline results in fewer spillage incidents and personal injuries than transporting them by road or rail."[363]

While Obama hesitated to act on the pipelines, President Trump made it a top priority. Just four days into his presidency, he reversed the federal government's positions on both pipelines. In an executive memorandum, Trump invited TransCanada, the owner of the Keystone pipeline system, to re-submit their application for a permit—which they accepted—and directed the Army Corps of Engineers to "to review and approve in an expedited manner" the Dakota Access pipeline.

This move enraged environmental activists, but not because they truly believed the pipeline was a threat to the environment. Even the former head of the State Department's energy bureau under Obama conceded that the Keystone XL pipeline "has never been a significant issue from an environmental point of view in substance, only in symbol."[364] A symbol of what, exactly? I submit that, in the minds of these environmental extremists, all oil is bad—the facts be damned.

By delaying his decision to approve the Keystone XL pipeline permit for seven years, Obama delayed economic growth during a time when our country desperately needed it…all to appease radical environmental groups that are too closed-minded to listen to facts about how pipelines are safer and better for the environment than the alternative methods of transporting oil and natural gas.

Pulling out of the Paris Climate Treaty

Just as the Iran Nuclear Deal was Obama's crowning foreign policy achievement (look how well that turned out), the Paris Climate Treaty was the *pièce de résistance* of his environmental legacy. There was no chance the US Senate would ratify the treaty, so Obama just ignored the Constitution. Todd Stern, Obama's Special Envoy for Climate Change, cooked up a scheme to bypass the US Senate. This must have seemed like a good strategy at the time. After all, the Obama administration assumed that Hillary Clinton would be his successor, and she'd leave his legacy in place. So, they didn't call it a treaty, they called it an "agreement" and carefully crafted the language of the treaty as an addendum to the United Nations Framework Convention on Climate

Change (UNFCCC), which the Senate ratified, and George H. W. Bush signed, in 1992.[365]

But the Paris Climate Treaty was its own separate treaty requiring Senate ratification, even if you called it an agreement. When the UNFCCC was ratified, the Bush administration "pledged to submit future protocols negotiated under the convention to the Senate for its advice and consent." Any protocols from future presidential administrations "containing targets and timetables"—which the Paris Climate Treaty does—would also be submitted to the Senate for advice and consent.[366] Also, *National Review* noted, "European signatories put it through their usual treaty-ratification protocols, but the United States did not."[367] Why? Because Obama knew the Senate would reject it.

The treaty was a financial boon to the United Nations. The United States would pay several billion dollars annually to the UN Green Climate Fund. In 2014, Barack Obama pledged $3 billion to the slush fund, though he only gave $1 billion before leaving office.[368] But putting that aside, the agreement was severely flawed in terms of its environmental objectives:

> *For example, limiting the amount of coal consumed by North American power plants would not necessarily reduce the amount of coal consumed on Earth—and climate change is, famously, a planetary issue—but would instead most likely result in shifting coal consumption from relatively clean North American facilities to relatively dirty ones in China—the U.S. already is a net exporter of coal, and China is the world's largest importer of it.[369]*

What about that bogeyman—greenhouse gases? "Two countries that are responsible for a large share of greenhouse-gas emissions—China and India, the world [sic] largest and fourth-largest carbon dioxide emitters, respectively—have made only modest commitments under the agreement, which puts most of the onus on the more developed nations of North America and Western Europe."[370]

The Green Climate Fund was also a magnet for corruption. Nicolas Loris of the Heritage Foundation explains that the treaty crafted the fund "as a tool for incentivizing developing country participation in the Paris accord, but in reality distorts energy markets and encourages corruption."[371] Even *Newsweek* described it as a "politically charged Kickstarter campaign," prone to the misuse of funds and lacking in anti-corruption safeguards and accountability.[372]

On the campaign trail, Trump also specifically promised to "cancel the Paris Climate Treaty" and put a stop to payments to the UN programs related to global warming. "We're going to put America first. That includes canceling billions in climate change spending for the United Nations, a number Hillary wants to increase, and instead use that money to provide for American infrastructure including clean water, clean air and safety," Trump said at a campaign rally in September 2016.[373] Thankfully, since the Senate never ratified the Paris Climate Treaty and Congress never authorized funding for the Green Climate Fund, President Trump was not obliged to stay in the treaty or fulfill Obama's $3 billion pledge. And he didn't.[374] In June 2017, President Trump withdrew from the Paris Climate Treaty. But, in an interview with Piers Morgan in January 2018, he signaled openness to reenter the deal. "First of all, it was a terrible deal for the US. If they made a good deal there's always a chance we'd get back. But it was a terrible deal for the US. It was unfair to the US."[375]

Despite their delusion that backing out of the Paris Climate Treaty would destroy the planet and that the United States no longer cared about the environment, green activists must now face the facts. It turns out that the US has done more to reduce greenhouse gas emissions than every major Paris Climate Treaty signatory. The *BP Statistical Review of World Energy for 2017* found, "America reduced its carbon emissions by 0.5 percent, the most of all major countries. That's especially impressive given that our economy grew by nearly 3 percent— so we had more growth and less pollution—the best of all worlds," wrote Stephen Moore of *The Washington Times*. "Meanwhile, as our emissions fell, the pollution levels rose internationally and by a larger amount than in previous years. So much for the rest of the world going green."[376] If other countries don't take reducing greenhouse gas emissions seriously, then why should we remain in the treaty in the first place? All it did was bankroll corrupt third-world dictators and unstable regimes who never intended to do a thing about climate. As Moore put it, this shows, "despite all of the criticism across the globe and in the American media, President Trump was completely right to pull the United States out of the flawed Paris accord. That might be one of the most universally violated treaties of all time—which is saying a lot."[377]

CHAPTER 6

DISMANTLING OBAMACARE

"The Affordable Care Act is a law that passed the House, that passed the Senate, the Supreme Court ruled constitutional," Obama declared in October 2013. "It is settled, and it is here to stay."[378] Except it's not…thanks to Donald Trump. It hasn't been easy, but President Trump has done what Obama said would be impossible: get rid of the so-called Patient Protection and Affordable Care Act, better known as Obamacare.

Obama promised that his health care solution would gain bipartisan support because he would include both parties in the process of crafting the legislation. But his takeover of one-sixth of the United States economy earned no Republican support in the US Senate, and only one Republican vote in the House. Why? Obama consulted precisely zero Republicans while he and the Democrats crafted the bill and ignored every expression of concern Republicans had for its likely consequences. The legislation came from secret negotiations held by Democrats and passed the Senate only by misleading Congress as to its projected cost to use the budget reconciliation process and escape the threat of a filibuster. "Lack of transparency is a huge political advantage," said Obamacare architect Jonathan Gruber. "And basically, call it the stupidity of the American voter or whatever, but basically that was really, really critical for the thing to pass."[379]

The bill called for the addition of tens of thousands of regulations, all to be written after it became law, leaving even Congress ignorant of what it entailed. "We have to pass the bill to find out what is in it," Nancy Pelosi notoriously said. We eventually found out—and we didn't like it. Obama promised that Obamacare wouldn't fund abortions, that if you liked your health care plan you could keep it, that premiums would go down $2,500 per family a year—every one of those promises was a lie. Despite the huge costs, Obamacare did little to improve access to health care. Sure, more people "had" coverage, but that coverage was more expensive, both in premiums and deductibles, and it granted access to fewer providers in most states. Young people weren't signing up in the numbers the Obama administration was counting on, making it unsustainable in the long term.[380] Even those that had insurance avoided using it in record numbers. According to Gallup surveys, more people delayed getting health care because of costs after Obamacare than before.[381] And many Americans had coverage from financially unstable cooperative health insurance groups. Twenty-three of these taxpayer-funded health care co-ops were created by Obamacare. Half had failed by January 2016, and only four remained in operation in 2018.[382]

Republican-controlled chambers of Congress tried and failed for seven years to repeal Obamacare.[383] Even with Trump at the helm, a bare two-vote majority in the Senate made an outright repeal of the law impossible, but Trump persisted. Immediate action was needed since the health insurance marketplace began a death spiral a year before he took office.[384] In August 2017, the Trump administration announced significant cuts for Obamacare outreach and promotion. That October, he signed an executive order instructing his administration to develop policies to improve competition, increase choices, improve the quality of health care and lower prices—all supposed objectives of Obamacare. His order promised it would help "millions of Americans with Obamacare relief."[385] Obamacare was officially on death watch. His subsequent efforts dismantled it to near irrelevance.

Thanks to Donald Trump, Obama's signature legislative achievement will soon be nothing but a bad memory.

Ending Illegal Obamacare Subsidies

Trump's first target within the Obamacare behemoth was a rarely mentioned financial sinkhole called Cost Sharing Reduction (CSR). The Obama administration created the CSR subsidies to reimburse health insurance companies for the costs of covering low-income Obamacare enrollees. According to Sally C. Pipes of the Pacific Research Institute, 6 million people qualified for these subsidies, which cost taxpayers about $7 billion in 2016. These subsidies were also unconstitutional. Congress never appropriated funds for this purpose.[386] What's worse, they didn't even help to rein in consumer costs. In fact, just before the 2016 election, insurers announced a calamitous average Obamacare premium hike of 25 percent for 2017.[387]

Thankfully, in October 2017, Trump announced that his administration would stop subsidizing insurers. Trump's press secretary, Sarah Huckabee Sanders, explained the decision. "Based on guidance from the Department of Justice, the Department of Health and Human Services has concluded that there is no appropriation for cost-sharing reduction payments to insurance companies under Obamacare. In light of this analysis, the Government cannot lawfully make the cost-sharing reduction payments." She added, "The bailout of insurance companies through these unlawful payments is yet another example of how the previous administration abused taxpayer dollars and skirted the law to prop up a broken system."[388] The *New York Times* noted that, without the subsidies, "insurance markets could quickly unravel."[389] But the Heritage Foundation countered that Obamacare premiums increased across the board, even in plans unaffected by the elimination of the subsidies, and that this increase was already underway before Trump arrived. "Providing CSR payments in 2018 will not dampen these premium increases. Nor do they address their underlying cause."[390]

> *Although the Administration's decision to terminate CSR payments has affected premiums for some plans,*

it is not the root cause of premium increases. Insurers in most states have substantially raised 2018 rates for policies that are unaffected by the CSR funding cutoff. These premium increases are more likely related to other factors, including declines in the number of people with individual coverage, the worsening of the insurance pool, and the withdrawal of insurers from the exchanges.[391]

Trump signaled a willingness to negotiate a legal new subsidy with both parties, tweeting, "The Democrats ObamaCare is imploding. Massive subsidy payments to their pet insurance companies has stopped. Dems should call me to fix!"[392] He knew Democrats wouldn't accept his overture. With Congress unwilling to do anything to fix or replace Obamacare or its many ad hoc regulatory additions, Trump did everything in his power to force their hand. But killing the illegal subsidies was just one tiny step; he wasn't finished yet.

Ending the Obamacare Individual Mandate

One of the most controversial aspects of Obamacare was the individual mandate. It's hard to believe the government could force anyone to buy something they either didn't want or didn't need in America, but Obama thought he knew better. So, under Obamacare, if you chose not to buy health insurance, you paid a crippling fine.

While he was running for president in 2008, Obama claimed he opposed an individual mandate to buy health insurance. "A mandate means that in some fashion, everybody will be forced to buy health insurance.... But I believe the problem is not that folks are trying to avoid getting health care. The problem is they can't afford it. And that's why my plan emphasizes lowering costs."[393] One can understand why he flip-flopped. It was a politically unpopular concept, and it was easily the least popular part of Obamacare, but if young, healthy Americans didn't buy insurance, the system would fail. Alas, the exchanges failed even with the mandate in place, and many people found that the fine was cheaper than Obamacare-compliant insurance. In 2016, 8 million people were fined under the Obamacare individual mandate, totaling

$3 billion in penalties, according to IRS data.[394] Who paid most of those fines? According to IRS data, eighty percent of taxpayers paying the mandate penalty made less than $50,000 a year.[395]

Conservatives criticized the mandate as unconstitutional and hoped that the Supreme Court would ultimately strike the mandate down and cripple the bill. But, in 2012, the Supreme Court bizarrely ruled that, although individual mandates weren't constitutional, Obamacare was. Chief Justice John G. Roberts Jr., nominated by President George W. Bush, joined the liberal wing of the court in crafting the majority decision. In his decision, Roberts wrote,

> The Affordable Care Act is constitutional in part and unconstitutional in part. The individual mandate cannot be upheld as an exercise of Congress's power under the Commerce Clause. That Clause authorizes Congress to regulate interstate commerce, not to order individuals to engage in it. In this case, however, it is reasonable to construe what Congress has done as increasing taxes on those who have a certain amount of income, but choose to go without health insurance. Such legislation is within Congress's power to tax.[396]

While many conservatives like me were upset that a Bush-appointed justice had saved Obamacare, he cleverly created a roadmap for killing it and got liberal justices to sign on. If the mandate was a tax levied by Congress, Congress could repeal it. When Donald Trump became president, he had majorities in the House and Senate and seized his chance.[397]

As part of the GOP tax reform, signed into law by President Trump on December 22, 2017, the individual mandate to purchase health insurance met its timely end. "The individual mandate was very unfair, because you're basically saying, pay for something in order to not have to get healthcare," Trump said when he signed the tax reform bill into law. "It was very unfair. Many people thought it should have been overturned at the Supreme Court."[398] The Congressional Budget Office forecasted that the repeal would cause 4 million people to forego coverage in 2019 (the year the repeal would take effect) and 13 million by 2027.[399] The left viewed this as a disaster, but here's another way of looking at it: that's a lot of people who would prefer not to have an expensive Obamacare plan. Thanks to Donald Trump and the Republican party, they no longer will have to pay a penalty for their choice.

Loosening Rules for Association Health Care Plans

In June 2018, Trump undercut Obamacare again by announcing new rules to expand association health plans (AHPs). The new rules made it easier for small businesses and trade groups to band together to purchase cheaper health coverage. Even sole proprietors could participate.[400] Justin Haskins of the Heartland Institute explained: "The expansion of association health plans is a truly remarkable improvement for the health insurance industry, one many insurance companies fought against because it gives significantly more power to millions of consumers across the country."[401]

Democrats were livid, accusing Trump of sabotaging the already failing Obamacare. AHPs are cheaper and offer less coverage than Obamacare-compliant plans, making it more attractive to younger and healthier people who don't need or want the more comprehensive insurance they can't afford. Business groups like the National Federation of Independent Business (NFIB) and the Chamber of Commerce cheered the new rules. "In the wake of the Senate's failure to repeal Obamacare, we are grateful to President Trump for addressing regulations that make it harder and costlier for small business owners to provide healthcare for themselves and their employees," NFIB CEO Juanita Duggan said in a statement.[402] Thomas J. Donohue, the president and CEO of the US Chamber of Commerce, concurred. "There is good news at last for the millions of small businesses nationwide that have struggled to find affordable health insurance. Previously, the unequal treatment of large and small companies left smaller employers with a stark choice: either pay for high-priced comprehensive plans or offer no health coverage at all. Is it any wonder that the number of small businesses offering coverage has fallen in recent years?"[403]

Democrats, as they so often do, pushed back hard. Attorneys general from eleven Democrat-led states and the District of Columbia sued the Trump administration, claiming they violated consumer protections under Obamacare.[404] This claim is laughable; AHPs still provide similar protections to Obamacare-compliant plans, explains Robert E. Moffit, a senior fellow in the Heritage Foundation's Center for Health Policy Studies.

> *Authorized under federal law, the rules governing association health plans are the same rules that exist today that enforce consumer protections in large group, or corporate health insurance. Persons with a pre-existing medical condition, for example, cannot be denied coverage, and federally regulated association health plans cannot drop persons from their coverage because they get sick, or charge them higher premiums because they have a pre-existing condition.[405]*

According to Moffit, the loosened rules could "reverse the continuing downward slide in the number of small businesses offering coverage." You'd think the left would be happy about this, but you'd be wrong. According to an NFIB report, from 2004 to 2016, "the number of small businesses offering insurance coverage fell from 42 percent to 29 percent. That decline sharply accelerated under Obamacare between 2013 and 2015."[406] In case you forgot, Obamacare was supposed to help people *afford* health insurance, not drive millions of people into expensive personal insurance plans when their small businesses couldn't offer them coverage.

According to Sally Pipes of the Pacific Research Institute, "AHP premiums are generally lower and more stable than small-group and individual market plans. Avalere, a health care consulting firm, projects that annual AHP premiums will be almost $3,000 lower than small group plans and nearly $10,000 lower than individual market plans by 2022."[407] Reaction to the new rules has been mixed. While the NFIB felt the Trump rules weren't workable for them, the Congressional Budget Office estimated 4 million Americans would enroll within five years, and approximately 400,000 of them "would otherwise have gone without insurance."[408] In other words, AHPs would increase access to care; something Obamacare failed to accomplish.

If you want to know why small business confidence reached its highest level ever in September 2018, Joseph Semprevivo, the president and CEO of Joseph's Lite Cookies, credited the new expansion of the association health plans, calling them a lifeline "for small businesses suffering from inflated health care costs."[409]

Rolling Back Limits on Short-Term Health Plans

In 2010, the Congressional Budget Office projected 21 million Americans would enroll in the Obamacare online marketplace by 2016. In reality, only 12.7 million actually purchased coverage. Obamacare plans were just too expensive, so rather than pay more than they could afford, they sought cheaper alternatives, like short-term health plans. Obama blamed the consumers rather than the inflated prices of his crippled marketplace and sought a way to seal that leak.

Shortly before leaving office, his administration imposed new restrictions on short-term health plans. The new rules cut the maximum duration of these plans down from one year to three months to make the more expensive Obamacare plans more attractive.[410] These plans have their disadvantages; they are bare bones plans and insurers can refuse to sell such plans to people who are sick. By reducing the maximum duration of these plans to three months, they became riskier for consumers.[411] Why let the rubes choose plans they could afford, even if they incurred risks with their purchase, when you can force them onto your overpriced government-subsidized insurance?

Predictably, the new rule backfired drastically.

With short-term plans rendered useless, and Obamacare-compliant plans increasingly unaffordable, many Americans decided to go without insurance. Only 11.8 million people enrolled in exchange plans for

2018. That's a 3.7 percent decrease from 2017 and nearly 1 million fewer enrollees than 2016. Forty-five percent of uninsured Americans cited cost as the reason they lack coverage, according to a recent Kaiser Family Foundation survey.[412]

To bring this affordable health insurance option back to the American people, the Trump administration restored the twelve-month enrollment period and allowed enrollees to renew their short-term coverage for up to three years. The Trump administration projected that the short-term health plan market would eventually grow to 1.6 million people.[413]

For healthier people who don't need comprehensive coverage that will bankrupt them, this is a good thing; short-term plans can cost about a tenth of Obamacare-compliant plans.[414] If the goal is to get people covered, and Obamacare was having the opposite effect in 2018, perhaps Obamacare's cheerleaders should get their priorities straight. Every time Americans find a cheaper way to get access to health care, Democrats cry foul, arguing that these "junk" plans didn't cover as much as Obamacare-compliant plans. Yet, these plans existed for decades, and Obama was unconcerned with them until the end of his final year in office.

"The Trump administration is right to provide more options to Americans who have suffered under Obamacare and, in many cases, been priced out of health coverage," said Marie Fishpaw, the director of domestic policy studies at the Heritage Foundation. "States should have more authority to regulate short-term, limited duration health plans."[415] A few liberal states like California banned short-term health plans soon after Trump's rollback was announced. Funny how those states didn't have a problem with these plans until the last year of Obama's term.[416]

The Trump administration acknowledged that short-term health insurance plans aren't for everyone. But, as Health and Human Services Secretary Alex M. Azar II told the *New York Times*, "they can provide a much more affordable option for millions of the forgotten men and women left out by the current system."[417] After all, what good is a comprehensive plan if you can't afford it?

Ending the Birth Control Mandate

The biggest problem with a government forcing its people to buy a service is that they must define what that service will entail. Invariably, this forces people to choose between their conscience and the law. For the left, one of the big selling points of Obamacare was guaranteed coverage of birth control and abortion-inducing drugs. But some religious charities, institutions, and for-profit businesses providing health insurance to their members felt their religious freedom was under attack. Only houses of worship and single-faith groups were exempt from the requirement, leading to dozens of lawsuits from groups not protected by that narrow exemption who felt that providing birth control coverage was counter to their faith.

Hobby Lobby, for example, is a successful national chain whose Christian owners want to run the business guided by their faith. "Our family is now being forced to choose between following the laws of the land that we love or maintaining the religious beliefs that have made our business successful and have supported our family and thousands of our employees and their families," said founder and CEO David Green. There was no exemption for Hobby Lobby or other for-profit businesses with religious principles. Not complying with the mandate would cost Hobby Lobby $1.3 million a day in fines.[418]

The United States Supreme Court ultimately agreed with Hobby Lobby, ruling, in June 2014, that certain for-profit businesses, "closely held corporations" run by a single family can be exempt from the mandate. This was a limited victory, however, since the contraception mandate would still apply to most employers.[419]

For example, the ruling did not apply to the Little Sisters of the Poor, a Roman Catholic women's institution. The group filed a complaint in federal court in 2013. In 2015, US Court of Appeals for the 10th District ruled against them because the mandate did not "substantially burden plaintiffs' religious exercise or violate the plaintiffs' First

Amendment rights." Mark Rienzi, lead attorney for the Little Sisters of the Poor, blasted the decision. "It is a national embarrassment that the world's most powerful government insists that, instead of providing contraceptives through its own existing exchanges and programs, it must crush the Little Sisters' faith and force them to participate."[420]

The Little Sisters of the Poor and other similar organizations achieved a major Supreme Court victory in May 2016 in a unanimous ruling vacating the lower courts' rulings against them, after the Obama administration acknowledged that women could get contraceptive coverage through the exchanges on their own. The Supreme Court ordered the lower courts to work out the details between all involved parties. According to David French of *National Review*, the ruling "provides a judicial roadmap for a national victory for religious liberty."[421]

But groups like the Little Sisters would see their religious liberty restored under President Trump. He promised to be an advocate for religious freedom and in the summer of 2017, he declared, "No American should be forced to choose between the dictates of the federal government and the tenets of their faith." In October of the same year, the Trump administration released two new rules allowing all employers and insurers to opt out of contraceptive coverage if they object based on "sincerely held religious beliefs," or have other "moral convictions" against covering such care.[422]

Liberals were furious and went to the courts to stop the rollback. There are plenty of left-wing activists sitting in federal district courts and two of them temporarily blocked the new rules.[423] This issue has continued to play out in the courts and will only be resolved by the Supreme Court. With Trump's Supreme Court nominees Neil Gorsuch and Brett Kavanaugh now hearing cases, there is little doubt that religious liberty will prevail. Had Hillary Clinton won in 2016, we wouldn't be so sure.

CHAPTER 7

TOUGH ON RUSSIA

Almost immediately after Donald Trump's surprise victory in the 2016 election, we were treated to a barrage of left-wing conspiracy theories and excuses to explain how he pulled it off. Polling outfits were putting Hillary's chances of victory at over 90 percent. Hillary's defeat was soul-crushing for those who had spent the past few years assuming Hillary's victory was a done deal, that the election was a waste of time when poll after poll showed her winning easily. There are compilation videos on YouTube showing liberal reactions to Hillary's defeat. I highly recommend watching some—they never get old.

So, what happened? The left wasn't short on absurd excuses. It was a white backlash, voter suppression, voter fraud, low voter turn-out, media bias, evil white women, white nationalism, James Comey reopening the investigation into Hillary's emails, bad polling, fake news bots, and so on, and so forth, ad nauseum. Everything short of alien mind control was on the table. The theory that gained the most traction was straight out of a James Bond plot: Trump colluded with his "good friend" Vladimir Putin to steal the election.

For most of Trump's first two years in office, all we heard from the media was: *"Russia! Russia! Russia!"*

We now know that the rogue agents within the FBI who advanced this theory were desperate to stop Donald Trump from becoming president and crafted an insurance policy just in case they didn't get their way on election day. A bogus dossier on Donald Trump compiled by a British spy was the key piece of "evidence" used to convince the Foreign Intelligence Surveillance Court to wiretap the Trump campaign and ultimately convince the Justice Department to appoint a Special Counsel to investigate alleged Russian collusion despite a lack of real evidence. Special counsel Robert Mueller's investigation has turned up nothing. Bob Woodward also looked into the allegations for his book on the Trump White House. Conservative radio host Hugh Hewitt asked him, "Did you, Bob Woodward, hear anything in your research, in your interviews, that sounded like espionage or collusion?" To which, Woodward replied, "I did not, and of course, I looked for it, looked for it hard."[424]

Despite the inability of the Mueller investigation to turn up any evidence of collusion, liberals and Never Trump conservatives, still unable to cope with the results of the 2016 election, have tried their best to claim Trump's actions as president prove he's a puppet of Putin. The narrative falls apart when you dig a little deeper—in fact, he's been tougher on Russia than Barack Obama was. Liberals don't want to admit this, but it's true.

Byron York theorizes that "some Trump critics appear to think of Russia only in terms of countering online election interference," but notes that Obama's actions in the aftermath of the 2016 election hardly prove Obama was tough on Russia—especially when you compare them to everything Trump has done.[425]

Let's not forget: it was the Obama administration that tried to reset relations with Russia. The Obama administration approved the sale of 20 percent of America's uranium to Russia—over Republican objections. Obama told Dmitry Medvedev he'd have "more flexibility" after his reelection to deal with more controversial issues with Russia. It was Obama who refused to enforce his red line with Syria, an ally of Russia. He also gave billions of dollars and a path to nuclear weapons to Iran, another strategic ally of Russia, even as they chanted "death to

America." It was Susan Rice, Obama's national security adviser, who ordered Michael Daniel, White House director of cybersecurity, to stand down and not work on options to counter Russian cyber-attacks during the 2016 election.[426]

Yes, you read that correctly. Obama was probably Russia's greatest ever patsy his entire tenure in office. He mocked Mitt Romney for saying Russia was America's number one geopolitical threat. In his last debate with Romney, Obama delivered the carefully scripted zinger, "The 1980s are now calling to ask for their foreign policy back." The Democrats and the media joined in the ridicule. Ultimately, it was Barack Obama who wound up with egg on his face.

Sanctions and More Sanctions

The first thing to look at are the sanctions imposed by the Trump administration against Russia. Liberals will be quick to point out that Obama sanctioned Russia too. Yes, Obama imposed sanctions on Russia and booted thirty-five Russian diplomats out of the United States...after Hillary Clinton lost the election.[427] Before the election, Obama gave no indication he considered Russia a serious threat; afterward, he needed a scapegoat.

Many on the left presumed that Trump, owing his victory to Russia, would be a reliable Russian puppet, doing Putin's bidding. But in his first month in office, he announced that existing sanctions against Russia for their annexation of Crimea from Ukraine would remain in place despite overtures of friendship from the White House. During her first appearance at the UN Security Council in February 2017, Trump's former UN Ambassador, Nikki Haley, condemned the "aggressive actions" of Russia. "We do want to better our relations with Russia. However, the dire situation in eastern Ukraine is one that demands clear and strong condemnation of Russian actions." She continued:

> *The United States stands with the people of Ukraine, who have suffered for nearly three years under Russian occupation and military intervention. Until Russia and*

the separatists it supports respect Ukraine's sovereignty and territorial integrity, this crisis will continue.

Eastern Ukraine, of course, is not the only part of the country suffering because of Russia's aggressive actions. The United States continues to condemn and call for an immediate end to the Russian occupation of Crimea. Crimea is a part of Ukraine. Our Crimea-related sanctions will remain in place until Russia returns control over the peninsula to Ukraine.[428]

In August 2017, Trump signed a bill imposing even more sanctions against Russia, targeting their energy and defense industries. The legislation even limited Trump's ability to undo the sanctions—but he still signed it.[429]

In April 2018, the US imposed new sanctions on Russia for their alleged attempts to interfere with US elections and "malign activity." Reuters reported the move was "aimed at seven Russian oligarchs and 12 companies they own or control, plus 17 senior Russian government officials. They freeze the U.S. assets of the people and companies named and forbid Americans in general from doing business with them."[430] Republican strategist Jennifer Kerns called the sanctions significant, and "among the toughest sanctions ever placed on individuals in a foreign country, with the exception of Iran and North Korea."[431] These sanctions hit Russia very hard, and Moscow was livid. "Washington once again struck at the Russian-American relations, now the captains of Russian business who refused to play by the Washington scenario got under the sanctions," the Russian Embassy wrote on its Facebook page. "The US made another erroneous step to destroy the freedom of entrepreneurship and competition, integration processes in the global economy."[432] Despite Russia's tough talk, Trump still wasn't done. In September 2018, he added thirty-three more Russian individuals and entities connected to Russia's defense and intelligence agencies to the US sanctions list.[433] And these tough sanctions are merely the tip of the iceberg.

Closing Russian Consulates and Expelling Diplomats

In response to the aforementioned sanctions imposed by Trump, the Kremlin ordered the United States to reduce its diplomatic presence in Russia, and Trump replied in equal measure. In August 2017, the Trump administration ordered the closures of the Russian consulate in San Francisco and the Russian diplomatic annexes in New York and Washington, D.C., giving them two days to comply. *The Chicago Tribune* described the closures as "perhaps the most drastic diplomatic measure by the United States against Russia since 1986, near the end of the Cold War."[434] Russia was furious over the closures, calling them "gross violation of international law," and vowed to respond. "We will have a tough response to the things that come totally out of the blue to hurt us and are driven solely by the desire to spoil our relations with the United States," promised Russian Foreign Minister Sergey Lavrov.

In March 2018, Trump announced the closure of the Russian consulate in Seattle, Washington, and the expulsion of sixty Russian diplomats nationwide as the punishment for Russia's role in a nerve agent attack on a former Russian spy in Britain. According to a report by *The Seattle Times*,

> Senior Trump administration officials said all 60 Russians ordered to leave were spies working in the U.S. under diplomatic cover, including a dozen at Russia's mission to the United Nations. The officials said the administration was acting jointly with European nations to send a message to Russia's leaders about the "unacceptably high" number of Russian intelligence operatives in the U.S.[435]

According to Jon Huntsman, the US ambassador to Russia, this was "the largest expulsion of Russian intelligence officers in United States history." Eighteen countries, including fourteen in the European Union, also announced plans to expel Russian diplomats—a hundred in total. Russia naturally denied having any role in the attack, and called the expulsions a "provocative gesture." If Putin recruited Trump to be his puppet, he must be very disappointed with the results.

Bombing Syria

On August 20, 2012, Barack Obama delivered his strongest words regarding how the United States would respond should Syria show signs of moving or using chemical weapons. In response to a question about the use of military force in Syria, Obama said, "We have been very clear to the Assad regime, but also to other players on the ground, that a red line for us is we start seeing a whole bunch of chemical weapons moving around or being utilized. That would change my calculus. That would change my equation." He later added, "We have communicated in no uncertain terms with every player in the region that that's a red line for us and that there would be enormous consequences if we start seeing movement on the chemical weapons front or the use of chemical weapons. That would change my calculations significantly." An administration official later added that this did not represent a change of policy, but that "there's a deterrent effect in making clear how seriously we take the use of chemical weapons or giving them to some proxy force."[436]

Syria was unmoved by Obama's red line. On August 21, 2013, one year and a day after Obama's "red line" statement, Assad used chemical weapons on his own people—killing nearly 1,500 civilians, including over 400 children, according to US intelligence analysts.[437] Assad knew Obama was all bark and no bite; the attack sent a message to America that Syria considered the threats empty. To the surprise of no one, Obama folded like a paper tiger, choosing, instead, to downplay his "red line" comments. During a joint press conference with Swedish Prime Minister John Fredrik Reinfeldt, Obama was asked, "Is a strike needed in order to preserve your credibility for when you set these sort of red lines?" He replied, "First of all, I didn't set a red line; the world set a red line. The world set a red line when governments representing 98 percent of the world's population said the use of chemical weapons are abhorrent and passed a treaty forbidding their use even when countries are engaged in war."[438]

It was a laughable excuse. Robert Farley of the left-leaning FactCheck.org reviewed Obama's original comment, the context, and his later equivocation, and concluded that there was no ambiguity in Obama's warning to Assad. "The decision to tie U.S. military involvement to Assad using chemical weapons was Obama's red line," Farley wrote.[439]

This begs the question: why would Obama undermine his credibility, and the credibility of the United States, by not enforcing the red line he made? Former State Department officials, speaking with *Foreign Policy* magazine, said that even though Obama and his advisers claimed to want to hold Assad accountable for attacking his own people, they feared reprisal from Russia. "The State Department's top brass balked when staff at the U.S. mission to the United Nations drafted a plan in the fall of 2014 to point the finger at the regime for a series of chlorine attacks in Syria, fearing it might upend efforts to secure Russia's support for peace in Syria and jeopardize an Iran nuclear pact."[440] Instead of enforcing his red line, Obama's administration struck a deal with Russia to remove Assad's chemical weapons— which turned out to be a huge mistake. "Not only did that deal fail to ensure the complete removal of Bashar Assad's stockpiles (as evidenced by the regime's repeated use of such weapons long after they were supposedly eliminated), it essentially opened the door to Russian military intervention two years later," explained James Kirchick, visiting fellow with the Brookings Institution.[441]

Lauren Fish, a research associate with the Defense Strategies and Assessments Program and the Future of Warfare Initiative at the Center for a New American Security, confirmed the Obama administration "was caught by strategic surprise when the leadership vacuum left by the United States led the Russians to enter the Syrian fray in the fall of 2015, bringing with them high-tech military equipment for battlefield testing and deployability and bolstering their standing on the world stage."[442]

Secretary of State John Kerry tried to claim the deal with Russia was a diplomatic victory for the United States, saying, "we got 100 percent of the chemical weapons out." Obama's national security adviser Susan Rice also claimed, in January 2017, that "we were able to get the Syrian government to voluntarily and verifiably give up its chemical weapons stockpile."[443] In April 2017, Assad attacked his people again…with chemical weapons the Obama administration claimed were gone. An estimated one hundred people were killed.[444] Within days, President Trump did what Obama refused to do: enforce the red line. He ordered a military strike targeting an airbase that housed the warplanes that carried out the chemical attacks.[445]

According to a report by *Politico*, several key Obama advisers cheered Trump's actions. "He's proved he's not Obama—and that's useful to him," said one former senior Obama official who supported Trump's Syria strike. "Our administration never would have gotten this done in 48 hours," said another former senior official of the Obama administration. "It's a complete indictment of Obama." Anne-Marie Slaughter, Obama's first-term chief of policy planning at the State Department, said, "I feel like finally we have done the right thing. The years of hypocrisy just hurt us all. It undermined the U.S., it undermined the world order."

Even John Kerry admits that not enforcing the red line was a big mistake. "I put several ideas on the table. The president was not persuaded by my argument. I believed that we had several options we could have done at very low risk to be able to make it clear to Assad that when we had a cease fire and when he said he was going to live by it, he had to live by it. And I thought we should have done that," Kerry said on CBS's *Face The Nation* in September 2018. "We paid a price for the way it played out without the red line being enforced by the bombing."[446]

Another chemical attack by the Assad regime came a year later.[447] And once again, President Trump enforced the red line Obama drew, striking three targets. According to Pentagon spokeswoman Dana White, the operation was a success. "We met our objectives. We hit the sites, the heart of the chem-weapons program. So it was mission accomplished."[448] Russia condemned the airstrike.[449] Putin probably got even madder when US forces killed at least one hundred Russian mercenaries and injured roughly 300 following a surprise attack on a US held base in Syria.[450] Trump has been a worse ally of Putin than Obama was of Benjamin Netanyahu.

Arming Ukraine

In March 2014, Russia unlawfully annexed Crimea. Vladimir Putin claimed, "Crimea has always been an integral part of Russia in the hearts and minds of people."[451] World leaders condemned these actions,[452] including the Obama administration. "We condemn Russia's moves to formally annex the Crimean region of Ukraine," said Obama press secretary Jay Carney. "Such action is a threat to international peace and security, and it is against international law. We would not recognize this attempted annexation."[453] Obama imposed some measured sanctions via executive order,[454] but that's pretty much all the help he offered Ukraine.

He didn't even offer much tough talk after his initial condemnation. When Russia sent soldiers, tanks, and heavy artillery into Ukraine that August, Obama refused to call it an invasion, even as US officials were privately doing so.[455] In response to the question from *Wall Street Journal* reporter Colleen Nelson, "Do you consider today's escalation in Ukraine an invasion?" Obama replied, "I consider the actions that we've seen in the last week a continuation of what's been taking place for months now."[456] A bipartisan congressional coalition called for Obama to arm Ukrainian forces.[457] Obama's Defense Secretary, Ash Carter, and key military leaders also wanted Obama to send weapons and military equipment to Ukraine.[458] Yet, when Congress authorized the sale of $41.5 million in military arms and equipment in 2014, the Obama administration did not approve it.[459]

Obama was apathetic about Russian aggression in Crimea, but Trump was not. In December 2017, he unequivocally defied Putin by approving the sale of lethal arms and ammunition to Ukraine—the same package approved by Congress in 2014.[460] "In addition to practical applications of these weapons there is also an important symbolism attached to this decision," said Luke Coffey, director of the Heritage Foundation's Foreign Policy Center. "It sends the right message to friend and foe that the U.S. is serious on trans-Atlantic security and that President Trump doesn't dither in these tough decisions."[461]

Russia was not happy about this and condemned the move.[462] That didn't stop Trump from approving another sale of arms to Ukraine. This $47 million sale included 210 Javelin anti-tank missiles and thirty-seven launch units in March 2018. According to a statement by the State Department, "This proposed sale will contribute to the foreign policy and national security of the United States by improving the security of Ukraine. The Javelin system will help Ukraine build its long-term defense capacity to defend its sovereignty and territorial integrity in order to meet its national defense requirements."[463] In July 2018, Trump sent another $200 million in non-lethal aid, including "secure communications, military mobility, night vision, and military medical treatment." Secretary of Defense James "Mad Dog" Mattis said, "Russia should suffer consequences for its aggressive, destabilizing behavior and its illegal occupation of Ukraine."[464]

Starting Research and Development on an INF Noncompliant Missile

In 2014, the Obama administration informed the North American Treaty Organization that Russia had tested a new ground-launched cruise missile in violation of the 1987 Intermediate Nuclear Forces Treaty between the United States and Russia. That treaty was instrumental in ending the Cold War, but Obama didn't seem to think so. The *New York Times* reported that the State Department was "trying to find a way to resolve the compliance issue, preserve the treaty and keep the door open to future arms control accords." But Obama's weak response reportedly frustrated administration officials and members of Congress.[465] By October 2016, Russia was still in violation of the treaty and American officials were concerned Russia was producing missiles for deployment, not just testing. The banned missiles could fly

300–3,400 miles and carry a nuclear warhead. Yet the Obama administration shrugged off concerns from lawmakers.[466]

Unlike Obama, Trump was not willing to ignore Russia's violation of the treaty. In December 2017, President Trump levied new sanctions it hoped would force Russia to comply with the Intermediate Nuclear Forces Treaty by targeting Russian companies providing the technology to develop the illegal missiles. The decision of the Trump administration came following a "lengthy review" by the National Security Council. According to an administration official who spoke with *Politico*, the goal was "to signal to Russia that the Trump administration will take treaty violations seriously," and to "change the economic calculus of Putin's government."[467]

A few days later, Trump signed a $700 billion defense bill, which included a $25 million appropriation for research and development of our own intermediate-range missile.

> *The research and development on the medium-range missile is intended to serve as a direct response to Russia's deployment in recent years of its own treaty-busting missile. U.S. intelligence first recognized Moscow's potential violation of the Intermediate-Range Nuclear Forces Treaty when the Russian missile was still in test phase. The Obama administration worked unsuccessfully to persuade the Kremlin to stand down the program. Now the Trump administration has decided to respond with a missile of its own.* [468]

"The research and development required by Trump's new law wouldn't in itself violate the treaty; only the development of a medium-range missile would," according to a Pentagon spokesman. "We are prepared to stop such research and development if Russia returns to verifiable compliance with the Treaty." [469]

Obama's soft response to Russia's violation of the thirty-year-old treaty allowed Russia to pursue development and produce deployable missiles. Trump, by comparison, answered Putin's treachery with a measured, proportional retaliation and an invitation to stand down delivered from a position of strength.

Increasing NATO Spending on Defense

The North Atlantic Treaty Organization (NATO) is an alliance of twenty-nine countries founded in 1949 "to protect the people and territory of its members." The NATO website explains the alliance was founded "on the principle of collective defence, meaning that if one NATO Ally is attacked, then all NATO Allies are attacked."[470] NATO's purpose was to counter the threat of the Soviet Union, but once the Cold War was over, most European countries slashed their spending on the program. The only time any NATO ally ever invoked the collective defense provision of the NATO treaty was after 9/11. NATO, as a defensive alliance, was nearly irrelevant…until Russia annexed Crimea.[471] Suddenly, Europe needed NATO to stand up to Russian aggression. In September 2014, NATO announced a rapid reaction force of 4,000 troops, and a pledge to increase annual defense spending to 2 percent of their GDP by 2024 to counter a potential Russian attack.[472] While running for president, Donald Trump was highly critical of NATO allies for not paying their fair share of joint defense costs. He even suggested he would make US military aid dependent on NATO members fulfilling their defense obligations. By June 2017, only six NATO nations met spending standards: the United States; Greece; the United Kingdom; Estonia; Poland; and Romania.[473]

The left cried out in horror at Trump's rhetoric, conveniently forgetting that Barack Obama, to his credit, also called out NATO allies for not spending enough. Perhaps they realized that Obama's words were meaningless, but Trump meant business. As soon as he tackled the issue, he got results. By the end of June 2017, NATO allies, in response to Trump's pressure, announced plans to boost their defense spending and "more fairly share the burden of our security," according to NATO Secretary General Jens Stoltenberg, who also called the increase "a clear demonstration that our alliance stands united in the face of any possible aggression."[474] According to *The Washington Post*, the increase for 2017 boosted "military spending by non-U.S. NATO members to about $295 billion, which is still far less than the United States spends alone."[475]

Unimpressed, Trump continued to pressure NATO allies to step up their defense spending. "I'm going to tell NATO, 'You gotta start paying your bills. The United States is not going to take care of everything,'" Trump said in July 2018 at a rally of supporters in Great Falls, Montana.[476] A few days later, NATO leaders agreed to increase defense spending "to bolster the alliance's deterrence and defense capabilities to counter Russian threats," according to CNN.[477] Trump also suggested that NATO leaders should increase their defense spending to 4 percent of GDP, double the original 2 percent goal from 2014.[478]

Besides pressuring NATO allies to increase their defense spending, Trump also signed defense cooperation agreements with NATO allies Lithuania and Estonia, deploying thousands of troops "to bolster NATO defenses in the face of a Russian threat of aggression."[479] Trump also agreed to sell Poland the Patriot missile system,[480] significantly modernizing their air defense capabilities, something Barack Obama had refused to do.[481]

Let's recap the story on this so-called bromance between Trump and Putin, shall we? Trump so loved his Russian masters that he hardened the defensive line along Russia's western border, took command of the Syrian battlefield when necessary—including by attacking Russians when they impeded US military actions in the country—levied unparalleled sanctions on Russian businesses and leadership, and threatened the development of intermediate-range nuclear missiles in response to similar illegal projects by the Kremlin. I don't know about you, but I don't feel the love.

CHAPTER 8

JUSTICE

Without a doubt, the Obama administration set the all-time record for corruption in the United States government. With the help of his Attorneys General Eric Holder and Loretta Lynch, Obama and his cronies forever erased the illusion of blind justice from the American psyche. They stonewalled every investigation into their dirty deals, got help from complicit journalists to bury every scandal, weaponized the executive agencies to target Obama's political enemies, and protected left-wing interests from scrutiny. Not once did Obama's DOJ appoint a special counsel; they instead conducted sham internal investigations. Predictably, they deemed themselves blameless of any wrongdoing. When the corruption got so blatant that a cover-up was impossible, those found responsible for various abuses were given slaps on the wrist and kept their pensions.

Incredibly, Barack Obama had the gall to accuse President Trump of politicizing the Department of Justice. In September 2018, Obama accepted an Ethics in Government award from the University of Illinois—an award he deserved even less than his bogus Nobel Peace Prize. In his speech, Obama told the audience they "should still be concerned with our current course and should still want to see a restoration of honesty and decency and lawfulness in our government." He later added, "it should not be a partisan issue to say that we do not pressure the attorney general or the FBI to use the criminal justice system as a cudgel to punish our political opponents."[482] If only he heeded his own advice, this chapter would not be necessary.

The lack of accountability in Obama's inner circle emboldened this culture of corruption, leading to some of the most egregious government racketeering in history. With Obama out of office, we've seen the depoliticization of the Department of Justice under Attorney General Jeff Sessions, who has begun the process of examining Obama era abuses of power. As special counsel Robert Mueller investigates Trump, Congress now oversees investigations into various rogue agents at the FBI, including Andrew McCabe, Peter Strzok, and Lisa Page among others. The House Oversight Committee has shown that the fake dossier these men and women commissioned was a part of a plot to undermine a Trump presidency, should he win the election.

It will take years to undo the damage done to the reputation of the Department of Justice, but President Trump deserves credit for reinforcing the credibility of federal law enforcement in ways even other Republicans might have avoided, had they been elected in his place. I share Trump's frustration with the lack of progress in the case against Hillary Clinton for her gross negligence in handling classified information. Given the lingering presence of Obama-era holdovers throughout the DOJ, Attorney General Jeff Sessions has acquitted himself remarkably well on matters of internal ethics, in stark contrast to his predecessors. What follows are some of Trump's most important successes in his battle to drain the swamp.

Reversing Obama's Fast and Furious Executive Privilege

Operation Fast and Furious was a horribly misguided gun-walking operation which sent 2,000 firearms from the United States to Mexico hoping to track them and capture Mexican drug cartel leaders. Most of the weapons disappeared. A few, though, found their way into the hands of men who murdered a Border Patrol agent and an Immigration and Customs Enforcement (ICE) agent. At least 150

Mexican civilians also died because of this folly while the FBI caught zero cartel leaders.[483]

Throughout the scandal that followed the murder of Border Patrol agent Brian Terry, Barack Obama and Attorney General Eric Holder had a symbiotic relationship. Holder protected Obama, and Obama protected Holder. Both denied advance knowledge of the operation. They even tried to blame the operation on George W. Bush, although the planning and execution of the operation happened after Obama took office. To further protect the Obama administration from accountability, Eric Holder lied under oath about his knowledge of Fast and Furious.[484] When Congress started their investigation, Obama's people systematically refused nearly every subpoena for documents or stalled for months before releasing that information. Obama claimed executive privilege to prevent documents from reaching the committee after Holder denied there was any attempt at a cover-up and said, "We're not going to be hiding behind any kind of privileges or anything." Oops.

Congress held Holder in contempt for his refusal to turn over documents. There was also a sham investigation that DOJ whistleblowers said was set up to absolve Holder and blame the entire operation on rogue employees. A congressional investigation determined that Holder had played a major role in the cover-up and in obstructing Congress.[485]

The Obama administration maintained executive privilege over critical Fast and Furious documents through the end of his presidency. There's no doubt that, had Hillary Clinton been elected president, those documents would still be under wraps. But with Trump in the Oval Office, things were different. On March 6, 2018, Kent Terry, Brian Terry's brother, appeared on "Fox & Friends" and urged President Trump to reopen the Fast and Furious case. "We need to find out the truth, exactly what happened, how it happened, why it happened. We need Mr. Trump, President Trump, to unseal the documents, reverse executive privilege so that we know what happened, and that we can hold the people accountable that are responsible," he said.[486]

The following day, the DOJ announced that it would turn over documents previously withheld by Attorney General Eric Holder to the House Oversight Committee. "The Department of Justice under my watch is committed to transparency and the rule of law," said Sessions in a statement. "This settlement agreement is an important step to make sure that the public finally receives all the facts related to Operation Fast and Furious."[487]

Margot Cleveland, a senior contributor at *The Federalist,* explained it will be awhile before we know the results of the investigation because "the DOJ demanded safeguards in the conditional settlement agreement to prevent leaks: The Committee agreed to store the documents exclusively on a computer not connected to either the internet or the House computer network, or on a removable digital media that will be kept in a locked container. The committee also agreed to give the DOJ seven-days' notice prior to releasing any newly unredacted material."[488] We don't know, yet, what Holder and Obama hid from the American people, but, sooner or later, we will. Obama and his allies can't be too happy about that.

Pardoning Dinesh D'Souza

In 2013, several months after Dinesh D'Souza's documentary, *2016: Obama's America,* became the second-most-popular political documentary in American history, the conservative author and filmmaker learned he was under federal investigation for campaign finance violations. In 2012, a college friend of the conservative author, filmmaker, and activist ran for the US Senate in the state of New York against Senator Kirsten Gillibrand. D'Souza, wanting to assist his longtime friend, arranged for $20,000 in straw donations to her campaign.[489] D'Souza was indicted in January 2014, and an immediate bipartisan uproar over the patently political indictment ensued. Famed lawyer and Harvard Law School professor Alan Dershowitz called the indictment "an outrageous prosecution" and a misuse of federal resources. "It raises the question of why he is being selected for prosecution among the many, many people who commit similar crimes." Dershowitz, a liberal supporter of Barack Obama, suspected the decision to indict D'Souza came from the top. "This sounds to me like it is coming from higher places. It is hard for me to believe this did not come out of Washington or at least get the approval of those in Washington." Other legal experts agreed. "What strikes me as unusual is that it involves a single donation made by an individual with no criminal record," said Joseph diGenova, a former US Attorney for the District of Columbia. He added, "It seems to me that a misdemeanor makes much more sense than a felony charge." David Mason, a commissioner of the Federal Election Commission from 1998 to 2008, also found the actions of the Obama administration troubling. "What struck me first was that it is unusual in cases like these for the FBI to go out and actually arrest someone, simply because it is not necessary." He added, "and even less so in this case because [D'Souza] has enough prominence that it is fairly obvious that he is not a flight risk. White collar indictments are made lots of times without an arrest being made." A $20,000 campaign finance donation, according to Mason, is trivial compared to most cases.[490] It's dwarfed by the nearly $2 million in irregular campaign donations Obama's 2008 presidential campaign accepted, which only resulted in a fine of $375,000, which, according to Politico, "was one of the largest fees ever levied against a presidential campaign."[491] The Obama campaign stonewalled the investigation, but no one suffered the wrath of government prosecution… and can you believe it, the Obama Justice Department chose not to prosecute anyone!

Andrew McCarthy, a former Assistant US Attorney and a contributor to *National Review*, also noted that the Obama administration piled on a second charge of making false statements to the government to maximize D'Souza's penalty. "You cannot commit the donation offense without simultaneously committing the false-statement offense. For the government to charge both smacks of double jeopardy: being twice prosecuted for the same, single offense," McCarthy explained. "By gratuitously piling on another felony, Obama and Holder portray D'Souza as a serious crook and subject him to the onerous potential of seven years in prison—all for an episode that ordinarily would not be prosecuted at all."[492]

D'Souza pleaded guilty, paid a $30,000 fine, and received five years of probation, which included eight months in a community confinement center. D'Souza served his time but finally got justice in May 2018 when President Trump announced he would grant him a full pardon. "I am thrilled and relieved and elated and as an immigrant in America, my American dream has been under something of a cloud, so I'm very relieved to have that cloud lifted," D'Souza told Fox News. Trump and D'Souza spoke on the phone for approximately ten minutes when Trump informed him of his decision to grant him a full pardon. "President Trump told me he felt I had been treated very unfairly and he felt that I was an important voice for America."[493] That such an injustice had to be fixed at all is a testament to just how politicized Obama's Justice Department was. Sadly, it wasn't the only example.

Pardoning Kristian Saucier

In 2009, then twenty-two-year-old US Navy sailor Kristian Saucier of Arlington, Vermont, took six photos in classified areas of the USS Alexandria, a nuclear submarine. He knew the areas were classified, but he wanted to show his family and future children what he did in the US Navy. "It was a foolish mistake by a very young man," said Saucier's lawyer. Federal prosecutors said Saucier was a national security risk and wanted to put him in prison for five years. Two other crew members of the nuclear submarine also took photos in the same classified areas Saucier did, but they faced only internal Naval discipline and avoided prosecution.

In August 2016, Saucier was sentenced to a year in federal prison. Saucier had asked the US district judge for probation, comparing his actions to those of Hillary Clinton, whom the FBI declined to prosecute despite her gross negligence in handling classified information, as part of his defense.[494] Federal prosecutors scoffed at the comparison and accused Saucier of "grasping at highly imaginative and speculative straws in trying to…draw a comparison to the matter of Sec. Hillary Clinton."[495] The prosecutors may have had a point; the *Washington*

Examiner noted that the six photos Saucier took "were deemed 'confidential,' the lowest level of classification […] Clinton, by contrast, sent and received highly classified information on a private email server,"[496] which may have been hacked by China.[497] So, what Hillary did was much, much worse.

Despite this, Hillary Clinton nearly became president of the United States while Saucier and his family went through hell. While he was in prison, his family accumulated massive debts leading to the repossession of his two cars and the foreclosure of his house. After leaving prison, Saucier found it difficult to find work. "No one will hire me because I'm a felon," he told the *Washington Examiner* in January 2018. "All the skills I worked so hard for in the military are useless." He found a job as a garbage man, but works seventy hours a week just to support his family.[498]

Donald Trump cited Saucier's case as a double standard of justice when compared to what Hillary Clinton did. A tweet on January 2, 2018, gave Saucier hope that Trump might give him justice. "Obviously with his tweet today he still recognizes my case, so hopefully he will do something about it. I think my family and I have been punished enough," Saucier said. "I made an innocent mistake as a kid, it wasn't planned like Hillary Clinton and them blatantly flouting the law."[499]

Saucier got his justice on March 9, 2018, when he received a pardon from Donald Trump. President Trump congratulated Saucier in a tweet the next day, "Congratulations to Kristian Saucier, a man who has served proudly in the Navy, on your newly found Freedom. Now you can go out and have the life you deserve!"[500] The Obama administration destroyed his life while they simultaneously excused Hillary Clinton's negligent mishandling of classified information to protect Barack Obama's presidential legacy. If Hillary Clinton had won, Saucier would never have been pardoned. It won't magically fix the damage done to his life, but it will make it easier for him going forward.

Ending Obama's Slush Funds

Obama probably wouldn't admit to this, but he was part of the problem that led to the 2007–2010 subprime mortgage crisis. Predatory lending practices disproportionately targeted minorities for subprime loans,[501] and, as a civil rights lawyer in Chicago in 1995, he sued Citibank for alleged racial discrimination in its lending practices on behalf of 186 African American clients. As far as Obama was concerned, banks had to give mortgages to minorities whether or not they could afford them. Most of Obama's clients could not. Only 6 percent still owned a home by 2012.[502] With lenders incentivized by Clinton-era regulations to give mortgages to people who couldn't afford them, and with lawyers like Obama suing them if they didn't hand out loans to minority applicants who fell well short of benchmarks, it was only a matter of time before the bubble burst.

Fast forward twelve years to when Obama was president in the midst of the crisis. He had to punish banks for doing exactly what he previously wanted them to do. Which he did…sort of. His Justice Department sued major lenders for their predatory lending and reached billion-dollar settlements with them.[503] But, if you think Obama cared about the victims who deserved compensation, you are wrong. By the summer of 2010, the Obama administration was steering leftover settlement money to select left-wing organizations instead of returning the money to the banks.[504] From there, it got shadier. The Obama administration started including language in settlement agreements that allowed banks to reduce their settlement obligations by two or more dollars for every one dollar they donated to left-wing groups approved by Obama that, George Will noted in *The Washington Post*, "were neither parties to the case nor victims of the banks' behaviors."[505] And they profited heavily from this slush fund scheme. Left-wing groups got millions of dollars that would have otherwise gone to victims of predatory lending.

So, what did Trump do when he took office? Did he attempt to direct millions of dollars to conservative organizations like Family Research Council, Judicial Watch, the Heritage Foundation,

Americans for Prosperity, and the like? Nope. Within six months, the Trump administration officially put an end to the practice. They banned settlement agreements that allowed large companies to reduce their settlement obligations by making donations to outside groups. Jeff Sessions sent a memo to ninety-four US attorneys' offices on June 7, 2017, prohibiting them from "entering into any agreement on behalf of the United States in settlement of federal claims or charges that directs or provides for a settlement payment to non-governmental, third parties that were not directly harmed by the conduct."[506]

"When the federal government settles a case against a corporate wrongdoer, any settlement funds should go first to the victims and then to the American people—not to bankroll third-party special interest groups or the political friends of whoever is in power," Sessions added. "Unfortunately, in recent years the Department of Justice has sometimes required or encouraged defendants to make these payments to third parties as a condition of settlement. With this directive, we are ending this practice and ensuring that settlement funds are only used to compensate victims, redress harm, and punish and deter unlawful conduct."[507]

Obama sought to enrich his allies at the expense of real victims. The Trump administration did the right thing instead. Which system do you prefer?

Pardoning Oregon Cattle Ranchers

In 2012, Oregon ranchers Dwight and Steven Hammond were charged with multiple counts of arson on federal land. In 2001 and 2006, controlled burns on their property inadvertently set fire to federal land. To avoid the statutory minimum of five years in prison under an anti-terrorism statute, the Hammonds entered into an agreement that gave them only a few months' jail time—which they served. But federal prosecutors challenged the decision to shorten their sentences, and the Ninth Circuit Court of Appeals decided, in 2015, to vacate their original sentence and re-sentenced the Hammonds to the mandatory minimum of five years in prison, less the time they had already served—essentially treating the ranchers like terrorists.[508]

The Hammonds returned to prison in January 2016.[509] Their case inspired a forty-one-day occupation of the Malheur National Wildlife Refuge by supporters who felt the Hammond family was being treated unfairly by the government. Ranchers commonly use controlled burns to reduce the risk of wildfires. Given that most western ranches are surrounded by vast tracts of federal land, the Hammonds' peers in the ranching industry had every reason to fear that they, too, might get targeted by the government and face unreasonable jail time.[510] Soon after the 2016 election, friends of the Hammonds started a petition on the White House website urging president-elect Donald Trump to pardon Dwight and Steven Hammond.[511] In July 2018, Trump gave the Hammonds the justice they deserved. "The Hammonds are multi-generation cattle ranchers in Oregon imprisoned in connection with a fire that leaked onto a small portion of neighboring public grazing land. The evidence at trial regarding the Hammonds' responsibility for the fire was conflicting, and the jury acquitted them on most of the charges," the White House said in a statement.[512] At the time of their release, Dwight Hammond was seventy-six years old and had served roughly three years in prison. His son Steven was forty-nine and had served roughly four years. They also paid $400,000 to settle a civil suit related to the case.

They'd served their time, but it wasn't enough for Obama, even though he used his clemency power more than any president since Harry Truman and commuted more sentences than any president in history,[513] including to FALN suspected terrorist Oscar López Rivera and former Army Private Bradley Manning, who leaked thousands of secret military documents through WikiLeaks but became a hero on the left for coming out as transgender. Obama claimed he was on a mission to right the wrongs of overly harsh prison sentences, yet he saw no need to help the Hammonds.

As the Trump White House noted, "At the Hammonds' original sentencing, the judge noted that they are respected in the community and that imposing the mandatory minimum, 5-year prison sentence would 'shock the conscience' and be 'grossly disproportionate to the severity' of their conduct. As a result, the judge imposed significantly lesser sentences. The [Obama] administration, however, filed an over-zealous appeal that resulted in the Hammonds being sentenced to five years in prison. This was unjust."[514] Indeed, it was, Mr. President.

Reversing Operation Choke Point

In 2013, the Obama administration launched an initiative called "Operation Choke Point" with a mandate to investigate banks that did business with companies considered high risk for fraud and money laundering. The partisan motives behind the initiative quickly surfaced as Obama's Justice Department used the initiative to pressure banks to terminate relationships with various businesses that were "entirely lawful and legitimate." They targeted politically incorrect industries like the adult entertainment industry, pawn shops, and pay-day lenders that Obama didn't like, even if they were doing perfectly legal business. But the firearms industry, in particular, felt the pinch. Thousands of properly licensed gun retailers reported being dropped by their banks or having their assets frozen, their lines of credit cancelled, even their ability to have an online presence restricted—due to pressure from the Obama administration.[515]

A Congressional investigation in 2014 determined that "Operation Choke Point was created by the Justice Department to 'choke out' companies the [Obama] Administration considers a 'high risk' or otherwise objectionable, despite the fact that they are legal businesses," and that the Justice Department lacked "adequate legal authority for the initiative." At the time the report came out, House Oversight and Government Reform Committee Chairman Darrell Issa called the initiative "the Justice Department's newest abuse of power." He added, "If the administration believes some businesses should be out of business, they should prosecute them before a judge and jury. By forcibly conscripting banks to do their bidding, the Justice Department has avoided any review and any check on their power."[516]

In January 2015, the Federal Deposit Insurance Corporation (FDIC) admitted in a statement that their actions on behalf of the

Obama administration were discriminatory and promised a more transparent process in the future.[517]

Despite the blatant abuse of power and Congress's recognition of that abuse, it took the Trump administration to end Operation Choke Point. Less than eight months into his presidency, Trump's Justice Department announced that it would end the controversial initiative. In a letter to Bob Goodlatte (R-VA), the House Judiciary Chairman, Assistant Attorney General Stephen Boyd explained the decision to end the program. "We share your view that law abiding businesses should not be targeted simply for operating in an industry that a particular administration might disfavor. Enforcement decisions should always be made based on facts and the applicable law," he wrote.

The National Rifle Association Institute for Legislative Action (NRA-ILA) cheered the decision. "On behalf of the NRA's five-million members, I want to thank President Trump and Attorney General Sessions for ending 'Operation Choke Point'," said Chris W. Cox, executive director of the NRA-ILA, in a statement. "President Obama's blatant attempt to misuse banking laws to destroy small firearm businesses was unconscionable. We appreciate the Trump administration's commitment to end it once and for all."[518]

Ending Abuse of Guidance Documents

We know that Obama abused his executive authority like none before him. Even the *New York Times* acknowledged that Obama's presidency "depended on bureaucratic bulldozing, rather than legislative transparency," and that Obama "pursued his executive power without apology, and in ways that will shape the presidency for decades to come."[519] When talking about Obama's abuse of executive powers, most will reference Obama's infamous threat: "I've got a pen and I've got a phone." They'll point to his various executive orders and the excessive regulations by various government departments designed to enact his domestic policy agenda without the consent of Congress. But he did far more than that. Obama also used guidance documents to thwart the will of Congress.

As I've previously mentioned in this book, Obama administration officials wrote guidance documents to threaten schools to use racial quotas in admissions and in their enforcement of discipline policies, and to force them to treat "gender identity" and sex as synonymous—meaning boys could use girls' bathrooms and locker rooms and even play on girls' sports teams—or risk losing Title IX funding.

I share the concerns of the *New York Times* that Obama's reshaping of executive power could transform the presidency into a position of unchecked power. When you think about it, can you imagine any president refusing a precedential power established by their predecessor? Imagine Hillary Clinton in the Oval Office doing all of her business with a pen and a phone. The Trump administration could easily cite Obama's executive overreach as precedent. Maybe he would do things I agree with ideologically, but the implications for the future of the republic would be disastrous. But instead of echoing the Obama strategy, Trump reversed it.

On November 17, 2017, Jeff Sessions issued a memo that put an end to the practice of using guidance documents to evade the rule-making process established by the Constitution. "Guidance documents can be used to explain existing law, but they should not be used to change the law or to impose new standards to determine compliance with the law," said Associate Attorney General Rachel Brand in a statement. Brand also promised that the Department of Justice would "proactively work to rescind existing guidance documents that go too far." The Trump administration had already been rescinding Obama-era guidance documents but would now "conduct a review of existing Department documents" and "recommend candidates for repeal or modification."[520] Associate Attorney General Brand reaffirmed the Trump administration's commitment to ending the abusive Obama-era practice in another memorandum declaring that "the department may not use its enforcement authority to effectively convert agency guidance documents into binding rules."[521]

The Attorney General's Regulatory Reform Task Force identified twenty-five guidance documents for repeal in December 2017, and another twenty-four in July 2018. "The American people deserve to have their voices heard and a government that is accountable to them. When issuing regulations, federal agencies must abide by constitutional principles and follow the rules set forth by Congress and the President," Sessions said in a statement. "In previous administrations, however, agencies often tried to impose new rules on the American people without any public notice or comment period, simply by sending a letter or posting a guidance document on a website. That's wrong, and it's not good government." He added, "In the Trump administration, we are restoring the rule of law."[522]

The rescinding of unconstitutional guidance documents by the Trump administration has not been without controversy, but one thing is for sure: Trump and his appointees put an end to guidance documents, curtailing their own power in favor of the Constitution.

Shifting the Judiciary Back to the Right

I've spent a lot of time carping about Obama's abuse of executive orders, the aggressive actions of his hand-picked regulators, and the broken nature of his few legislative accomplishments. But as we've seen, executive orders can be rescinded as easily as they were enacted. Regulations can be reversed. Even legislation can be superseded by new legislation. But judicial appointments are a whole other animal. Presidential appointments to the judiciary are for life. Thus, they are typically the most enduring aspects of a president's legacy and, without a doubt, the hardest to reverse.

By 2014, Barack Obama had already appointed more judges to the federal courts than George W. Bush, shifting the judiciary dramatically to the left. The Alliance for Justice, a left-wing legal organization, claimed Obama had shifted the circuits from 38.7 percent liberal when he took office to 53.5 percent liberal by June 2014.[523] Obama couldn't have done it without Harry Reid. For years, presidents were unable to get the justices they wished to appoint onto the bench when they faced an opposition party in control of the Senate. Many of President George W. Bush's appellate court nominees were blocked by unprecedented Democrat filibusters. But when the tables were turned, the Republican minority in the Senate returned the favor when Obama was president. But after Democrats grew tired of being stymied by the GOP minority, Reid nuked the filibuster for judicial appointments, a move Senate Democrats would later regret. Once Republicans took command of the Senate in 2015, Obama's ability to pack the courts collapsed.

Despite Obama's success shifting the circuits leftward, President Trump inherited over one hundred court vacancies—nearly double the vacancies Obama inherited.[524] Without the filibuster, Democrats relied on the abuse of an old parliamentary tradition commonly called the "blue slip." Each Senator hailing from the state that housed a court with a vacancy could block any nomination by deploying their "blue slip" veto. But Democrats unleashed a beast when they nuked the filibuster and abandoned centuries of Senate tradition meant to protect the minority. Senate Majority Leader Mitch McConnell, feeling no urge to live by rules the Democrats no longer honored, declared in October 2017, that blue slips would no longer be honored as a device to block judicial nominees.[525]

Trump took it from there and filled vacancies with gusto. The Senate confirmed more US Circuit Court judges in his first year in office than that of any other president, and his record pace continued through his second year.[526] Trump flipped two federal circuits, the Sixth and Seventh Circuit Courts of Appeals, from liberal to conservative, and the Eighth and Eleventh Circuit Courts are also on the verge of flipping conservative. Incredibly, the notoriously liberal Ninth Circuit is also under the gun, as Trump has nominated three hard conservatives to fill vacancies that would shift the California court to, at worst, roughly ideologically even.[527] Since Republicans increased their Senate majority in the 2018 midterm elections, it's safe to say Trump will have an even easier time getting judges confirmed.

Besides nominating qualified originalist judges to the courts, Trump also tends to nominate younger judges. *The Washington Post* studied the recent history of court appointments and found, "the median age of Trump's circuit court judges is about 49 years old, younger than the judges put forward by the past five presidents."[528]

Trump's commitment to nominating young conservative judges will have a long-lasting impact on the judiciary—and not just with the appellate courts.

Trump's Supreme Court Nominees

I still remember the moment I found out that Supreme Court Justice Antonin Scalia had unexpectedly passed away and the indescribable panic I had that Barack Obama would get to appoint his replacement. It was bad enough he already got two…but now he'd get a third? I couldn't contain my dread. Obama's previous Supreme Court picks, Sonia Sotomayor and Elena Kagan, ascended the bench despite neither being in the mainstream. Aside from extreme liberal voting records, there were other concerns with both that I considered disqualifying. Sotomayor's past public comments on race and gender in the judiciary exposed her reliance on identity politics over the Constitution in her decision-making. I was also troubled by Elena Kagan's anti-military activism. But both were confirmed with bipartisan majorities; Sotomayor was confirmed 68-31, and Kagan 63-37.

Republicans finally showed backbone after Scalia's passing. They vowed not to hold any hearings or consider any nominee put forth by Obama in his final year of office. To justify this strategy, they pointed to a 1992 floor speech by then-Senator Joe Biden, the chairman of the Judiciary Committee, who argued that if a Supreme Court vacancy occurred before the presidential election, a president should delay any nomination until after the election. "It is my view that if a Supreme Court Justice resigns tomorrow, or within the next several weeks, or resigns at the end of the summer, President Bush should consider following the practice of a majority of his predecessors and not - and *not* - name a nominee until after the November election is completed." Without a doubt, Democrats—who controlled the Senate in 1992— would have blocked any nominee put forth by President George H. W. Bush had a vacancy occurred.

Knowing what the Republican strategy would be, Barack Obama nominated Merrick Garland to fill Scalia's seat about a month after

Scalia's passing. To counter the Republican strategy of not giving Obama's nominee a vote, Obama and the Democrats tried to present Garland as a "consensus nominee" and a "moderate." The media was more than willing to echo this fantasy as they did with Kagan, Sotomayor, Breyer, and Ginsburg—all of whom they branded centrists,[529] and were more than willing to repeat the same lies for Garland.

The *Los Angeles Times* called Garland a moderate and a centrist, but also acknowledged that if Garland were confirmed, "the court would tip to the left on several key issues, like abortion, affirmative action, the death penalty, gun control, campaign spending, immigration and environmental protection."[530] The same day their editorial board called Garland "the ideal moderate Supreme Court nominee" with a "solidly centrist voting record,"[531] the *New York Times* published an extensive analysis of Garland's record placing him ideologically firmly on the left, right between Ginsburg and Kagan. "If Judge Garland is confirmed, he could tip the ideological balance to create the most liberal Supreme Court in 50 years."[532] Analysis by *The Washington Post* also conceded that, despite his reputation for being a moderate, Garland "would shift the court—and the court's median ideology—significantly to the left."[533] So not only had we lost Antonin Scalia, but Obama was about to put a liberal in his place. The future of the Supreme Court relied not only upon the resolve of Senate Republicans to keep the seat open for nearly a year, but on the results of the presidential election. If Hillary Clinton won, the Supreme Court would be lost.

Many on the right, myself included, were not convinced that then-frontrunner for the Republican nomination for president, Donald Trump, was a true conservative who would nominate conservatives to the judiciary, let alone the Supreme Court. Ben Shapiro, the editor-in-chief of *The Daily Wire,* declared, "there is no shot – *zero shot* – that Trump will appoint a conservative."[534] This was months after Trump released a list of potential Supreme Court nominees generated with the guidance of the Federalist Society and the Heritage Foundation.[535] This was a smart move on Trump's part, as polling showed that the Supreme Court was the most important factor for GOP voters turning out for Trump on Election Day.[536]

Trump proved his conservative critics wrong when he nominated Neil Gorsuch to the Supreme Court on January 31, 2017. Conservatives were thrilled. Liberals were outraged, immediately going into attack mode. Democrats falsely accused Gorsuch of every "ism" under the sun, then filibustered Gorsuch hoping to block his confirmation, forcing Republicans to nuke the filibuster and clear a path for his confirmation. Gorsuch was confirmed on April 7, 2017, in a 54–45 vote, with three Democrats supporting his confirmation.[537] Scalia's seat on the court was saved, thanks to Donald Trump and Republican unity against Obama.

The liberal media criticized Democrats for overplaying their hand. Their abuse of the filibuster had precluded all procedural means to block any future Supreme Court nominee by Trump. So when Justice Anthony Kennedy announced his retirement in the summer of 2018, the left panicked. Kennedy, though nominated by President Reagan, became the court's ideological swing vote. His retirement meant that the nomination of a conservative judge to replace him would shift the court further to the right. Liberals immediately vowed to block his nominee, whoever it was.

On July 9, 2018, President Trump nominated Brett Kavanaugh, who was on Trump's list of twenty-five potential Supreme Court picks. Before the ink was dry on his nomination, Senate Democrats denounced Kavanaugh. Senator Chuck Schumer declared he would fight the nomination "with everything I have." Other Democrats expressed similar sentiments. They tried everything in their dirty bag of tricks. They invoked the Biden Rule, arguing that a Supreme Court nomination should not be considered during a midterm election year. That excuse fell flat because Elena Kagan had been nominated and confirmed in a midterm election year. They argued that the Mueller investigation into bogus claims of Russian collusion should prevent Trump from being able to make the nomination. This excuse also fell flat because Bill Clinton got two Supreme Court picks while under investigation. They argued that Kavanaugh withheld key information from the committee despite the fact that the Senate received more material on Kavanaugh's legal record than the past five nominees combined.[538] Every excuse offered by the Democrats failed to stop Kavanaugh, and upon completion of his confirmation hearings, it was all but certain that Kavanaugh would be confirmed.

On July 30, 2018, Senator Dianne Feinstein received a letter from a California woman who alleged that Kavanaugh had assaulted her at a high school party in the 1980s. Rather than bringing this letter to the attention of the committee to have it investigated privately, Feinstein held on to the letter, never mentioning it to Senate Republicans, or even Brett Kavanaugh when they met privately on August 20, 2018. On September 10, the Senate Judiciary Committee hearings concluded. Three days later, Feinstein, knowing that Kavanaugh's confirmation was inevitable without a Hail Mary, referred the letter to the FBI, and on September 16, 2018, *The Washington Post* unmasked the identity of Kavanaugh's accuser and the details of her allegations.

The Senate Judiciary Committee investigated, but the Democrats on the committee refused to participate.[539] The allegations against Kavanaugh were weak, and all the alleged witnesses to the event denied it or had no memory of the party in question. Between the lack of corroboration, the holes in the story, and the lack of similar accusations against Kavanaugh, who had passed six previous FBI background checks with no red flags, it seemed this smear tactic would also fizzle out.

But then, on September 23, *The New Yorker* published a story detailing another allegation of sexual misconduct. This allegation was even weaker than the previous one. It alleged drunken sexual misconduct during Kavanaugh's time at Yale. Despite an incident allegedly witnessed by dozens at a dorm party, there were, once again, no corroborating witnesses, and the accuser herself wasn't even sure Kavanaugh was the one who had committed the alleged acts.[540] The story was so weak that even the *New York Times* chose not to run with the story because it lacked corroboration.[541] A third accuser offered the even more ridiculous accusation that Brett Kavanaugh and his friend had orchestrated gang rapes at high school parties. For many

Americans, the increasingly circus-like atmosphere surrounding the nomination process smelled like a desperate ploy by Democrats. As polls showed they might win back the Senate, they sought to either force Kavanaugh to withdraw, or force a long enough delay in confirmation that they could ensure his defeat after the midterms. In so doing, they destroyed his good name and the lives of his family and the families of his accusers.

After a series of delay tactics by legal teams representing his first accuser, she and Kavanaugh testified before the Senate Judiciary Committee on September 27, 2018. Her testimony, despite its emotion, was full of holes and lacked corroboration. Brett Kavanaugh forcefully denied the allegations and had evidence to support that he was never at a party like the one she described. Kavanaugh also gave his own emotional testimony. In his opening statement, Kavanaugh decried the ten-day delay in getting a new hearing. "As I predicted, my family and my name have been totally and permanently destroyed by vicious and false additional accusations," he said. "This confirmation process has become a national disgrace. The Constitution gives the Senate an important role in the confirmation process. But you have replaced 'advice and consent' with 'search and destroy.'" But Kavanaugh promised to fight to clear his name. "I will not be intimidated into withdrawing from this process. You have tried hard. You've given it your all. No one can question your efforts. Your coordinated and well-funded efforts to destroy my good name and destroy my family will not drag me out. The vile threats of violence against my family will not drive me out. You may defeat me in the final vote, but you'll never get me to quit. Never."

Kavanaugh's testimony was persuasive, so Democrats once again stalled for time. They asked for a short investigation, limited in scope to the two most credible accusations, and eventually got Republican Senator Jeff Flake of Arizona to back the plan. The Senate Judiciary Committee voted to recommend Kavanaugh for a final vote on the Senate floor on the condition that the FBI completed a seventh week-long background check on Kavanaugh. The only thing the new investigation revealed was witness tampering by the team representing Kavanaugh's first accuser.[542]

Democrats knew this extra investigation would go nowhere and tried to hammer Kavanaugh with other charges, including bogus allegations of perjury and absurd suggestions that his testimony showed he lacked the temperament and impartiality to serve on the Supreme Court. Despite their best efforts, Kavanaugh was ultimately confirmed on Saturday, October 6, 2018. The aggressive and shameful tactics of the Democrats didn't work, but it often seemed like Kavanaugh's confirmation was in doubt. Through it all, President Trump confidently stood by him rather than withdrawing his nomination. "President Trump stood by Brett Kavanaugh throughout this whole process, I don't know if any other Republican president would have done so," said Mercedes Schlapp, the White House Director of Strategic Communications.[543] I couldn't agree more.

Thanks to President Trump, we have a 5-4 conservative majority on the Supreme Court, instead of a 6-3 left-wing Court under Hillary Clinton. With any luck, he'll have at least one more chance to cement this most crucial legacy.

CONCLUSION

No one can deny that over the course of Obama's two terms in the White House, he fulfilled his promise to fundamentally transform America. The list of major policy shifts is long: Obamacare, Dodd-Frank, racial quotas for college admissions, gun control, net neutrality, open borders, executive amnesty, purging the Guantánamo Bay terrorist prison, the war on coal, the war on oil, the Paris Climate Accord, the Iran Deal, assaults on religious liberty…need I go on? In his quest to make America more acceptable to his milieu, he didn't ask what we wanted. Apart from asking for our vote, he showed no concern at all for denigrating and dismissing the half of America that didn't care for his meddling. When Democrats got shellacked in the midterm election in 2014, for the second time in his presidency, he refused to back down from his radical agenda. "For those of you who voted today, I hear you," he said. "To the two-thirds of voters who chose not to participate in the process yesterday, I hear you, too."[544] For Obama, the Republican wave that saw him lose both Houses of Congress was not a signal to change course, but a call to double down on his radical agenda.

Obama surveyed the international landscape with misplaced optimism and, by the time he was done, left us with a world on fire. His misadventures in Libya, Yemen, Syria, and Ukraine emboldened

133

Russia, enabled the rise of ISIS, fortified Al-Qaeda, left our allies cold and our military in disarray. Jihadis carried out hundreds of terror attacks around the globe, including a dozen successful terror attacks on American soil. Obama kowtowed to America-hating dictators at the expense of American national security. His nuclear deal with Iran left the mullahs in a great position to become the dominant regional power and to gain nuclear weapons. Trump, on the other hand, passed a budget deal that included a massive increase in defense spending, pressured NATO allies to do more to stabilize Eastern Europe, began the construction of a missile defense system in Ukraine and Poland, utterly decimated ISIS, and pushed back against Chinese aggression both economic and diplomatic. He obliterated the deal with Iran, and he reined in North Korea so completely that Kim Jong Un is helping to dismantle the demilitarized zone along the southern border, signaling a new era of cooperation with South Korea.

Obama's answer to the health care crisis was a juggernaut of regulatory strangulation, commandeering one-sixth of the economy with a partisan bill so bloated that no one knew what they were voting for. Obama promised if we liked our doctors, we could keep them; he lied. Obama promised if we liked our existing health care plans, we could keep them; he lied. He said our premiums would drop by $2,500 a year; he lied. Obamacare made matters far worse for most Americans and came at a great cost, not just to our wallets but to our civil liberties. Trump promised to stop the bleeding, and he has done more to render Obamacare inert than most thought possible. He repealed the individual mandate to buy health insurance, improved drug price transparency, and whittled away many of the regulations that most threaten the economy.

Obama believed the bill of rights was merely a guideline and worked to undermine it where it allowed for behavior he deemed unacceptable. He bowed to extremists among grievance activists by forcing religious institutions' health insurance policies to cover birth control, states to pay for abortion, colleges and high schools to engage in biased disciplinary policies intended to correct perceived injustices to women and minorities, and the military to allow women and gender dysphoria sufferers to fight on the front lines. He grabbed for every measure he could find to restrict Americans from owning guns, attacked the fourth amendment's guarantee of privacy, and interfered with states' rights to choose how to run their elections. Trump has righted many of these wrongs and returned the right of all Americans to decide how they will live, to the states and the people.

Obama once claimed a GDP growth rate of 2 percent was "the new normal," and that 4 percent growth was impossible in the 21st century. His executive branch agencies stymied businesses at every turn, making it difficult for them to hire new workers or turn a profit. Trump saw the potential to be better than what they could manage. Within three months of taking office, the *Wall Street Journal* noted that President Trump was "rolling back more regulations than any President in history."[545] In fact, Trump has used the Congressional Review Act to repeal more regulations than any other president in history. Trump's unprecedented deregulation saved billions in lifetime net regulatory costs.[546] Thanks to Trump's tax cuts, median household income is at its highest since the recession. Wages and paychecks are growing faster than they were under Obama. The Trump economy has lifted 4 million Americans off of food stamps. American optimism is at historic highs.[547] Trump has successfully negotiated new trade deals with Japan, South Korea, the European Union, and our North American neighbors. He renegotiated NAFTA into the new USMCA with Canada and Mexico. He crippled the Consumer Financial Protection Bureau. The manufacturing industry has experienced job growth under Trump not seen since 1995.[548] Small business and consumer confidence are at record highs, and, for the first time since George W. Bush was president, the United States reclaimed its spot as the number one most economically competitive country in the world.[549] The economy under Trump has done so well that, in the summer of 2018, there were more job openings than workers to fill them. Jobless claims fell to the lowest level in forty-nine years, and African-American, Hispanic, Asian-American, woman, and youth unemployment have all hit historic lows. Veterans unemployment hit a two-decade low. Without a doubt, Americans across the board have benefited in the Trump economy.[550]

Obama imposed a radical environmental agenda, without regard for efficacy, economic impact, or the Constitution. He saw climate change as an immediate national security threat, justifying exceeding his authority to do as he pleased. Rather than seek the approval of Congress, he enriched his green energy backers and attacked the fossil fuel industry with his Clean Power Plan. He ignored the Senate's role in ratifying treaties to get the United States to agree to the fraudulent Paris Climate Treaty. Obama's EPA spent more time covering up scandals than cleaning up environmental disasters. Under Donald Trump, the Paris Climate Treaty is no more, our military is no longer a tool for environmental extremism, and America can once again take advantage of all its energy resources. America and the world still survive. In fact, the United States, despite its economic growth, reduced carbon emissions more than any Paris Climate Treaty signatory, and total greenhouse gas emissions have declined on Trump's watch despite the repeal of Obama's Clean Power Plan regulations.[551]

Obama sought to pack the federal judiciary with activist judges who would reinterpret laws and ignore the Constitution to favor liberal causes. When Senate Republicans tried to halt Obama's court-packing, Senate Democrats obliterated all protections for the minority party and rammed through dozens of appointees. Trump and his Republican allies saw Obama's bet and raised him. He nominated conservative judges to the courts at a record pace and added two judges to the US Supreme Court, both of whom had a history of interpreting the laws as written: Neil Gorsuch and Brett Kavanaugh. The latter faced an all-out assault on his character but had Trump in his corner all the way. Trump still has over a hundred additional vacancies to fill.

There's more to Trump's legacy than just what he's done to erase Obama's. He's committed billions to fight the opioid epidemic and is aggressively fighting the flow of illegal drugs into the United States from Mexico. Trump signed a law to combat sex trafficking. He also signed the "right to try" bill, allowing terminally ill patients to have access to experimental medical treatments that haven't yet been approved by the Food and Drug Administration (FDA).[552] Trump worked hard to modernize our military and increase pay and access to care for soldiers and veterans. He moved the US Embassy in Israel from Tel Aviv to its capital, Jerusalem.[553] His education department is fighting for school choice. The Trump administration counted 289 accomplishments (most of which I have not previously covered in this book) during Trump's presidency up through the confirmation of Brett Kavanaugh to the Supreme Court.[554] For a man the media assured us wasn't qualified to lead, Trump has been shockingly productive on the job.

If you disliked Obama's confused, yet officious leadership style, if you thought his presidency was a disaster for America, as I did, then Trump is your answer. Contrary to fears he would govern like a New York liberal, Donald Trump has been a very effective president for the conservative movement. More effective, in many ways, than Ronald Reagan—albeit without the class. He's a bare-knuckle brawler who makes up for his lack of decorum with his abundance of results. He's brash, cocksure, boastful, and rude; oh, and he has a nasty tendency to exaggerate and speak off-the-cuff. He cares only for what works, not for how others feel about it. He's a bully and knows how to get what he wants in rooms full of other bullies and has shown the Republican Party that when you fight for conservative causes, you win.

Donald Trump was not the champion of conservatism many of us wanted in 2016, but he proved to be the fighter we needed to protect liberty and freedom after eight years of seeing our rights and freedoms chipped away by a thin-skinned narcissist-in-chief. And you should be glad he's on our side. I hope that President Trump won't be remembered merely for saving us from Barack Obama's legacy of failure and radical policy, but for the conservative foundation he's built and for teaching Republicans how to stand and fight for America.

Democrats continue to divide the country and counter Trump's policy ideas with white-hot rage and hatred, and it cost them in the 2018 midterms. Although they gained a slim majority in the House, those gains were weak compared to historical precedent. Meanwhile,

Republicans gained seats in the Senate and those gains will translate into a more conservative judiciary. Patriotic Americans have Trump to thank for our strong position as he skillfully highlights media dishonesty, liberal hypocrisy, and the contrasting success of his tenure. He deserves the support of every conservative and Republican as he runs for reelection in 2020; he certainly has mine.

ENDNOTES

Introduction

1. Jennifer Agiesta, "Most See a Clinton Victory and a Fair Count Ahead," CNN, October 25, 2016, accessed October 9, 2018, https://www.cnn.com/2016/10/25/politics/hillary-clinton-2016-election-poll/index.html.

2. Peter Baker, "Can Trump Destroy Obama's Legacy?" *New York Times*, June 23, 2017, accessed October 9, 2018, https://www.nytimes.com/2017/06/23/sunday-review/donald-trump-barack-obama.html.

3. Graham Lanktree, "Trump Is Trying to Undo Obama's Presidency, Says Biden—but He Can't," *Newsweek*, February 7, 2018, accessed October 9, 2018, http://www.newsweek.com/trump-trying-undo-obamas-presidency-says-biden-he-cant-800628.

4. Andrew Sullivan, "Andrew Sullivan: Obama's Legacy Has Already Been Destroyed," *Daily Intelligencer*, May 18, 2018, accessed October 9, 2018, http://nymag.com/daily/intelligencer/2018/05/obamas-legacy-has-already-been-destroyed.html.

5. Fred Barnes, "The Wipeout of Obama's Legacy," *The Weekly Standard*, May 11, 2018, accessed October 9, 2018, https://www.weeklystandard.com/fred-barnes/the-wipeout-of-obamas-legacy.

Chapter 1

6   Paul Kengor, "How Barack Obama Fundamentally Transformed the United States," *National Catholic Register*, January 12, 2017, accessed October 16, 2018, http://www.ncregister.com/daily-news/how-barack-obama-fundamentally-transformed-the-united-states.

7   Ibid.

8   Katie Pavlich, "Mark Levin Unloads: Trump Is 'Pretty Damn Close' to Sounding Like a 9/11 Truther," Townhall, February 16, 2016, accessed October 16, 2018, https://townhall.com/tipsheet/katiepavlich/2016/02/16/mark-levin-unloads-on-donald-trumps-debate-comments-n2120124.

9   Wikipedia, s.v. "Mexico City Policy," modified August 14, 2018, accessed August 17, 2018, https://en.wikipedia.org/wiki/Mexico_City_policy.

10   Laura Koran and James Masters, "Trump Reverses Abortion Policy for Aid to NGOs," CNN, January 24, 2017, accessed August 17, 2018, https://www.cnn.com/2017/01/23/politics/trump-mexico-city-policy/index.html.

11   Nicole Hong and Melissa Korn, "Court Filings Detail Role of Race in Harvard Undergraduate Admissions," *Wall Street Journal*, June 15, 2018, accessed August 8, 2018, https://www.wsj.com/articles/filings-provide-look-at-how-harvard-uses-race-in-admissions-1529068477.

12   Melissa Korn, Nicole Hong, and Beth Reinhard, "Justice Department Seeks to Hire Attorneys for Affirmative Action Review," *Wall Street Journal*, August 2, 2017, accessed August 8, 2018, https://www.wsj.com/articles/justice-department-seeks-to-hire-attorneys-for-affirmative-action-review-1501710345?mod=article_inline.

13   Michelle Hackman, "Trump Administration to Rescind Obama Guidelines on Race in College Admissions," *Wall Street Journal*, July 3, 2018, accessed August 8, 2018, https://www.wsj.com/articles/trump-administration-to-rescind-obama-era-guidelines-on-race-in-college-admissions-1530619273.

14 S. A. Miller, "Trump Administration Pushes Colleges to Drop Race from Admissions Process," *The Washington Times*, July 3, 2018, accessed September 30, 2018, https://www.washingtontimes.com/news/2018/jul/3/trump-administration-pushes-colleges-drop-race-adm/.

15 "Race-Neutral College Admissions Action Applauded by Black Activists," National Center for Public Policy Research, July 5, 2018, accessed September 30, 2018, https://nationalcenter.org/project21/2018/07/05/race-neutral-college-admissions-action-applauded-by-black-activists/.

16 Ibid.

17 Jessica Chasmar, "Obama Pushing for 'Largest Gun Grab in American History': NRA," *The Washington Times*, July 27, 2015, accessed August 9, 2018, https://www.washingtontimes.com/news/2015/jul/27/obama-pushing-for-largest-gun-grab-in-american-his/?cache.

18 "Grandma Got Run Over by Obama: SSA Finalizes New Gun Prohibition Rule," NRA-ILA, December 23, 2016, accessed August 9, 2018, https://www.nraila.org/articles/20161223/grandma-got-run-over-by-obama-ssa-finalizes-new-gun-prohibition-rule.

19 Charles C. W. Cooke, "No, the GOP Did Not Just Repeal the Background Check System or Give Guns to the Mentally Ill," *National Review*, February 3, 2017, accessed August 9, 2018, https://www.nationalreview.com/corner/no-gop-did-not-just-repeal-background-check-system-or-give-guns-mentally-ill/.

20 Lois Beckett, "NRA and Republicans Find Unlikely Ally on Rollback of Gun Control Rule: Science," *The Guardian,* February 16, 2017, accessed August 9, 2018, https://www.theguardian.com/us-news/2017/feb/16/nra-republicans-gun-control-science.

21 Ibid.

22 Ibid.

23 Dave Umhoefer, "Glenn Grothman Says Planned Parenthood is Leading Abortion Provider," *Politifact*, May 15, 2017, accessed August 9, 2018, https://www.politifact.com/wisconsin/statements/2017/may/15/glenn-grothman/glenn-grothman-says-planned-parenthood-leading-abo/.

24   Leah Jessen, "Planned Parenthood Entities Spend Over $38 Million to Elect Democrats," *The Daily Signal,* November 3, 2016, accessed August 9, 2018, https://www.dailysignal.com/2016/11/03/planned-parenthood-arms-spend-over-38-million-to-elect-democrats/.

25   Jackie Calmes, "Obama Bars States From Denying Federal Money to Planned Parenthood," *New York Times,* December 14, 2016, accessed August 9, 2018, https://www.nytimes.com/2016/12/14/us/politics/obama–administration-planned-parenthood.html.

26   Colin Dwyer, "Trump Signs Law Giving States Option to Deny Funding For Planned Parenthood," NPR, April 13, 2017, accessed August 9, 2018, https://www.npr.org/sections/thetwo-way/2017/04/13/523795052/trump-signs-law-giving-states-option-to-deny-funding-for-planned-parenthood.

27   Mark Mix, "Barack Obama: 'I Owe Those Unions,'" *The Washington Times*, August 31, 2012, accessed October 7, 2018 https://www.washingtontimes.com/news/2012/aug/31/barack-obama-i-owe-those-unions/.

28   Alex Swoyer, "Trump's Justice Department Reverses Obama Stance on Requiring Union Dues," *Washington Times*, February 12, 2018, accessed October 7, 2018, https://www.washingtontimes.com/news/2018/feb/12/justice-department-reverses-stance-on-paying-union/.

29   Bill Mears, "Supreme Court Deals Blow to Unions, Rules against Forced Fees for Government Workers," Fox News. June 27, 2018, accessed October 7, 2018, https://www.foxnews.com/politics/supreme-court-deals-blow-to-unions-rules-against-forced-fees-for-government-workers.

30   Gregg Re, "Trump Administration to Dump Obama-era Rule Allowing Unions to Siphon Medicaid Money," Fox News, July 10, 2018, accessed October 7, 2018, https://www.foxnews.com/politics/trump-administration-to-dump-obama-era-rule-allowing-unions-to-siphon-medicaid-money.

31   Lydia Wheeler, "Labor Board Burns through Obama-era Rules," *The Hill*, December 20, 2017, accessed October 7, 2018, https://the-

hill.com/regulation/365707-labor-board-burns-through-obama-era-rules.

32 J. Bryan Lowder, "Holder Interprets Title VII Protections To Cover Transgender Workers," *Slate Magazine*, December 19, 2014, accessed August 8, 2018, http://www.slate.com/blogs/outward/2014/12/19/holder_says_title_vii_sex_discrimination_protections_now_cover_trans_workers.html.

33 Ryan T. Anderson, "Trump Should Rescind Obama's Transgender Agenda and Protect Religious Liberty," *The Daily Signal*, January 31, 2017, accessed August 9, 2018, https://www.dailysignal.com/2017/01/31/trump-should-rescind-obamas-transgender-agenda-and-protect-religious-liberty/.

34 Mark Abadi, "US Justice Department: North Carolina's 'Bathroom Law' Violates the Civil Rights Act," *Business Insider*, May 4, 2016, accessed August 8, 2018, https://www.businessinsider.com/ncs-hb2-violates-civil-rights-act-2016-5.

35 Andrea Noble, "Jeff Sessions Rolls Back Obama-era Work Protections for Transgender Employees," *Washington Times*, October 5, 2017, accessed August 8, 2018, https://www.washingtontimes.com/news/2017/oct/5/jeff-sessions-rolls-back-obama-era-work-protection/.

36 "U.S. Departments of Education and Justice Release Joint Guidance to Help Schools Ensure the Civil Rights of Transgender Students," U.S. Department of Education, May 13, 2016, accessed August 9, 2018, https://www.ed.gov/news/press-releases/us-departments-education-and-justice-release-joint-guidance-help-schools-ensure-civil-rights-transgender-students.

37 Ibid.

38 David Montgomery and Alan Blinder, "States Sue Obama Administration Over Transgender Bathroom Policy," *New York Times*, May 25, 2016, accessed August 9, 2018, https://www.nytimes.com/2016/05/26/us/states-texas-sue-obama-administration-over-transgender-bathroom-policy.html.

39 Camila Domonoske, "U.S. Judge Grants Nationwide Injunction Blocking White House Transgender Policy," NPR, August 22,

2016, accessed August 9, 2018, https://www.npr.org/sections/ thetwo-way/2016/08/22/490915833/u-s-judge-grants-nation- wide-injunction-blocking-white-house-transgender-policy.

40   Ryan T. Anderson, "Trump Right to Undo Transgender Mandate for Schools," *The Daily Signal*, February 23, 2017, accessed August 9, 2018, https://www.dailysignal.com/2017/02/22/trump-right- to-fix-obamas-unlawful-transgender-school-policies/.

41   Chris Brooke, "Transgender Prisoner Rapist Who Identifies as a Woman Admits Sexually Assaulting Fellow Inmates," *Daily Mail Online*, September 7, 2018, accessed September 30, 2018, https:// www.dailymail.co.uk/news/article-6139305/Transgender- prisoner-rapist-identifies-woman-admits-sexually-assaulting- fellow-inmates.html.

42   German Lopez, "The Trump Administration Just Rescinded Obama-era Protections for Transgender Prisoners," *Vox*, May 14, 2018, accessed August 11, 2018, https://www.vox.com/ policy-and-politics/2018/5/14/17351636/trump-transgender- prison-lgbtq.

43   Ibid.

44   "Pentagon to Move 'Expeditiously' to Lift Ban on Women in Combat Roles," *The Washington Post*, January 24, 2013, accessed August 21, 2018, https://www.washingtonpost.com/world/ national-security/pentagon-to-move-expeditiously-to-lift-ban- on-women-in-combat-roles/2013/01/24/f9fd6244-665d-11e2- 85f5-a8a9228e55e7_story.html.

45   Ernesto Londoño, "Pentagon to Move 'Expeditiously' to Lift Ban on Women in Combat Roles," *The Washington Post,* January 24, 2013, accessed August 21, 2018, https://www.washingtonpost. com/world/national-security/pentagon-to-move-expeditiously- to-lift-ban-on-women-in-combat-roles/2013/01/24/f9fd6244- 665d-11e2-85f5-a8a9228e55e7_story.html.

46   Ash Carter, "Remarks on the Women-in-Service Review," U.S. Department of Defense, December 3, 2015, accessed August 21, 2018, https://www.defense.gov/News/Speeches/Speech-View/ Article/632495/remarks-on-the-women-in-service-review/.

[47] Associated Press, "Half of Female Marines Fail 3-Pullup Requirement," CBS, January 2, 2014, accessed August 21, 2018, https://www.cbsnews.com/news/most-female-soldiers-fail-3-pullup-requirement/.

[48] Rowan Scarborough, "Pressure Grows on Marines to Consider Lowering Combat Standards for Women," *Washington Times*, April 19, 2015, accessed August 21, 2018, https://www.washingtontimes.com/news/2015/apr/19/marine-corps-weighs-lower-standards-for-women-afte/.

[49] Lolita C. Baldor, "Pentagon Chief to Military: Open All Combat Jobs to Women," AP News, December 3, 2015, accessed August 21, 2018, https://apnews.com/051710452d6f47388f0cf54f99726adf/carter-telling-military-open-all-combat-jobs-women.

[50] Maya Rhodan, "Obama Compares Letting Women in Combat Role to Desegregation, Gays in the Military," *Time*, December 3, 2015, accessed August 21, 2018, http://time.com/4135757/obama-compares-allowing-women-in-combat-roles-to-desegregation-gays-in-the-military/.

[51] Jennifer Rizzo and Zachary Cohen, "Pentagon Ends Transgender Ban," CNN, last modified June 30, 2016, accessed August 20, 2018, https://www.cnn.com/2016/06/30/politics/transgender-ban-lifted-us-military/index.html.

[52] Mary Emily O'Hara, "Trump Slammed for Controversial Response to Trans Military Question," NBC, October 4, 2016, accessed August 20, 2018, https://www.nbcnews.com/feature/nbc-out/trump-slammed-controversial-response-trans-military-question-n659521.

[53] Baldor, "Mattis Delays New Transgender Policy for US Military," *Military Times,* August 8, 2017, accessed August 21, 2018, https://www.militarytimes.com/news/pentagon-congress/2017/07/01/mattis-delays-new-transgender-policy-for-us-military/.

[54] Elizabeth Harrington, "Here's the Astronomical Cost Taxpayers Would Pay for Transgender Surgeries in the Military," *Washington Free Beacon*, July 28, 2017, accessed August 21, 2018, https://free-

beacon.com/issues/transgender-surgeries-would-cost-pentagon-1-3-billion/.

55 Domonoske, "Federal Judge Blocks Trump's Ban on Transgender Service Members," NPR, October 30, 2017, accessed August 21, 2018, https://www.npr.org/sections/thetwo-way/2017/10/30/560847850/federal-judge-blocks-trumps-ban-on-transgender-service-members.

56 "Trump Signs New Transgender Military Ban," BBC News, March 24, 2018, accessed August 21, 2018, https://www.bbc.com/news/world-us-canada-43525549.

57 Ibid.

58 Thomas Spoehr, "Pentagon's New Transgender Policy Strikes Right Balance for Military," The Heritage Foundation, June 7, 2018, accessed August 21, 2018, https://www.heritage.org/defense/commentary/pentagons-new-transgender-policy-strikes-right-balance-military.

59 Claudia Grisales, "Trump's Attempted Ban of Transgender Military Service Remains Steeped in Confusion, Chaos," *Stars and Stripes*, July 25, 2018, accessed August 21, 2018, https://www.stripes.com/news/us/trump-s-attempted-ban-of-transgender-military-service-remains-steeped-in-confusion-chaos-1.539500.

60 Phyllis Schlafly and George Neumayr, *No Higher Power: Obama's War on Religious Freedom* (Washington, D.C: Regnery Publishing, 2012).

61 "President Donald J. Trump Stands Up for Religious Freedom in The United States," The White House, accessed August 9, 2018, https://www.whitehouse.gov/briefings-statements/president-donald-j-trump-stands-religious-freedom-united-states/.

62 Margot Cleveland, "ACLU Distorts the Purpose of a Federal Effort to Protect Religious Liberty," *National Review*, January 19, 2018, accessed September 30, 2018, https://www.nationalreview.com/2018/01/conscience-religious-freedom-division-health-human-service-office-civil-rights-aclu-threatens-lawsuit/.

63 Fred Lucas, "Trump Order Creates White House Initiative on Protecting Religious Freedom," *The Daily Signal*, May 3, 2018, accessed August 9, 2018, https://www.dailysignal.

com/2018/05/03/trump-order-creates-white-house-initiative-on-protecting-religious-freedom/.

64 Ibid.

65 Paul Bedard, "Report: Trump Ends Obama's 'War' on Religious Liberty, Helping Millions," *Washington Examiner*, May 2, 2018, accessed August 8, 2018, https://www.washingtonexaminer.com/washington-secrets/report-trump-ends-obamas-war-on-religious-liberty-helping-millions.

66 John Malcolm, "Why Trump Was Right to Reverse Obama's Policy on Military Gear for Police," The Heritage Foundation, accessed August 26, 2018, https://www.heritage.org/homeland-security/commentary/why-trump-was-right-reverse-obamas-policy-military-gear-police.

67 Ibid.

68 Vincenzo Bove and Evelina Gavrilova, "Police Officer on the Frontline or a Soldier? The Effect of Police Militarization on Crime," *American Economic Journal: Economic Policy* 9, no. 3 (2017): 1–18.

69 Barack Obama, "Executive Order: White House Initiative on Educational Excellence for African Americans," National Archives and Records Administration, July 26, 2012, accessed August 10, 2018, https://obamawhitehouse.archives.gov/the-press-office/2012/07/26/executive-order-white-house-initiative-educational-excellence-african-am.

70 Hans A. von Spakovsky and Roger Clegg, "Withdraw the Obama Administration's 'Dear Colleague' Letter on School Discipline," The Heritage Foundation, accessed August 10, 2018, https://www.heritage.org/education/commentary/withdraw-the-obama-administrations-dear-colleague-letter-school-discipline.

71 Ibid.

72 Kelsey Harkness, "Their Son Is Suicidal Because of Bullying. They Blame an Obama Policy," *The Daily Signal,* June 3, 2018, accessed August 10, 2018, https://www.dailysignal.com/2018/06/03/their-son-is-suicidal-because-of-bullying-they-blame-an-obama-era-school-discipline-policy/.

73 Paul Sperry, "Trump 'Plans to Scrap' Obama-era Rule That Turned Schools into War Zones," *New York Post,* March 26, 2018, accessed August 10, 2018, https://nypost.com/2018/03/24/trump-scrapping-obama-era-rule-that-turned-schools-into-war-zones/.

74 Sperry, "Obama's Lax Discipline Policies Made Schools Dangerous," *New York Post*, December 23, 2017, accessed August 10, 2018, https://nypost.com/2017/12/23/obamas-lax-discipline-policies-made-schools-dangerous/.

75 Debra Heine, "Heather Mac Donald Blasts 'Ludicrous' Obama-Era School Discipline Policy That Turned Schools into War Zones," PJ Media, April 6, 2018, accessed August 10, 2018, https://pjmedia.com/trending/heather-mac-donald-blasts-ludicrous-obama-era-school-discipline-policy-turned-schools-war-zones/.

76 Frederick Hess, "The Public Agrees With Teachers . . . And Betsy DeVos?!" *Forbes*, August 21, 2018, accessed October 3, 2018, https://www.forbes.com/sites/frederickhess/2018/08/21/the-public-agrees-with-teachers-and-betsy-devos.

77 Greg Toppo, "DeVos Commission Eyes Obama School Discipline Rules," *USA Today,* March 12, 2018, accessed August 10, 2018, https://www.usatoday.com/story/news/2018/03/12/devos-commission-eyes-obama-school-discipline-rules/418147002/.

78 John Fund, "Obama's Final Whopper as President," *National Review*, January 24, 2017, accessed August 10, 2018, https://www.nationalreview.com/2017/01/obama-lies-voter-id-many-countries-require-it/.

79 "Voter Fraud Map Page," The Heritage Foundation, accessed August 11, 2018, https://www.heritage.org/voterfraud.

80 Fund, "Obama's Final Whopper as President," *National Review*.

81 Ibid.

82 Jeremy Pelofsky, "Obama Administration Blocks Texas Voter ID Law," Reuters, March 12, 2012, accessed August 10, 2018, https://www.reuters.com/article/us-usa-politics-texas-idUSBRE82B0XA20120312.

83 Pam Fessler, "Justice Department Reverses Position on Texas Voter ID Law Case," NPR, February 27, 2017, accessed August

11, 2018, https://www.npr.org/2017/02/27/517558469/justice-department-reverses-position-on-texas-voter-id-law-case.

84 Jessie Balmert, "Trump's Justice Dept. Reverses Obama's Stance on Ohio's Voter Purge," Cincinnati.com, August 8, 2017, accessed August 10, 2018, https://www.cincinnati.com/story/news/politics/2017/08/08/trump-justice-dept-reverses-obama-ohio-voter-purge/548549001/.

85 Adam Liptak, "Supreme Court Upholds Ohio's Purge of Voting Rolls," *New York Times*, June 11, 2018, accessed August 11, 2018, https://www.nytimes.com/2018/06/11/us/politics/supreme-court-upholds-ohios-purge-of-voting-rolls.html.

86 "'The Time Has Come for Voter ID': Trump Rips 'Crazy' Voting Rules," Fox News, August 1, 2018, accessed August 11, 2018, http://insider.foxnews.com/2018/07/31/donald-trump-rally-tampa-desantis-rips-voter-id-rules.

Chapter 2

87 Kevin Boyd, "Barack Obama Has Imposed More Regulations than Any Other President in History," Rare, October 13, 2016, accessed August 11, 2018, https://rare.us/rare politics/issues/regulation-nation/barack-obama-has-imposed-more-regulations-than-any-other-president-in-history/.

88 Dave Boyer, "The 'Most Transparent' President in History Issues Record Number of 'Midnight' Regulations," *Washington Times*, January 5, 2017, accessed August 11, 2018, https://www.washingtontimes.com/news/2017/jan/5/obama-issuing-record-number-midnight-regulations/.

89 Wayne Crews, "Trump Is Least-Regulatory President Since Reagan in First Six Months," CNS, July 20, 2017, accessed August 11, 2018, https://www.cnsnews.com/commentary/wayne-crews/trump-least-regulatory-president-reagan-first-six-months.

90 David Shepardson and Valerie Volcovici, "White House Deregulation Push Clears Out Hundreds of Proposed Rules," Reuters, July 20, 2017, accessed August 11, 2018, https://www.reuters.com/arti-

cle/us-usa-trump-regulation/white-house-makes-broad-deregu-latory-push-idUSKBN1A51O1.

91 Crews, "Trump Is Least-Regulatory."

92 Paul Bedard, "Boom: Team Trump Cuts Nearly Twice as Many Regulations as Promised," *Washington Examiner,* May 20, 2018, accessed August 11, 2018, https://www.washingtonexaminer.com/washington-secrets/boom-team-trump-cuts-nearly-twice-as-many-regulations-as-promised.

93 Matthew J. Belvedere, "Reagan Would Have Supported Trump Tax Reform Despite Its Flaws, Says Reagan Budget Director," CNBC, December 22, 2017, accessed October 18, 2018, https://www.cnbc.com/2017/12/22/reagan-would-have-supported-trump-tax-reform-reagan-budget-director.html.

94 "GOP Better Remind Forgetful Voters: Tax Cuts Are Huge Boost to Middle Class," *Investor's Business Daily*, September 23, 2018, accessed October 18, 2018, https://www.investors.com/politics/editorials/gop-tax-cuts-middle-class/.

95 Roberto A. Ferdman, "School Kids Are Blaming Michelle Obama for Their 'Gross' School Lunches," *The Washington Post*, November 24, 2014, accessed August 9, 2018, https://www.washingtonpost.com/news/wonk/wp/2014/11/24/students-are-blaming-michelle-obama-for-their-gross-school-lunches/.

96 Paul Bedard, "Schools Want Out of Michelle Obama's Lunch Rules, Kids Say 'Yuck,'" *Washington Examiner,* March 13, 2017, accessed August 9, 2018, https://www.washingtonexaminer.com/schools-want-out-of-michelle-obamas-lunch-rules-kids-say-yuck.

97 Mariam Khan and Stephanie Ebbs, "Trump Administration Relaxing Obama-era School Lunch Standards," ABC, May 1, 2017, accessed August 9, 2018, https://abcnews.go.com/Politics/trump-ad-ministration-relaxing-obama-era-school-lunch-standards/story?id=47134641.

98 Elizabeth Nolan Brown, "Nutrition Studies That Backed Obama-Era School Lunch Programs Get Retracted: Reason Roundup," Reason.com, September 20, 2018, accessed October

3, 2018, https://reason.com/blog/2018/09/20/brian-wansink-nutrition-papers-retracted.

[99] "The Dodd-Frank Act," The Heritage Foundation, accessed August 20, 2018, https://www.heritage.org/markets-and-finance/heritage-explains/the-dodd-frank-act.

[100] Veronique De Rugy, "The Dodd-Frank Five-Year Anniversary Is as Bad as We Thought It Would Be," *National Review*, October 10, 2017, accessed August 8, 2018, https://www.nationalreview.com/corner/dodd-frank-five-year-anniversary/.

[101] Norbert Michel and Salim Furth, "The Macroeconomic Impact of Dodd Frank-and of Its Repeal," The Heritage Foundation, April 13, 2017, accessed August 20, 2018, https://www.heritage.org/markets-and-finance/report/the-macroeconomic-impact-dodd-frank-and-its-repeal.

[102] "The Dodd-Frank Act," The Heritage Foundation, accessed August 20, 2018, https://www.heritage.org/markets-and-finance/heritage-explains/the-dodd-frank-act.

[103] Jeb Hensarling, "After Five Years, Dodd-Frank Is a Failure," *Wall Street Journal*, July 19, 2015, accessed August 8, 2018, http://www.wsj.com/articles/after-five-years-dodd-frank-is-a-failure-1437342607.

[104] Ibid.

[105] Reuters, "Donald Trump Says He Would Dismantle Dodd-Frank Wall Street Regulation," *Fortune*, May 18, 2016, accessed August 8, 2018, http://fortune.com/2016/05/18/trump-dodd-frank-wall-street/.

[106] Antoine Gara, "With A Stroke of The Pen, Donald Trump Aims to Wave Goodbye to the Dodd Frank Act," *Forbes*, February 3, 2017, accessed August 8, 2018, https://www.forbes.com/sites/antoine-gara/2017/02/03/with-a-stroke-of-the-pen-donald-trump-will-wave-goodbye-to-the-dodd-frank-act/#6f98ad521148.

[107] Donna Borak, "Trump Signs Orders That Take Aim at Dodd-Frank," CNN, April 21, 2017, accessed August 8, 2018, https://money.cnn.com/2017/04/21/news/trump-executive-order-taxes/index.html.

[108] David Jackson, "Obama Endorses Net Neutrality," *USA Today*, November 11, 2014, accessed August 9, 2018, https://www.usatoday.com/story/news/nation/2014/11/10/obama-internet-net-neutrality/18793429/.

[109] Ian Tuttle, "The FCC's 'Open Internet Rules' Make the Internet Less Open," *National Review*, May 23, 2017, accessed August 9, 2018, https://www.nationalreview.com/2017/05/fcc-open-internet-rules-make-internet-less-open/.

[110] Aaron Bandler, "7 Reasons Net Neutrality Is Idiotic," *Daily Wire*, July 14, 2017, accessed August 9, 2018, https://www.dailywire.com/news/18613/7-reasons-net-neutrality-idiotic-aaron-bandler.

[111] Ibid.

[112] Jesse Hathaway and Justin Haskins, "Ending Net Neutrality Will Save the Internet, Not Destroy It," Fox News, December 16, 2017, accessed August 9, 2018, http://www.foxnews.com/opinion/2017/12/16/ending-net-neutrality-will-save-internet-not-destroy-it.html.

[113] Margaret Harding McGill, "Man Charged with Threatening to Kill Ajit Pai's Family," *Politico*, June 29, 2018, accessed August 9, 2018, https://www.politico.com/story/2018/06/29/ajit-pai-family-death-threat-man-charged-688040.

[114] Emily Tillett, "22 States and D.C. Urge Court to Vacate and Reverse FCC Rollback of Net Neutrality," CBS News, August 21, 2018, accessed October 3, 2018, https://www.cbsnews.com/news/22-states-and-d-c-urge-court-to-vacate-and-reverse-fcc-rollback-of-net-neutrality/.

[115] Cecilia Kang, "Justice Department Sues to Stop California Net Neutrality Law," *New York Times*, September 30, 2018, accessed October 3, 2018, https://www.nytimes.com/2018/09/30/technology/net-neutrality-california.html.

[116] Daniel Wiessner, "States, Business Groups Sue U.S. Government on Overtime Pay Rule," Reuters, September 20, 2016, accessed August 10, 2018, https://www.reuters.com/article/us-overtime-lawsuit/states-business-groups-sue-u-s-government-on-overtime-pay-rule-idUSKCN11Q2E2.

117 Brakkton Booker, "Federal Judge Blocks Obama Administration's Overtime Pay Rule," NPR, November 22, 2016, accessed August 10, 2018, https://www.npr.org/sections/thetwo-way/2016/11/22/503081151/federal-judge-blocks-obama-administrations-overtime-pay-rule.

118 John Bowden, "Justice Department Drops Appeal to save Obama Overtime Rule," The Hill, September 5, 2017, accessed August 10, 2018, http://thehill.com/homenews/administration/349221-justice-department-drops-appeal-to-save-obama-overtime-rule.

119 Sean Higgins, "Trump Administration Won't save Obama-era Overtime Rule," Washington Examiner, September 5, 2017, accessed August 10, 2018, https://www.washingtonexaminer.com/trump-administration-wont-save-obama-era-overtime-rule.

120 Glenn Kessler, "President Obama's Persistent '77-cent' Claim on the Wage Gap Gets a New Pinocchio Rating," The Washington Post, April 9, 2014, accessed August 10, 2018, https://www.washingtonpost.com/news/fact-checker/wp/2014/04/09/president-obamas-persistent-77-cent-claim-on-the-wage-gap-gets-a-new-pinocchio-rating/.

121 Zachary A. Goldfarb, "Male-female Pay Gap Remains Entrenched at White House," The Washington Post, July 1, 2014, accessed August 10, 2018, https://www.washingtonpost.com/politics/male-female-pay-gap-remains-entrenched-at-white-house/2014/07/01/dbc6c088-0155-11e4-8fd0-3a663dfa68ac_story.html.

122 Romina Boccia, "Trump's Reversal of Obama Pay Gap Rule Is Good News for Women, Minorities," The Heritage Foundation, August 31, 2017, accessed August 10, 2018, https://www.heritage.org/economic-and-property-rights/commentary/trumps-reversal-obama-pay-gap-rule-good-news-women.

123 Ibid.

124 Erik Ortiz, "Obama Announces Rules for Closing Gender Pay Gap," NBC, January 29, 2016, accessed August 10, 2018, https://www.nbcnews.com/news/us-news/obama-announce-new-rules-closing-gender-pay-gap-n506941.

[125] Nicole Gaudiano, "Business Groups Try to Quash Federal Equal Pay Project," *USA Today*, March 31, 2017, accessed August 10, 2018, https://www.usatoday.com/story/news/politics/2017/03/31/business-groups-try-quash-federal-equal-pay-project/99874422/.

[126] Boccia, "Trump's Reversal of Obama Pay Gap."

[127] Ibid.

[128] Ibid.

[129] Alden Abbott, "Time to Get Rid of the Consumer Financial Protection Bureau," The Heritage Foundation, February 17, 2016, accessed August 8, 2018, https://www.heritage.org/economic-and-property-rights/commentary/time-get-rid-the-consumer-financial-protection-bureau.

[130] Iain Murray, "The Case against the Consumer Financial Protection Bureau," Competitive Enterprise Institute, September 21, 2017, accessed August 11, 2018, https://cei.org/content/case-against-cfpb.

[131] Donald J. Trump (@realDonaldTrump), "The Consumer Financial Protection Bureau, or CFPB, has been a total disaster as run by the previous Administrations pick. Financial Institutions have been devastated and unable to properly serve the public. We will bring it back to life!" Twitter, November 25, 2017, 1:48 p.m., https://twitter.com/realDonaldTrump/status/934539256940417024.

[132] Elizabeth Zwirz, "Trump Calls CFPB 'a Total Disaster' in a Tweet following Cordray's Resignation," Fox News, November 25, 2017, accessed August 8, 2018, http://www.foxnews.com/politics/2017/11/25/trump-calls-cfpb-total-disaster-in-tweet-following-cordrays-resignation.html.

[133] Zack Friedman, "Trump Administration Requests $0 In Funding for Consumer Protection Agency," *Forbes*, January 19, 2018, accessed August 8, 2018, https://www.forbes.com/sites/zackfriedman/2018/01/19/cfpb-funding-trump/#2a931acd1826.

[134] Chris Arnold, "Trump Official Wants to Put Tight Leash On Consumer Watchdog Agency," NPR, April 2, 2018, accessed August 8, 2018, https://www.npr.org/sections/thet-

wo-way/2018/04/02/598820472/trump-official-wants-to-put-tight-leash-on-consumer-watchdog-agency.

135 Gabby Morrongiello, "Mulvaney Fires All 25 Members of CFPB's Advisory Board," *Washington Examiner*, June 6, 2018, accessed August 8, 2018, https://www.washingtonexaminer.com/news/mulvaney-fires-all-25-members-of-consumer-financial-protection-bureaus-advisory-board.

Chapter 3

136 "President Obama's Record of Dismantling Immigration Enforcement," Federation for American Immigration Reform, accessed August 13, 2018, http://www.fairus.org/issue/publications-resources/president-obamas-record-dismantling-immigration-enforcement.

137 Ibid.

138 Rick Noack, "Sweden Proposes Tough Sexual Assault Law," *The Washington Post,* December 20, 2017, accessed August 13, 2018, https://www.washingtonpost.com/news/worldviews/wp/2017/12/20/amid-metoo-movement-and-fear-of-immigrants-sweden-proposes-tough-sexual-assault-law/.

139 Soeren Kern, "Germany's Migrant Rape Crisis: January 2017," Gatestone Institute, February 13, 2017, accessed August 13, 2018, https://www.gatestoneinstitute.org/9934/germany-rape-january.

140 Anthony Faiola and Souad Mekhennet, "Tracing the Path of Four Terrorists Sent to Europe by the Islamic State," *The Washington Post*, April 22, 2016, accessed August 16, 2018, https://www.washingtonpost.com/world/national-security/how-europes-migrant-crisis-became-an-opportunity-for-isis/2016/04/21/ec8a7231-062d-4185-bb27-cc7295d35415_story.html.

141 Maxim Lott, "Fact Check: Claims 'No Refugees' Since 9/11 Took Part in Terror Plots Ring False," Fox News, accessed August 16, 2018, http://www.foxnews.com/us/2015/11/24/fact-check-claims-no-refugees-since-11-took-part-in-terror-plots-ring-false.html.

142 Faiola and Mekhennet, "Tracing the Path."

143 Matthew O'Brien and Spencer Raley, "The Fiscal Cost of Resettling Refugees in the United States," Federation for American Immigration Reform, February 5, 2018, accessed August 16, 2018, https://fairus.org/issue/legal-immigration/fiscal-cost-resettling-refugees-united-states.

144 Ibid.

145 Stephen Dinan, "Trump Signs Memo Vowing End to 'Catch-and-Release' of Illegal Immigrants," *The Washington Times*, April 6, 2018, accessed August 14, 2018, https://www.washington-times.com/news/2018/apr/6/trump-signs-memo-vowing-end-to-catch-and-release-o/.

146 Dinan, "Obama Reinstates 'Catch-and-Release' Policy for Illegal Immigrants," *The Washington Times*, February 4, 2016, accessed August 14, 2018, https://www.washingtontimes.com/news/2016/feb/4/obama-reinstates-catch-and-release-policy-illegals/.

147 Donald J. Trump, "Executive Order: Border Security and Immigration Enforcement Improvements," The White House, January 25, 2017, accessed August 13, 2018, https://www.white-house.gov/presidential-actions/executive-order-border-security-immigration-enforcement-improvements/.

148 "Border Patrol Council VP: 'Obama Holdovers' Keeping 'Catch & Release' Alive and Well," Fox News, April 2, 2018, accessed August 14, 2018, http://insider.foxnews.com/2018/04/02/illegal-immigration-obama-border-patrol-holdovers-using-catch-and-release-policies.

149 Dinan, "Trump Signs Memo."

150 Trump, "Executive Order: Border Security."

151 Michelle Mark, "Trump Is Visiting the 8 Prototypes for His Border Wall—See What They Look Like," *Business Insider*, March 13, 2018, https://www.businessinsider.com/trump-border-wall-construction-prototypes-photos-cbp-2017-10.

152 Associated Press, "Trump's Border Wall Prototypes Pass Tests by Military Special Forces," *Los Angeles Times*, January 19, 2018,

https://www.latimes.com/local/lanow/la-me-border-wall-test-20180119-story.html.

153 Chantal Da Silva, "Is Donald Trump's Border Wall Already Being Built?" *Newsweek*, September 24, 2018, https://www.newsweek.com/donald-trumps-border-wall-already-being-built-construction-begins-texas-4-1135603.

154 Trump, "Executive Order: Enhancing Public Safety in the Interior of the United States," The White House, January 25, 2017, accessed August 14, 2018, https://www.whitehouse.gov/presidential-actions/executive-order-enhancing-public-safety-interior-united-states/.

155 Jessica M. Vaughan, "Restoring Enforcement of Our Nation's Immigration Laws," Center for Immigration Studies, March 27, 2017, accessed August 17, 2018, https://cis.org/Restoring-Enforcement-Our-Nations-Immigration-Laws.

156 Alex Nowrasteh, "Trump Administration Expands Interior Immigration Enforcement," Cato Institute, December 5, 2017, accessed August 14, 2018, https://www.cato.org/blog/trump-administration-expands-interior-immigration-enforcement.

157 Barbara Boland, "Homeland Sec. Chairman: ISIS Will Use Refugee Crisis to Infiltrate West," *Washington Examiner*, September 13, 2015, accessed August 14, 2018, https://www.washingtonexaminer.com/homeland-sec-chairman-isis-will-use-refugee-crisis-to-infiltrate-west.

158 Rowan Scarborough, "Islamic State Finds Success Infiltrating Its Terrorists into Refugee Flows to West," *The Washington Times*, January 29, 2017, accessed August 14, 2018, https://www.washingtontimes.com/news/2017/jan/29/isis-finds-success-infiltrating-terrorists-into-re/.

159 Nick Gutteridge, "Rise of EUROPEAN Jihadis: EU Admits ISIS Is Exploiting Refugee Crisis to Infiltrate Europe," Express.co.uk, April 6, 2016, accessed August 14, 2018, https://www.express.co.uk/news/world/658508/EU-migrant-crisis-Islamic-State-ISIS-refugees-Syria-Greece-Italy-terror-Paris-attacks.

160 Associated Press, "ISIS Working to Send Operatives to the West, CIA Director John Brennan Says," CBS, June 16, 2016, accessed August 14, 2018, https://www.cbsnews.com/news/isis-operatives-west-cia-director-john-brennan/.

161 Nahal Toosi and Seung Min Kim, "Obama Raises Refugee Goal to 110,000, Infuriating GOP," *Politico*, September 13, 2016, accessed August 14, 2018, https://www.politico.com/story/2016/09/obama-refugees-228134.

162 "Trump's Executive Order: Who Does Travel Ban Affect?" BBC News, February 10, 2017, accessed August 14, 2018, https://www.bbc.com/news/world-us-canada-38781302.

163 Gregory Korte, "Trump Signs Order Cutting Refugee Quota to Lowest Level since 1980," *USA Today*, September 29, 2017, accessed August 14, 2018, https://www.usatoday.com/story/news/politics/2017/09/29/trump-set-cut-refugee-quota-lowest-level-since-1980/713463001/.

164 "United States Ends Participation in Global Compact on Migration," U.S. Department of State, accessed August 17, 2018, https://usun.state.gov/remarks/8197.

165 Olivia Beavers, "US Pulls out of Global Compact on Migration," *The Hill*, December 3, 2017, accessed August 17, 2018, http://thehill.com/homenews/administration/363014-us-pulls-out-of-global-compact-on-migration.

166 Jose A. DelReal, "Trump Says His Proposed Ban on Refugees Is a 'matter of Quality of Life,'" *The Washington Post*, September 21, 2016, accessed August 14, 2018, https://www.washingtonpost.com/news/post-politics/wp/2016/09/21/trump-calls-proposed-ban-on-refugees-a-matter-of-quality-of-life/.

167 Richard Wolf, "Supreme Court Upholds President Trumps Travel Ban against Majority-Muslim Countries," *USA Today*, June 26, 2018, accessed August 14, 2018, https://www.usatoday.com/story/news/politics/2018/06/26/supreme-court-upholds-president-trump-immigration-travel-ban/701110002/.

168 Alan Gomez, "Refugee Admissions to U.S. Plummet in 2017," *USA Today*, January 3, 2018, accessed August 14, 2018,

https://www.usatoday.com/story/news/world/2018/01/03/
refugee-admissions-u-s-plummet-2017/999903001/.

169 Steve Almasy and Cheri Mossburg, "Iraqi Refugee Accused of
Being ISIS Killer Arrested in California," CNN, August 16, 2018,
accessed August 17, 2018, https://www.cnn.com/2018/08/16/
us/iraqi-national-suspected-isis-member/index.html.

170 Phillip Connor and Jens Manuel Krogstad, "For the First Time,
U.S. Resettles Fewer Refugees Than the Rest of the World," Pew
Research Center, July 5, 2018, accessed August 16, 2018, http://
www.pewresearch.org/fact tank/2018/07/05/for-the-first-time-
u-s-resettles-fewer-refugees-than-the-rest-of-the-world/.

171 Jan C. Ting, "Obama's Own Words Refute His Stand on Immigration
Authority," *New York Times*, July 8, 2015, accessed August 15,
2018, https://www.nytimes.com/roomfordebate/2014/11/18/
constitutional-limits-of-presidential-action-on-immigration-12/
obamas-own-words-refute-his-stand-on-immigration-authority.

172 Barack Obama, "Remarks by the President on Immigration,"
National Archives and Records Administration, June 15, 2012,
accessed August 15, 2018, https://obamawhitehouse.archives.gov/
the-press-office/2012/06/15/remarks-president-immigration.

173 Jeffrey S. Passel and Mark Hugo Lopez, "Up to 1.7 Million
Unauthorized Immigrant Youth May Benefit from New
Deportation Rules," Pew Research Center's Hispanic Trends
Project, August 14, 2012, accessed August 15, 2018, http://www.
pewhispanic.org/2012/08/14/up-to-1-7-million-unauthorized-
immigrant-youth-may-benefit-from-new-deportation-rules/.

174 Tal Kopan, "Trump Ends DACA but Gives Congress Window
to Save It," CNN, September 6, 2017, accessed August 15, 2018,
https://www.cnn.com/2017/09/05/politics/daca-trump-con-
gress/index.html.

175 Trump, "Statement from President Donald J. Trump," The
White House, September 5, 2017, accessed August 15, 2018,
https://www.whitehouse.gov/briefings-statements/statement-
president-donald-j-trump-7/.

176 Ibid.

177 Alexander Burns and Vivian Yee, "Democrats Begin Legal Assault on Trump's Move to End 'Dreamer' Program," *New York Times*, September 6, 2017, accessed August 15, 2018, https://www.nytimes.com/2017/09/06/us/daca-lawsuits-trump.html.

178 Maria Sacchetti, "Federal Judge Gives Respite to 'Dreamers', Says DACA Can't End While Lawsuit Is Pending," *The Washington Post*, January 10, 2018, accessed August 15, 2018, https://www.washingtonpost.com/local/immigration/federal-judge-says-daca-cant-end-while-lawsuit-is-pending/2018/01/09/715745a8-f5ba-11e7-a9e3-ab18ce41436a_story.html.

179 "President Donald J. Trump's State of the Union Address," The White House, accessed August 16, 2018, https://www.whitehouse.gov/briefings-statements/president-donald-j-trumps-state-union-address/.

180 Alan Feuer, "Second Federal Judge Issues Injunction to Keep DACA in Place," *New York Times*, February 13, 2018, accessed August 16, 2018, https://www.nytimes.com/2018/02/13/nyregion/daca-dreamers-injunction-trump.html.

181 Miriam Jordan, "Judge Upholds Order for Trump Administration to Restore DACA," *New York Times*, August 4, 2018, accessed August 16, 2018, https://www.nytimes.com/2018/08/03/us/federal-judge-daca.html.

182 Joel Rose, "Texas Judge Says DACA Is Probably Illegal, But Leaves It in Place," NPR, August 31, 2018, www.npr.org/2018/08/31/643814735/texas-judge-says-daca-is-probably-illegal-but-leaves-it-in-place.

183 Elise Foley, "Obama Moves to Protect Millions From Deportation," *The Huffington Post*, November 20, 2014, accessed October 8, 2018, https://www.huffingtonpost.com/2014/11/20/obama-immigration-plan_n_6178774.html.

184 Terrance P. Jeffrey, "Obama Claims Power to Make Illegal Immigrants Eligible for Social Security, Disability," CNS News, April 6, 2016, accessed October 8, 2018, https://www.cnsnews.com/commentary/terence-p-jeffrey/obama-claims-power-make-illegal-immigrants-eligible-social-security.

185 Bill Chappell, "Federal Judge Blocks Obama's Executive Actions On Immigration," NPR, February 17, 2015, accessed August 15, 2018, https://www.npr.org/sections/thetwo-way/2015/02/17/386905806/federal-judge-blocks-obama-s-executive-actions-on-immigration.

186 Sacchetti, "Kelly Revokes Obama Order Shielding Immigrant Parents of U.S. Citizens," *The Washington Post*, June 15, 2017, accessed October 8, 2018, https://www.washingtonpost.com/local/social-issues/kelly-revokes-obama-order-shielding-immigrant-parents-of-us-citizens/2017/06/15/d3b4db62-5244-11e7-91eb-9611861a988f_story.html.

187 Renuka Rayasam, "Trump Official Halts Abortions among Undocumented, Pregnant Teens," *Politico*, October 16, 2017, accessed August 16, 2018, https://www.politico.com/story/2017/10/16/undocumented-pregnant-girl-trump-abortion-texas-243844.

188 Ibid.

189 Ann E. Marimow, Spencer S. Hsu, and Sacchetti, "U.S. Government Ordered to Allow Abortion Access to Detained Immigrant Teens," *The Washington Post*, March 30, 2018, accessed August 16, 2018, https://www.washingtonpost.com/local/public-safety/us-judge-orders-government-to-allow-abortion-access-to-detained-immigrant-teens/2018/03/30/19e9fcf8-3128-11e8-94fa-32d48460b955_story.html.

190 Lawrence Hurley, "U.S. High Court Throws Out Immigrant Teen Abortion Ruling," Reuters, June 4, 2018, accessed August 16, 2018, https://www.reuters.com/article/us-usa-court-abortion-immigrant/u-s-high-court-throws-out-immigrant-teen-abortion-ruling-idUSKCN1J01RB.

Chapter 4

191 Christian Datoc, "Obama: 'Hopefully, We Can Learn From' Cuba About Improving Human Rights in America," *The Daily Caller*, March 21, 2016 accessed August 5, 2018, http://dailycaller.

com/2016/03/21/obama-hopefully-we-can-learn-from-cuba-about-improving- human-rights-in-america-video/.

192 "Statement by the President on the Passing of Fidel Castro," National Archives and Records Administration, accessed August 5, 2018, https://obamawhitehouse.archives.gov/the-press-office/2016/11/26/statement-president-passing-fidel-castro.

193 Brian Ross et al., "ISIS 2 Years Later: From 'JV Team' to International Killers," ABC, June 29, 2016, accessed October 16, 2018, https://abcnews.go.com/International/isis-years-jv-team-international-killers/story?id=40214844.

194 Matt Margolis and Mark Noonan, *The Worst President in History: The Legacy of Barack Obama* (New York: Bombardier Books, 2018).

195 Max Ehrenfreund, "How the TPP Became the Most Divisive Policy in the Democratic Party," *The Washington Post*, July 26, 2016, accessed October 7, 2018, https://www.washingtonpost.com/news/wonk/wp/2016/07/26/how-the-tpp-became-the-most-divisive-policy-in-the-democratic-party/.

196 S. A. Miller, "Donald Trump Keeps Campaign Promise to Abandon Trans-Pacific Partnership," *Washington Times*, January 23, 2017, accessed October 7, 2018, https://www.washingtontimes.com/news/2017/jan/23/trump-pull-out-trans-pacific-partnership/.

197 Iain Murray, "Trump Moves on Trade: TPP and NAFTA," Competitive Enterprise Institute, January 23, 2018, accessed October 7, 2018, https://cei.org/blog/trump-moves-trade-tpp-and-nafta.

198 Kevin D. Williamson, "A Free Trader's Argument Against TPP," *National Review*, June 30, 2016, accessed October 7, 2018, https://www.nationalreview.com/2015/12/anti-tpp-free-trade-argument/.

199 Steven Nelson, "Trump Says Bilateral Deals Are Better Than TPP," *Washington Examiner*, April 18, 2018, accessed October 7, 2018, https://www.washingtonexaminer.com/news/white-house/trump-says-bilateral-deals-are-better-than-tpp.

200 Ben Kamisar, "Trump Bashes UN," *The Hill*, March 21, 2016, accessed August 17, 2018, http://thehill.com/blogs/ballot-box/presidential-races/273826-trump-bashes-un.

201 Ian Johnston, "Donald Trump Just Dismissed the Planet's Most Important Organisation," *The Independent*, December 27, 2016, accessed August 17, 2018, https://www.independent.co.uk/news/world/americas/donald-trump-united-nations-club-have-good-time-barack-obama-israel-settlements-a7496786.html.

202 "Remarks by President Trump to the 72nd Session of the United Nations General Assembly," The White House, accessed August 17, 2018, https://www.whitehouse.gov/briefings-statements/remarks-president-trump-72nd-session-united-nations-general-assembly/.

203 Brett Schaefer, "America, We Pay Way Too Much for the United Nations," Fox News, June 16, 2015, accessed August 17, 2018, http://www.foxnews.com/opinion/2015/06/16/america-pay-way-too-much-for-united-nations.html.

204 George Russell, "Obama's Last Money Shower for the UN: Some $9.2 Billion," Fox News, February 3, 2017, accessed August 17, 2018, http://www.foxnews.com/politics/2017/02/03/obamas-last-money-shower-for-un-some-9-2-billion.html.

205 Schaefer, "Congress Should Learn from Obama's UN Spending Binge," *The Daily Signal*, January 25, 2017, accessed August 17, 2018, https://www.dailysignal.com/2017/01/25/congress-should-learn-from-obamas-last-minute-un-spending-binge/.

206 Robert Gearty, "Haley Announces $285M Cut in 2018-19 UN Operating Budget," Fox News, December 25, 2017, accessed August 17, 2018, http://www.foxnews.com/world/2017/12/25/haley-announces-285m-cut-in-2018-19-un-operating-budget.html.

207 Peter Baker, "U.S. to Restore Full Relations with Cuba, Erasing a Last Trace of Cold War Hostility," *New York Times*, December 17, 2014, accessed August 19, 2018, https://www.nytimes.com/2014/12/18/world/americas/us-cuba-relations.html.

208 "Lawmakers Slam Obama Over Cuba Relations," NBC, December 17, 2014, accessed August 18, 2018, https://www.nbcnews.com/storyline/u-s--cuba-relations/lawmakers-slam-obama-over-cuba-relations-n270076.

209 Ana Quintana, "Congressional Oversight Needed as Obama Administration Moves to Remove Cuba from State Sponsors of Terrorism List," The Heritage Foundation, January 29, 2015, accessed August 18, 2018, https://www.heritage.org/americas/report/congressional-oversight-needed-obama-administration-moves-remove-cuba-state.

210 David Wright, "Trump Threatens to Reverse Diplomatic Relations with Cuba," CNN, October 24, 2016, accessed August 18, 2018, https://www.cnn.com/2016/10/24/politics/trump-miami-interview-cuba-relations-trade-embargo/index.html.

211 Joe DePaolo, "Trump Reinstates Cuba Embargo: 'I Am Canceling, Immediately, the Previous Administration's One-Sided Deal,'" Mediaite, June 16, 2017, accessed August 18, 2018, https://www.mediaite.com/online/trump-reinstates-cuba-embargo-i-am-canceling-immediately-the-previous-adminstrations-one-sided-deal/.

212 Franco Ordoñez, "U.S. to Expel Two-thirds of Cuban Diplomats Amid Sonic Attack Probe," *McClatchy*, October 2, 2017, accessed August 19, 2018, https://www.mcclatchydc.com/news/politics-government/white-house/article176682381.html.

213 Alan Gomez, "Trump Cracks down on U.S. Business and Travel to Cuba. Here's What's Changing," *USA Today*, November 9, 2017, accessed August 19, 2018, https://www.usatoday.com/story/news/world/2017/11/08/trump-cracks-down-u-s-business-and-travel-cuba/843419001/.

214 Will Racke, "Trump Reverses Obama Policy on Cuba Embargo," *The Daily Caller*, October 31, 2017, accessed August 19, 2018, http://dailycaller.com/2017/10/31/trump-reverses-obama-policy-on-cuba-embargo/.

215 Eli Lake, "Why Obama Let Iran's Green Revolution Fail," *Bloomberg*, August 24, 2016, accessed August 19, 2018, https://www.bloomberg.com/view/articles/2016-08-24/why-obama-let-iran-s-green-revolution-fail.

216 Philip Klein and Ronald Zak, "6 Major U.S. Concessions in Iran Nuke Deal," *Washington Examiner*, July 14, 2015,

accessed August 19, 2018, https://www.washingtonexaminer.com/6-major-us-concessions-in-iran-nuke-deal.

217 Russ Read, "Kerry Thanks Iran Following Humiliation of US Sailors," *The Daily Caller*, accessed August 19, 2018, http://dailycaller.com/2016/01/14/kerry-thanks-iran-following-humiliation-of-us-sailors/.

218 Louis Nelson, "State Dept. Confirms $400 Million Iran Payment Conditioned on Prisoner Release," *Politico*, August 18, 2016, accessed August 19, 2018, https://www.politico.com/story/2016/08/iran-payment-hostage-release-227170.

219 Julian Hattem, "Obama: Iran Not following 'Spirit' of Deal," *The Hill*, April 1, 2016, accessed August 19, 2018, http://thehill.com/policy/national-security/274954-obama-iran-has-followed-letter-but-not-spirit-of-nuke-deal.

220 Patrick Goodenough, "State Dept. on Iran's 'Death to America' Chants: 'Like Any Country, There's Heated Political Rhetoric,'" CNS News, November 4, 2016, accessed August 19, 2018, https://www.cnsnews.com/news/article/patrick-goodenough/state-dept-irans-death-america-chants-any-country-theres-heated.

221 Katie Zezima, "Donald Trump, Ted Cruz Headline Capitol Rally against Iran Nuclear Deal," *The Washington Post*, September 9, 2015, accessed August 19, 2018, https://www.washingtonpost.com/news/post-politics/wp/2015/09/09/donald-trump-ted-cruz-to-headline-capitol-rally-against-iran-nuclear-deal/.

222 Jacob Kornbluh, "Trump: Obama's 'Like a Baby' on Iran Deal," *Haaretz*, April 10, 2018, accessed August 19, 2018, https://www.haaretz.com/world-news/trump-obama-s-like-a-baby-on-iran-deal-1.5426058.

223 Louis Nelson, "State Dept. Confirms $400 Million Iran Payment Conditioned on Prisoner Release," *Politico*, August 18, 2016, accessed August 19, 2018, https://www.politico.com/story/2016/08/iran-payment-hostage-release-227170.

224 Nelson and Nahal Toosi, "Trump Slaps New Sanctions on Iran after Missile Test," *Politico*, February 3, 2017, accessed

August 19, 2018, https://www.politico.com/story/2017/02/iran-sanctions-234604.

[225] Katie Bo Williams, "Trump Administration Unveils New Iran Sanctions," *The Hill*, July 18, 2017, accessed August 19, 2018, http://thehill.com/policy/national-security/342505-us-hits-iran-with-new-sanctions-over-ballistic-missiles.

[226] Adam Edelman, "Trump Threatens to Cancel Iran Nuclear Deal If It's Not Strengthened," NBC, accessed August 19, 2018, https://www.nbcnews.com/politics/donald-trump/trump-puts-iran-nuclear-deal-hands-congress-n810366.

[227] "Remarks by President Trump on the Joint Comprehensive Plan of Action," The White House, May 8, 2018, accessed August 20, 2018, https://www.whitehouse.gov/briefings-statements/remarks-president-trump-joint-comprehensive-plan-action/.

[228] "Trump Administration to Reinstate All Iran Sanctions," BBC News, November 2, 2018, accessed November 4, 2018, https://www.bbc.com/news/world-us-canada-46071747.

[229] Ibid.

[230] Rowan Scarborough, "Ex-defense Secretaries among Toughest Critics of Obama's Military Strategy," *Washington Times*, January 3, 2016, accessed August 21, 2018, https://www.washingtontimes.com/news/2016/jan/3/obama-military-strategy-blasted-by-robert-gates-le/.

[231] Ibid.

[232] Ibid.

[233] Ibid.

[234] Richard Sisk, "Gates and Panetta Blast Obama for Micromanaging Military," Military.com, accessed August 21, 2018, https://www.military.com/daily-news/2014/11/17/gates-and-panetta-blast-obama-for-micromanaging-military.html.

[235] Michael R. Gordon, "Trump Shifting Authority Over Military Operations Back to Pentagon," *New York Times*, March 19, 2017, accessed August 21, 2018, https://www.nytimes.com/2017/03/19/us/trump-shifting-authority-over-military-operations-back-to-pentagon.html.

236 W. J. Hennigan and Brian Bennett, "Trump Doesn't Micromanage the Military - But That Could Backfire," *Los Angeles Times*, June 7, 2017, accessed August 21, 2018, http://www.latimes.com/nation/la-na-trump-military-20170602-story.html.

237 Gordon, "Trump Shifting Authority Over Military Operations Back to Pentagon," *New York Times*, March 19, 2017, accessed August 21, 2018, https://www.nytimes.com/2017/03/19/us/trump-shifting-authority-over-military-operations-back-to-pentagon.html.

238 "President Obama Signs Executive Orders on Detention and Interrogation Policy," National Archives and Records Administration, accessed August 23, 2018, https://obamawhitehouse.archives.gov/realitycheck/the-press-office/background-president-obama-signs-executive-orders-detention-and-interrogation-polic.

239 Charlie Savage, "Plan to Move Guantánamo Detainees Faces New Delay," *New York Times,* December 22, 2009, accessed August 23, 2018, https://www.nytimes.com/2009/12/23/us/politics/23gitmo.html.

240 Michael Dorstewitz, "'Extraordinary Admission' by Chuck Hagel as He Exits; He Was Pressured by WH to Release Terrorists," *Conservative News Today*, February 1, 2015, accessed August 23, 2018, https://www.bizpacreview.com/2015/01/31/extraordinary-admission-by-chuck-hagel-as-he-exits-he-was-pressured-by-wh-to-release-terrorists-176765.

241 Susan Crabtree, "WH Brags: Only 5 Percent of Gitmo Detainees Return to Terrorism," *Washington Examiner,* March 8, 2016, accessed August 23, 2018, https://www.washingtonexaminer.com/wh-brags-only-5-percent-of-gitmo-detainees-return-to-terrorism.

242 "Former CIA Officer: Admin's Release of Gitmo Prisoners Is 'Insane'," Fox News. January 17, 2015, accessed August 23, 2018, http://insider.foxnews.com/2015/01/17/former-cia-officer-obama-administrations-release-guantanamo-bay-terror-prisoners-insane.

[243] Stephen F. Hayes and Thomas Joscelyn, "The Disgraceful Gitmo Exodus," *The Weekly Standard,* September 16, 2016, accessed August 23, 2018, https://www.weeklystandard.com/stephen-f-hayes-and-thomas-joscelyn/the-disgraceful-gitmo-exodus.

[244] Adam Goldman, "Former Guantanamo Detainee Implicated in Benghazi Attack," *The Washington Post,* January 7, 2014, accessed August 23, 2018, https://www.washingtonpost.com/world/national-security/former-guantanamo-detainee-implicated-in-benghazi-attack/2014/01/07/c73fdf78-77d5-11e3-8963-b4b654bcc9b2_story.html.

[245] Tim Stelloh, "Americans 'Died Because Of' Released Gitmo Detainees: Envoy," NBC, March 24, 2016, accessed August 23, 2018, https://www.nbcnews.com/news/us-news/americans-died-because-released-gitmo-detainees-pentagon-official-n544536.

[246] Ryan Browne, "Obama's Last Transfer of Gitmo Detainees, Trump Inherits 41," CNN, January 20, 2017, accessed August 23, 2018, https://www.cnn.com/2017/01/19/politics/obama-final-guantanamo-bay-transfer/index.html.

[247] Tim Lister et al., "ISIS: 143 Attacks in 29 Countries Have Killed 2,043," CNN, February 12, 2018, accessed August 24, 2018, https://www.cnn.com/2015/12/17/world/mapping-isis-attacks-around-the-world/index.html.

[248] Danielle Kurtzleben, "CHART: How the U.S. Troop Levels in Afghanistan Have Changed Under Obama," NPR, July 6, 2016, accessed August 24, 2018, https://www.npr.org/2016/07/06/484979294/chart-how-the-u-s-troop-levels-in-afghanistan-have-changed-under-obama.

[249] James Warren, "President Obama Lost Faith in Afghanistan Mission, Can't Stand Afghan President Karzai: Robert Gates' Memoir - NY Daily News," *New York Daily News,* January 7, 2014, accessed August 24, 2018, http://www.nydailynews.com/news/politics/president-obama-lost-faith-afghanistan-mission-article-1.1569274.

250 Scarborough, "Shades of Vietnam: Spike in U.S. Troop Deaths Tied to Stricter Rules of Engagement," *Washington Times*, December 5, 2013, accessed August 24, 2018, https://www.washingtontimes.com/news/2013/dec/5/increase-in-battlefield-deaths-linked-to-new-rules/.

251 Elise Jordan, "How Obama Lost Afghanistan," *The Daily Beast*, April 5, 2014, accessed August 24, 2018, https://www.thedaily-beast.com/how-obama-lost-afghanistan.

252 Mark Thompson, "Afghanistan Troop Pullout Slowed by President Obama," *Time*, July 6, 2016, accessed August 24, 2018, http://time.com/4394955/afghanistan-barack-obama-troops-pullout/.

253 Kristina Wong, "GOP Questions Obama's Afghanistan Troop Withdrawal," *The Hill*, July 7, 2016, accessed August 24, 2018, http://thehill.com/policy/defense/286787-gops-question-obamas-decision-to-withdraw-1400-troops-from-afghanistan.

254 Politico Staff, "Full Text: Trump's Speech on Afghanistan," *Politico*, August 21, 2017, accessed August 24, 2018, https://www.politico.com/story/2017/08/21/trump-afghanistan-speech-text-241882?cmpid=sf.

255 Ibid.

256 The Editorial Board, "Trump's Afghan Commitment," *Wall Street Journal*, August 22, 2017, accessed August 24, 2018, https://www.wsj.com/articles/trumps-afghan-commitment-1503430721.

257 Zalmay Khalilzad, "Why Trump Is Right to Get Tough With Pakistan," *New York Times*, August 23, 2017, accessed August 24, 2018, https://www.nytimes.com/2017/08/23/opinion/trump-afghanistan-pakistan-strategy.html.

258 Gen. John Allen and Michael O'Hanlon, "Donald Trump Makes Right Moves in Afghanistan: Gen. John Allen and Michael O'Hanlon," *USA Today*, August 22, 2017, accessed August 24, 2018, https://www.usatoday.com/story/opinion/2017/08/22/trumps-afghanistan-moves-will-prevent-new-terror-safe-haven-column/588142001/.

259 Dianna Cahn, "Nicholson: 'Strategy Is Working' in Afghanistan," *Stars and Stripes*, August 22, 2018, accessed August 24, 2018, https://

www.stripes.com/nicholson-strategy-is-working-in-afghanistan-1.543828.

[260] Matt Margolis and Mark Noonan, *The Worst President in History: The Legacy of Barack Obama* (New York: Bombardier Books, 2018).

[261] "Obama 'Snubbed' Israel, Treated Iran with 'Tender Love and Care,' Trump Charges," *The Times of Israel,* April 27, 2016, accessed August 24, 2018, https://www.timesofisrael.com/obama-snubbed-israel-treated-iran-with-tender-love-and-care-trump-charges/.

[262] Avi Issacharoff and AP, "Palestinians Say Obama's Last-minute $221 Million Payout Frozen by Trump," *The Times of Israel*, January 25, 2017, accessed August 24, 2018, https://www.timesofisrael.com/palestinians-say-trump-freezes-obamas-last-minute-221-million-payout/.

[263] Amir Tibon, "U.S. Officially Cuts Funding to Palestinian Authority over Payments to Terrorists and Their Families," *Haaretz*, March 24, 2018, accessed August 24, 2018, https://www.haaretz.com/us-news/.premium-u-s-cuts-funding-to-pa-over-payments-to-terrorists-families-1.5937745.

[264] Katie Zezima, "Netanyahu Warns That Nuclear Deal 'Paves Iran's Path' to a Bomb," *The Washington Post*, March 3, 2015, accessed August 24, 2018, https://www.washingtonpost.com/news/post-politics/wp/2015/03/03/in-much-anticipated-speech-netanyahu-to-address-congress-tuesday/.

[265] Gareth Davies, "Iran Vows 'Death to Israel' as It Unveils Latest Missiles," *Daily Mail Online*, April 18, 2017, accessed August 24, 2018, http://www.dailymail.co.uk/news/article-4421410/Iran-vows-Death-Israel-unveils-latest-missiles.html.

[266] Eliott C. McLaughlin, "Netanyahu Says He Has Proof of Secret Iranian Nuclear Program," CNN, May 1, 2018, accessed August 24, 2018, https://www.cnn.com/2018/04/30/middleeast/netanyahu-iran-nuclear-program/index.html.

[267] Yoel Goldman, "Despite Amended Party Platform, Obama Administration Refuses to Name Israel's Capital," *The Times of Israel*, September 7, 2012, accessed August 24, 2018, http://www.

timesofisrael.com/despite-amended-party-platform-obama-administration-refuses-to-name-israels-capital/?fb_comment_id=222023247925686_773856.

268 "Full Video and Transcript: Trump's Speech Recognizing Jerusalem as the Capital of Israel," *New York Times*, December 6, 2017, accessed August 24, 2018, https://www.nytimes.com/2017/12/06/world/middleeast/trump-israel-speech-transcript.html.

269 Garance Burke, "AP INVESTIGATION: Feds' Failures Imperil Migrant Children," AP News, January 25, 2016, accessed August 27, 2018, https://apnews.com/cc07b82ec58145cca37d6ff952f334c1/ap-investigation-feds-failures-imperil-migrant-children.

270 Abbie VanSickle, "Obama Administration Placed Children with Human Traffickers, Report Says," *The Washington Post*, January 28, 2016, accessed August 27, 2018, https://www.washingtonpost.com/national/obama-administration-placed-children-with-human-traffickers-report-says/2016/01/28/39465050-c542-11e5-9693-933a4d31bcc8_story.html.

271 Ibid.

272 Ibid.

273 AP Staff, "Trump Vows to Fight 'Epidemic' of Human Trafficking," AP News, February 23, 2017, accessed August 27, 2018, https://apnews.com/9517fb5ec44e4e93a275cc0722abd6a1/trump-vows-fight-epidemic-human-trafficking.

274 Liz Crokin, "Why the MSM Is Ignoring Trump's Sex Trafficking Busts," Townhall, February 25, 2017, accessed August 27, 2018, https://townhall.com/columnists/lizcrokin/2017/02/25/why-the-msm-is-ignoring-trumps-sex-trafficking-busts-n2290379.

275 Conchita Sarnoff, "Finally! President Trump Freezes Assets of Human Traffickers," *The Daily Caller*, January 1, 2018, accessed August 27, 2018, https://dailycaller.com/2018/01/01/finally-president-trump-freezes-assets-of-human-traffickers/.

276 Brett Samuels, "Trump Signs Online Sex Trafficking Bill," *The Hill*, April 11, 2018, accessed August 27, 2018, http://thehill.com/policy/technology/382664-trump-signs-online-sex-trafficking-bill.

277 Josh Rogin, "Exclusive: Obama Declines to Add Names to Russian Sanction List," *The Daily Beast*, December 19, 2013, accessed August 27, 2018, https://www.thedailybeast.com/exclusive-obama-declines-to-add-names-to-russian-sanction-list.

278 Mark Najarian, "U.S. Sanctions 52 People for Abuses Related to Global Magnitsky Act," RadioFreeEurope/RadioLiberty, December 21, 2017, accessed August 27, 2018, https://www.rferl.org/a/magnitsky-52-sanctioned-karimova-chaika/28931607.html.

279 Jason Szep and Matt Spetalnick, "Special Report: State Department Watered Down Human Trafficking Report," Reuters, August 3, 2015, accessed August 27, 2018, https://www.reuters.com/article/us-usa-humantrafficking-disputes-special/special-report-state-department-watered-down-human-trafficking-report-idUSKCN-0Q821Y20150803.

280 Beh Lih Yi and agencies in Wang Kelian, "Malaysia Migrant Mass Graves: Police Reveal 139 Sites, Some with Multiple Corpses," *The Guardian*, May 25, 2015, accessed August 27, 2018, https://www.theguardian.com/world/2015/may/25/malaysia-migrant-mass-graves-police-reveal-139-sites-some-with-multiple-corpses.

281 Jeff Conant, "The Obama Administration Just Blew Off Human Trafficking Concerns to Pass the TPP-FPIF," Foreign Policy In Focus, August 6, 2015, accessed August 27, 2018, https://fpif.org/the-obama-administration-just-blew-off-human-trafficking-concerns-to-pass-the-tpp/.

282 Zach Carter, "Obama Shrugs Off Global Slavery to Protect Trade Deal," *The Huffington Post*, July 27, 2015, accessed August 27, 2018, https://www.huffingtonpost.com/entry/malaysia-human-trafficking-tpp_us_55b66521e4b0224d8832fe28.

283 Clark Mindock, "Trump Attacked the UN Human Rights Council for including Abusive Regimes—Like US Ally Saudi Arabia," *Independent*, September 19, 2017, accessed August 27, 2018, https://www.independent.co.uk/news/world/americas/us-politics/trump-saudi-arabia-un-human-rights-council-attack-a7955996.html.

284 Nick Wadhams, "U.S. Quits UN Human Rights Council, Saying It's Anti-Israel," *Bloomberg*, June 19, 2018, accessed August 27, 2018, http://www.bloomberg.com/news/articles/2018-06-19/trump-is-said-ready-to-pull-u-s-from-un-s-human-rights-council.

285 Matt Margolis, *The Scandalous Presidency of Barack Obama* (New York: Bombardier Books, 2018).

286 Ken Dilanian and Kevin Monahan, "Obama Nixed CIA Plan for Syria: Officials," NBC, April 2, 2016, accessed August 21, 2018, https://www.nbcnews.com/news/us-news/obama-nixed-cia-plan-could-have-stopped-isis-officials-n549111.

287 Tim Lister et al., "ISIS: 143 Attacks in 29 Countries Have Killed 2,043," CNN, February 12, 2018, accessed August 21, 2018, https://www.cnn.com/2015/12/17/world/mapping-isis-attacks-around-the-world/index.html.

288 Jim Sciutto et al., "Obama Declared ISIS 'Contained' Day Before Paris Attack," CNN, November 16, 2015, accessed August 21, 2018, https://www.cnn.com/2015/11/14/politics/paris-terror-attacks-obama-isis-contained/index.html.

289 Robin Simcox, "Did Trump Really Beat ISIS?" The Heritage Foundation, accessed August 21, 2018, https://www.heritage.org/middle-east/commentary/did-trump-really-beat-isis.

290 Ibid.

291 Eric Levenson and Jomana Karadsheh, "Iraq Is 'Fully Liberated' from ISIS, Its Military Says," CNN, December 9, 2017, accessed October 16, 2018, https://www.cnn.com/2017/12/09/middleeast/iraq-isis-military-liberated/index.html.

292 "Department of Defense Press Briefing by Secretary Mattis, General Dunford," U.S. Department of Defense, May 19, 2017, accessed August 21, 2018, https://www.defense.gov/News/Transcripts/Transcript-View/Article/1188225/department-of-defense-press-briefing-by-secretary-mattis-general-dunford-and-sp/.

293 Aaron Mehta, "Mattis Reveals New Rules of Engagement," *Military Times*, October 3, 2017, accessed October 16, 2018,

https://www.militarytimes.com/flashpoints/2017/10/03/mattis-reveals-new-rules-of-engagement/.

[294] Ross Douthat, "A War Trump Won," *New York Times*, December 16, 2017, accessed August 21, 2018, https://www.nytimes.com/2017/12/16/opinion/sunday/war-trump-islamic-state.html.

Chapter 5

[295] Nico Pitney, "Obama's Nomination Victory Speech in St. Paul," *The Huffington Post*, last updated May 25, 2011, accessed September 10, 2018, https://www.huffingtonpost.com/2008/06/03/obamas-nomination-victory_n_105028.html.

[296] Timothy Cama, "Trump EPA to Keep and Defend Obama Smog Rule," *The Hill,* August 1, 2018, accessed August 5, 2018, http://thehill.com/policy/energy-environment/399974-trump-epa-wont-change-obama-smog-rule.

[297] Kevin Mooney, "Trump's EPA Outpaces Obama in Cleaning Up Hazardous Waste Sites," *The Daily Signal*, July 24, 2018, accessed August 31, 2018, https://www.dailysignal.com/2018/07/24/trumps-epa-outpaces-obama-in-cleaning-up-hazardous-sites/.

[298] "American Antiquities Act of 1906 (16USC431-433)," National Parks Service, accessed August 10, 2018, https://www.nps.gov/history/local-law/anti1906.htm.

[299] Jonathan Wood, "Let's Halt Antiquities Act Abuse," Reason.com, May 3, 2017, accessed August 10, 2018, http://reason.com/archives/2017/05/03/lets-put-a-stop-to-antiquities-act-abuse.

[300] H. Sterling Burnett, "Obama's Dangerous Use of The National Monument Law," *Forbes*, October 12, 2016, accessed August 10, 2018, https://www.forbes.com/sites/realspin/2016/10/12/obamas-dangerous-use-of-the-national-monument-law/.

[301] Ibid.

[302] Doug G. Ware, "Trump to Review National Monuments Designated by Clinton, Bush, Obama," UPI, April 25, 2017, accessed August 10, 2018, https://www.upi.com/Trump-to-

review-national-monuments-designated-by-Clinton-Bush-
Obama/7431493160397/.

303 Michael Bastasch, "Obama Puts 1.6 Million Acres Under Stricter
Federal Control Despite Intense Local Opposition," *The Daily
Caller,* December 28, 2016, accessed August 10, 2018, http://dai-
lycaller.com/2016/12/28/ obama-puts-1-6-million-acres-under-
stricter-federal-control- despite-intense-local-opposition/.

304 Gregory Korte, "Trump Shrinks Bears Ears, Grand Staircase-
Escalante Monuments in Historic Proclamations," *USA Today,*
December 4, 2017, accessed August 10, 2018, https://www.
usatoday.com/story/news/politics/2017/12/04/trump-trav-
els-utah-historic-rollback-national-monuments/919209001/.

305 Jeffrey Goldberg, "The Obama Doctrine," *The Atlantic* (April
2016), accessed September 14, 2018, https://www.theatlantic.
com/magazine/archive/2016/04/the-obama-doctrine/471525/.

306 Theodore R. Bromund, "Climate Change Is Not a National
Security Threat," The Heritage Foundation, June 4, 2015, accessed
September 14, 2018, https://www.heritage.org/environment/
commentary/climate-change-not-national-security-threat.

307 Ibid.

308 Pete Kasperowicz, "Kerry Concedes: Terrorism Is a Bigger Threat
Than Climate Change," *Washington Examiner,* June 17, 2016, accessed
September 14, 2018, https://www.washingtonexaminer.com/
kerry-concedes-terrorism-is-a-bigger-threat-than-climate-change.

309 Keith Johnson, "Obama Says Climate Change Is a Security
Risk. Why Are Republicans Laughing?" *Foreign Policy,* March
21, 2016, accessed September 13, 2018, https://foreignpolicy.
com/2016/03/21/obama-says-climate-change-is-a-security-risk-
why-are-republicans-laughing/.

310 Erika Bolstad, "Obama Demands That Security Agencies
Consider Climate Change," *Scientific American,* September 22,
2016, accessed September 13, 2018, https://www.scientificamer-
ican.com/article/obama-demands-that-security-agencies-consid-
er-climate-change/.

311 Goldberg, "The Obama Doctrine."

312 Tim Lister et al., "ISIS: 143 Attacks in 29 Countries Have Killed 2,043," CNN, February 12, 2018, accessed September 13, 2018, https://www.cnn.com/2015/12/17/world/mapping-isis-attacks-around-the-world/index.html.

313 Matt Margolis and Mark Noonan, *The Worst President in History: The Legacy of Barack Obama* (New York: Bombardier Books, 2018).

314 Darryl Fears and Juliet Eilperin, "President Obama Bans Oil Drilling in Large Areas of Atlantic and Arctic Oceans," *The Washington Post*, December 20, 2016, accessed August 31, 2018, https://www.washingtonpost.com/news/energy-environment/wp/2016/12/20/president-obama-expected-to-ban-oil-drilling-in-large-areas-of-atlantic-and-arctic-oceans/.

315 "Remarks by President Trump at Signing of Executive Order on an America-First Offshore Energy Strategy," The White House, April 28, 2017, accessed August 31, 2018, https://www.white-house.gov/briefings-statements/remarks-president-trump-sign-ing-executive-order-america-first-offshore-energy-strategy/.

316 Bonner T. Cohen, "News—Trump Removes Offshore Drilling Restrictions," Heartland Institute, June 9, 2017, accessed August 31, 2018, https://www.heartland.org/news-opinion/news/trump-removes-offshore-drilling-restrictions.

317 Ibid.

318 Evan Lehman, "Senate Abandons Climate Effort, Dealing Blow to President," *New York Times*, July 23, 2010, accessed September 2, 2018, https://archive.nytimes.com/www.nytimes.com/cwire/2010/07/23/23climatewire-senate-abandons-climate-effort-deal-ing-blow-88864.html.

319 Meghan Drake, "New EPA Rules Cast Cloud Over Coal Industry," *The Washington Times*, June 2, 2014, accessed September 2, 2018, https://www.washingtontimes.com/news/2014/jun/2/new-epa-rules-cast-cloud-over-coal-industry/.

320 Cassandra Carroll, "More Evidence That EPA's Clean Power Plan Is Economically Irresponsible," Americans for Tax Reform, October 21, 2014, accessed September 2, 2018, https://www.atr.

org/more-evidence-epa's-clean-power-plan-economically-irre-sponsible.

321 Jonathan H. Adler, "Supreme Court Puts the Brakes on the EPA's Clean Power Plan," *The Washington Post*, February 9, 2016, accessed September 2, 2018, https://www.washingtonpost.com/news/volokh-conspiracy/wp/2016/02/09/supreme-court-puts-the-brakes-on-the-epas-clean-power-plan/.

322 H. Sterling Burnett, "Trump and the End of Obama's Bitter 'War on Coal,'" *The Hill*, September 30, 2017, accessed September 2, 2018, http://thehill.com/opinion/energy-environment/353232-trump-and-the-end-of-obamas-bitter-war-on-coal.

323 "Trump Signs Order Undoing Obama Climate Change Policies," BBC News, March 29, 2017, accessed September 2, 2018, https://www.bbc.com/news/world-us-canada-39415631.

324 Burnett, "Trump and the End."

325 Associated Press in Hazard, Kentucky, "'The War on Coal Is Over': EPA Boss to Roll Back Obama's Clean Power Rules," *The Guardian*, October 9, 2017, accessed September 2, 2018, https://www.theguardian.com/environment/2017/oct/09/epa-scott-pruitt-abandon-clean-power-plan-obama.

326 Matthew Kandrach, "Protecting Affordable, Reliable Power," *Washington Times*, August 28, 2018, accessed September 2, 2018, https://www.washingtontimes.com/news/2018/aug/28/the-trump-administration-replaces-obamas-clean-pow/.

327 Steve Everley, "'Promised Land' Offers a False Choice," *Politico*, January 11, 2013, accessed September 5, 2018, https://www.politico.com/story/2013/01/promised-land-offers-a-false-choice-on-shale-development-086018.

328 Ben Geman, "Energy Secretary: Natural Gas Helps Battle Climate Change—for Now," *The Hill*, August 1, 2013, accessed September 5, 2018, http://thehill.com/policy/energy-environment/315009-energy-secretary-natural-gas-helps-battle-climate-change-for-now.

329 Rock Zierman, "Why Such Hysteria Over Fracking?" *Los Angeles Times*, June 21, 2013, accessed September 5, 2018, http://articles.

latimes.com/2013/jun/21/opinion/la-oe-zierman-california-fracking-moratorium-20130621.

330 Robert Rapier, "No, The EPA Has Not Actually Changed Its Conclusion on Risks of Fracking to Drinking Water," *Forbes*, December 15, 2016, accessed September 5, 2018, https://www.forbes.com/sites/rrapier/2016/12/15/yes-direct-injection-of-fracking-fluid-into-groundwater-causes-contamination/#389f146119d3.

331 AP, "Study Finds Fracking Chemicals Didn't Pollute Water: AP," CBS, July 19, 2013, accessed September 5, 2018, https://www.cbsnews.com/news/study-finds-fracking-chemicals-didnt-pollute-water-ap/.

332 Sean Hackbarth, "Yale Study: Hydraulic Fracturing Doesn't Contaminate Drinking Water," U.S. Chamber of Commerce, October 15, 2015, accessed September 5, 2018, https://www.uschamber.com/above-the-fold/yale-study-hydraulic-fracturing-doesn-t-contaminate-drinking-water.

333 "Innovative Strategy Would Allow U.S. to Capitalize on America's New Energy Advantage While Protecting the Environment and Speeding the Transition to a Lower-Carbon Energy Future," Harvard Business School, June 11, 2015, accessed September 5, 2018, https://www.hbs.edu/news/releases/Pages/innovative-strategy-low-carbon-energy.aspx.

334 Kevin Liptak, "Obama Administration Puts New Rules on Fracking," CNN, March 20, 2015, accessed September 5, 2018, https://www.cnn.com/2015/03/20/politics/fracking-rules-white-house/index.html.

335 Reuters, "Oil and Gas Industry Groups Sue over U.S. Fracking Rules," *Fortune*, March 20, 2015, accessed September 5, 2018, http://fortune.com/2015/03/20/fracking-lawsuit-obama/.

336 Coral Davenport, "Obama Fracking Rule Is Struck Down by Court," *New York Times*, June 22, 2016, accessed September 5, 2018, https://www.nytimes.com/2016/06/23/us/politics/hydraulic-fracturing-interior-department-regulations.html.

337 Valerie Richardson, "Interior Department Repeals Never-Used Regulations on Hydraulic Fracturing," *The Washington Times*, December 31, 2017, accessed September 5, 2018, https://www.washingtontimes.com/news/2017/dec/31/trump-administration-kills-obama-era-fracking-rule/.

338 Lachlan Markay, "Report: 80% of DOE Green Energy Loans Went to Obama Backers," *The Daily Signal*, November 14, 2011, accessed September 6, 2018, https://www.dailysignal.com/2011/11/14/report-80-of-doe-green-energy-loans-went-to-obama-backers/.

339 John-Michael Seibler, "This Bird Regulation Might Have Made You a Criminal. Not Anymore," The Heritage Foundation, January 18, 2018, accessed September 6, 2018, https://www.heritage.org/crime-and-justice/commentary/bird-regulation-might-have-made-you-criminal not-anymore.

340 Jennifer A. Dlouhy, "Trump Administration Reverses Obama-Era Policy on Accidental Bird Deaths," *Bloomberg*, December 22, 2017, accessed September 6, 2018, https://www.bloomberg.com/news/articles/2017-12-22/trump-is-said-to-reverse-strict-obama-era-policy-on-bird-deaths-jbi84akp.

341 Ibid.

342 Barbara Hollingsworth, "Federal Permits Will Allow Wind Farms to Kill More Bald Eagles," CNS News, December 21, 2016, accessed September 6, 2018, https://www.cnsnews.com/news/article/barbara-hollingsworth/new-regulations-will-allow-wind-farms-kill-4200-bald-eaglesyear.

343 Douglas Ernst, "Obama Admin Regulation Allows Wind Turbines to Kill up to 4,200 Bald Eagles Per Company," *The Washington Times*, December 14, 2016, accessed September 6, 2018, https://www.washingtontimes.com/news/2016/dec/14/obama-admin-regulation-allows-wind-turbines-kill-4/.

344 "Obama Looks the Other Way When Wind & Solar Power Kill Birds & Bats," Institute for Energy Research, September 2, 2014, accessed September 6, 2018, https://www.instituteforenergyresearch.org/renewable/wind/obama-administration-ignores-wind-solar-power-killing-birds-bats/.

[345] Michael Bastasch, "Trump Will Reverse Obama's Policy of Prosecuting Unintentional Bird Killings," *The Daily Caller*, December 22, 2017, accessed September 6, 2018, http://dailycaller.com/2017/12/22/trump-will-reverse-obamas-policy-of-prosecuting-unintentional-bird-killings/.

[346] Ibid.

[347] Peter Baker, "Obama Mandates Rules to Raise Fuel Standards," *New York Times*, May 21, 2010, accessed September 10, 2018, https://www.nytimes.com/2010/05/22/business/energy-environment/22fuel.html.

[348] "Obama Administration Finalizes Historic 54.5 MPG Fuel Efficiency Standards," National Archives and Records Administration, August 28, 2012, accessed September 10, 2018, https://obamawhitehouse.archives.gov/the-press-office/2012/08/28/obama-administration-finalizes-historic-545-mpg-fuel-efficiency-standard.

[349] Larry Bell, "New Auto Fuel Economy Standards Will Regulate Us to Death," *Forbes*, August 16, 2011, accessed September 10, 2018, https://www.forbes.com/sites/larrybell/2011/08/16/new-auto-fuel-economy-standards-will-regulate-us-to-death/.

[350] Ibid.

[351] Ibid.

[352] Nicolas Loris, "Trump's Rollback of CAFE Mandates Is a Big Win for Car Buyers, Consumer Choice," The Heritage Foundation, August 16, 2018, accessed September 10, 2018, https://www.heritage.org/energy-economics/commentary/trumps-rollback-cafe-mandates-big-win-car-buyers-consumer-choice.

[353] Bell, "New Auto Fuel Economy Standards Will Regulate Us to Death."

[354] Ibid.

[355] Peter Valdes-Dapena, "Clunkers: Taxpayers Paid $24,000 per Car," CNN, October 29, 2009, accessed September 11, 2018, https://money.cnn.com/2009/10/28/autos/clunkers_analysis/index.htm.

[356] Bill Vlasic, "E.P.A. Affirms Fuel-Economy Goals, Frustrating Automakers," *New York Times*, January 13, 2017, accessed

September 11, 2018, https://www.nytimes.com/2017/01/13/business/fuel-economy-standards.html.

357 "Trump's Fuel Economy Plan Is A No Brainer—It Saves Money and Lives," *Investor's Business Daily*, August 6, 2018, accessed September 12, 2018, https://www.investors.com/politics/editorials/trumps-fuel-economy-plan/.

358 Marlo Lewis Jr., "Trump Revision of Obama-era Fuel Economy Rules Is No Climate Disaster," Competitive Enterprise Institute, August 10, 2018, accessed September 12, 2018, https://cei.org/blog/trump-revision-obama-era-fuel-economy-rules-no-climate-disaster.

359 Ibid.

360 Elise Labott and Dan Berman, "Obama Rejects Keystone XL Pipeline," CNN, November 6, 2015, accessed September 12, 2018, https://www.cnn.com/2015/11/06/politics/keystone-xl-pipeline-decision-rejection-kerry/index.html.

361 Robinson Meyer, "The Obama Administration Temporarily Blocks the Dakota Access Pipeline," *The Atlantic*, September 9, 2016, accessed September 12, 2018, https://www.theatlantic.com/science/archive/2016/09/the-obama-administration-temporarily-blocks-the-dakota-access-pipeline/499454/.

362 "Benefits of Keystone XL," Global Energy Institute, August 17, 2017, accessed September 12, 2018, https://www.globalenergyinstitute.org/benefits-keystone-xl.

363 Diana Furchtgott-Roth, "Pipeline Safety," Manhattan Institute, December 14, 2015, accessed September 12, 2018, https://www.manhattan-institute.org/html/pipeline-safety-4253.html.

364 Baker and Davenport, "Trump Revives Keystone Pipeline Rejected by Obama," *New York Times*, January 24, 2017, accessed September 13, 2018, https://www.nytimes.com/2017/01/24/us/politics/keystone-dakota-pipeline-trump.html.

365 "George Bush: Statement on Signing the Instrument of Ratification for the United Nations Framework Convention on Climate Change—October 13, 1992," The American Presidency

Project, accessed August 20, 2018, https://www.presidency.ucsb.edu/node/266987.

[366] Steven Groves, "The Paris Agreement Is a Treaty and Should Be Submitted to the Senate," The Heritage Foundation, March 15, 2016, accessed August 20, 2018, https://www.heritage.org/environment/report/the-paris-agreement-treaty-and-should-be-submitted-the-senate.

[367] The Editors, "We'll Never Have Paris," *National Review*, June 1, 2017, accessed August 20, 2018, https://www.nationalreview.com/2017/06/paris-agreement-withdrawal-trump/.

[368] "Obama Administration Gives $500m to UN Climate Change Fund," BBC News, January 18, 2017, accessed August 17, 2018, https://www.bbc.com/news/world-us-canada-38661259.

[369] The Editors, "We'll Never Have Paris."

[370] Ibid.

[371] Loris, "After Paris: Next Steps for the Trump Administration's International Climate Agenda," The Heritage Foundation, accessed August 17, 2018, https://www.heritage.org/energy-economics/report/after-paris-next-steps-the-trump-administrations-international-climate.

[372] Ben Wolford, "Green Climate Fund Must Fight Corruption Before It Can Beat Global Warming," *Newsweek*, April 30, 2016, accessed August 17, 2018, https://www.newsweek.com/2015/11/20/green-climate-fund-must-fight-corruption-it-can-beat-global-warming-391771.html.

[373] Kate Sheppard, "Donald Trump Finally Said Something Concrete About Climate Policy," *The Huffington Post*, November 6, 2016, accessed August 17, 2018, https://www.huffingtonpost.com/entry/donald-trump-climate-change-policy_us_581f57bde-4b0e80b02caa351.

[374] Jason Hopkins, "President Trump Has Rendered the Green Climate Fund Nearly Useless," *The Daily Caller*, July 11, 2018, accessed August 17, 2018, http://dailycaller.com/2018/07/11/green-climate-fund-trump/.

375 Graham Ruddick, "Donald Trump Says US Could Re-enter Paris Climate Deal," *The Guardian*, January 29, 2018, accessed August 20, 2018, https://www.theguardian.com/us-news/2018/jan/28/donald-trump-says-us-could-re-enter-paris-climate-deal-itv-interview.

376 Stephen Moore, "'Who's the Cleanest of Them All,'" *The Washington Times*, August 19, 2018, accessed August 31, 2018, https://www.washingtontimes.com/news/2018/aug/19/the-united-states-didnt-sign-the-paris-climate-acc/.

377 Ibid.

Chapter 6

378 "Read a Transcript of Obama's Remarks on the Shutdown and Obamacare," *The Washington Post*, October 1, 2013, accessed August 5, 2018, http://www.washingtonpost.com/politics/transcript-president-obamas-oct-1-remarks-on-obamacare-and-the-government-shutdown/2013/10/01/2f7d071c-2ab7-11e3-97a3-ff2758228523_story.html.

379 Lucy McCalmont, "New Video Surfaces of Obamacare Architect," *Politico*, November 12, 2014, accessed October 9, 2018, https://www.politico.com/story/2014/11/jonathan-gruber-obamacare-voters-112812.

380 Bob Bryan, "Obamacare Has Gone from the President's Greatest Achievement to a 'Slow-Motion Death Spiral'," *Business Insider*, August 21, 2016, accessed September 16, 2018, https://www.businessinsider.com/obamacare-is-in-slow-motion-death-spiral-2016-8.

381 Matt Margolis and Mark Noonan, *The Worst President in History: The Legacy of Barack Obama* (New York: Bombardier Books, 2018).

382 Ali Meyer, "19th ObamaCare Co-op Folds, Leaving Only 4 Operating in 2018," Fox News, June 28, 2017, accessed September 16, 2018, http://www.foxnews.com/politics/2017/06/28/19th-obamacare-co-op-folds-leaving-only-4-operating-in-2018.html.

383 MJ Lee and Lauren Fox, "GOP Regroups After Obamacare Repeal Fail," CNN, September 27, 2017, accessed August 5, 2018,

https://www.cnn.com/2017/09/27/politics/bruised-republi-cans-regroup-after-obamacare-repeal-fail/index.html.

384 Post Editorial Board, "Now, Even Democrats Can See the ObamaCare Death Spiral," *New York Post*, October 17, 2016, accessed August 5, 2018, https://nypost.com/2016/10/16/now-even-democrats-can-see-the-obamacare-death-spiral/.

385 Kevin Liptak, "Trump Begins Obamacare Dismantling with Executive Order," CNN, October 12, 2017, accessed September 21, 2018, https://www.cnn.com/2017/10/12/politics/trump-obamacare-executive-order/index.html.

386 Sally C. Pipes, "Column: Trump Right to End Obamacare Subsidies," *Detroit News*, December 11, 2017, accessed September 16, 2018, https://www.detroitnews.com/story/opinion/2017/12/10/sally-pipes-end-obamacare-subsidies/108493784/.

387 Reuters, "Obamacare Premiums for 2017 Jumped 25% on Healthcare.gov," *Fortune*, October 25, 2016, accessed September 16, 2018, http://fortune.com/2016/10/25/obamacare-insurance-premiums-2017-healthcare/.

388 Josh Dawsey and Paul Demko, "Trump Will Scrap Critical Obamacare Subsidies," *Politico*, October 13, 2017, accessed September 17, 2018, https://www.politico.com/story/2017/10/12/trump-obamacare-subsidy-243736.

389 Robert Pear, Maggie Haberman, and Reed Abelson, "Trump to Scrap Critical Health Care Subsidies, Hitting Obamacare Again," *New York Times*, October 12, 2017, accessed September 17, 2018, https://www.nytimes.com/2017/10/12/us/politics/trump-obamacare-executive-order-health-insurance.html.

390 Doug Badger, "How Lawmakers Should Deal with Obamacare Cost-Sharing-Reduction Payments," The Heritage Foundation, December 18, 2017, accessed September 17, 2018, https://www.heritage.org/health-care-reform/report/how-lawmakers-should-deal-obamacare-cost-sharing-reduction-payments.

391 Ibid.

392 Dawsey and Demko, "Trump Will Scrap Critical Obamacare Subsidies."

393 Angie Drobnic Holan, "Obama Flip-Flops on Requiring People to Buy Health Care," *Politifact*, July 20, 2009, accessed September 20, 2018, https://www.politifact.com/truth-o-meter/statements/2009/jul/20/barack-obama/obama-flip-flops-requiring-people-buy-health-care/.

394 Jed Graham, "ObamaCare Individual Mandate Fine Hit 8 Million People In 2016," *Investor's Business Daily*, September 19, 2016, accessed September 20, 2018, https://www.investors.com/news/obamacare-individual-mandate-fine-hit-8-million-people-in-2016/.

395 Ryan Ellis, "Individual Mandate Repeal Is a Middle Class Tax Cut," *Forbes*, November 15, 2017, accessed September 21, 2018, https://www.forbes.com/sites/ryanellis/2017/11/15/individual-mandate-repeal-is-a-middle-class-tax-cut/#5c2425a34b80.

396 "Supreme Court Upholds Individual Mandate, ObamaCare Survives," Fox News, accessed September 20, 2018, http://www.foxnews.com/politics/2012/06/28/supreme-court-upholds-individual-mandate-obamacare-survives.html.

397 Tom Howell Jr., "Roberts' Obamacare Argument Being Used by GOP to Undo Individual Mandate Requirement," *The Washington Times*, December 3, 2017, accessed September 20, 2018, https://www.washingtontimes.com/news/2017/dec/3/roberts-obamacare-argument-used-to-undo-individual/.

398 Philip Klein and Evan Vucci, "Trump Declares Obamacare Is 'Over' as He Signs Individual Mandate Repeal into Law," *Washington Examiner*, December 22, 2017, accessed September 20, 2018, https://www.washingtonexaminer.com/trump-declares-obamacare-is-over-as-he-signs-individual-mandate-repeal-into-law.

399 Robert King, "The Obamacare Individual Mandate Is Repealed. Here's What's Next," *Washington Examiner*, January 13, 2018, accessed September 21, 2018, https://www.washingtonexaminer.com/the-obamacare-individual-mandate-is-repealed-heres-whats-next.

400 Paul Demko and Adam Cancryn. "Trump's New Health Insurance Rules Expected to Hurt Obamacare," *Politico*, June 19,

2018, accessed September 17, 2018, https://www.politico.com/story/2018/06/19/trumps-new-health-insurance-rules-535846.

401 Justin Haskins, "Trump and Sen. Rand Paul Lead the Way on Health-care Reform," *Washington Examiner*, June 21, 2018, accessed September 18, 2018, https://www.washingtonexaminer.com/opinion/trump-and-sen-rand-paul-lead-the-way-on-healthcare-reform.

402 Demko and Cancryn. "Trump's New Health Insurance Rules Expected to Hurt Obamacare."

403 Thomas J. Donohue, "A Health Care Victory for Small Businesses," U.S. Chamber of Commerce, June 25, 2018, accessed September 17, 2018, https://www.uschamber.com/series/above-the-fold/health-care-victory-small-businesses.

404 Allison Inserro, "Democratic-Led States Sue Trump Administration Over Association Health Plans," AJMC, July 27, 2018, accessed September 17, 2018, https://www.ajmc.com/newsroom/democraticled-states-sue-trump-administration-over-association-health-plans.

405 Robert E. Moffit, "Trump's New Health Initiative Will Spell Relief for Americans," The Heritage Foundation, June 19, 2018, accessed September 17, 2018, https://www.heritage.org/health-care-reform/commentary/trumps-new-health-initiative-will-spell-relief-americans.

406 Ibid.

407 Sally C. Pipes, "Providing Better Deals for Health Coverage," *The Washington Times*, August 19, 2018, accessed September 17, 2018, https://www.washingtontimes.com/news/2018/aug/19/ahps-offer-small-businesses-sole-proprietors-big-h/.

408 Ibid.

409 Joseph Semprevivo, "This 1 Move by the Trump Administration Is Boosting My Small Business," *The Daily Signal*, September 13, 2018, accessed September 17, 2018, https://www.dailysignal.com/2018/09/13/this-1-move-by-the-trump-administration-is-boosting-my-small-business/.

410 Whitney Jones, "New Trump Health Policy Would Make Coverage Options More Affordable," *The Daily Signal*, February

21, 2018, accessed September 19, 2018, https://www.dailysignal. com/2018/02/20/new-trump-health-policy-make-coverage-options-affordable/.

411 Sally C. Pipes, "Trump's Short-Term Health Plans Will Legalize Affordable Care," *Forbes*, March 5, 2018, accessed September 17, 2018, https://www.forbes.com/sites/sallypipes/2018/03/05/trumps -short-term-health-plans-will-legalize-affordable-care/#22b7746f7683.

412 Ibid.

413 Demko, "Trump Whacks Obamacare by Boosting Short-term Health Plans," *Politico*, August 1, 2018, accessed September 19, 2018, https:// www.politico.com/story/2018/08/01/trump-obamacare-short-term-plans-689126.

414 Vann R. Newkirk II, "The True Cost of Cheap Health Insurance," *The Atlantic*, April 25, 2018, accessed September 19, 2018, https://www.theatlantic.com/politics/archive/2018/04/ short-term-insurance-trump-proposed-rule/558743/.

415 "Heritage Expert on HHS Rule Regarding Short-Term Health Plans," The Heritage Foundation, August 1, 2018, accessed September 19, 2018, https://www.heritage.org/press/ heritage-expert-hhs-rule-regarding-short-term-health-plans.

416 Rachel Del Guidice, "California on Cusp of Banning Short-Term Health Coverage," *The Daily Signal*, September 5, 2018, accessed September 19, 2018, https://www.dailysignal.com/2018/09/04/ california-on-cusp-of-banning-short-term-health-coverage/.

417 Robert Pear, "'Short Term' Health Insurance? Up to 3 Years Under New Trump Policy," *New York Times*, August 1, 2018, accessed September 19, 2018, https://www.nytimes.com/2018/08/01/us/ politics/trump-short-term-health-insurance.html.

418 Julie Royner, "Businesses Sue Government Over Birth Control Mandate," NPR, January 11, 2013, accessed September 19, 2018, https://www.npr.org/sections/health-shots/2013/01/11/ 169136510/businesses-sue-government-over-birth-control-man-date.

[419] Dan Mangan, "Court Rules for Certain Companies over Obamacare Mandate," CNBC, July 21, 2014, accessed September 19, 2018, https://www.cnbc.com/2014/06/30/supreme-court-for-profit-companies-can-claim-a-religious-exemption-to-the-contraceptive-insurance-mandate-of-obamacare.html.

[420] Sarah Ferris, "Court: Nuns Must Comply with Obamacare's Birth Control Mandate," *The Hill*, February 4, 2016, accessed September 19, 2018, https://thehill.com/policy/healthcare/247850-court-rules-nuns-group-must-comply-with-obamacare-birth-control-mandate.

[421] David French, "The Little Sisters of the Poor Just Beat the Obama Administration at the Supreme Court," *National Review*, October 10, 2017, accessed September 19, 2018, https://www.nationalreview.com/corner/little-sisters-poor-just-beat-obama-administration-supreme-court/.

[422] Pear, "Trump Administration Rolls Back Birth Control Mandate," *New York Times*, October 6, 2017, accessed September 20, 2018, https://www.nytimes.com/2017/10/06/us/politics/trump-contraception-birth-control.html.

[423] Victoria Colliver, "Second Federal Judge Halts Trump's Birth Control Rule," *Politico*, December 21, 2017, accessed September 20, 2018, https://www.politico.com/story/2017/12/21/second-federal-judge-halts-trumps-birth-control-rule-312405.

Chapter 7

[424] Ian Schwartz, "Woodward: No Evidence Of Trump-Russia Collusion, I Searched For Two Years," RealClearPolitics, September 14, 2018, accessed September 23, 2018, https://www.realclearpolitics.com/video/2018/09/14/woodward_no_evidence_of_collusion_between_trump_and_russia_i_searched_for_two_years.html.

[425] Byron York, "Byron York: Trump and Obama: Who's Really Tougher on Russia?" *Washington Examiner*, February 27, 2018, accessed

September 30, 2018, https://www.washingtonexaminer.com/byron-york-trump-and-obama-whos-really-tougher-on-russia.

426 Michael Isikoff, "Obama Cyber Chief Confirms 'Stand Down' Order Against Russian Cyberattacks in Summer 2016," *Yahoo! News*, June 20, 2018, accessed August 2, 2018, https://www.yahoo.com/news/obama-cyber-chief-confirms-stand-order-russian-cyberattacks-summer-2016-204935758.html.

427 Lauren Gambino, Sabrina Siddiqui, and Shaun Walker, "Obama Expels 35 Russian Diplomats in Retaliation for US Election Hacking," *The Guardian*, December 30, 2016, accessed August 2, 2018, https://www.theguardian.com/us-news/2016/dec/29/barack-obama-sanctions-russia-election-hack.

428 Nikki Haley, "Remarks at a UN Security Council Briefing on Ukraine," U.S. Department of State, February 2, 2017, accessed September 23, 2018, https://usun.state.gov/remarks/7668.

429 Jen Kerns, "President Trump Is Tougher on Russia in 18 Months than Obama in Eight Years," *The Hill*, July 16, 2018, https://thehill.com/opinion/white-house/397212-president-trump-is-tougher-on-russia-in-18-months-than-obama-in-eight.

430 Lesley Wroughton and Patricia Zengerle, "U.S. Slaps Sanctions on Putin Cronies for Russia's 'Malign Activity,'" Reuters, April 6, 2018, https://www.reuters.com/article/us-usa-russia-sanctions-announcement/u-s-slaps-sanctions-on-putin-cronies-for-russias-malign-activity-idUSKCN1HD1O0.

431 Kerns, "President Trump Is Tougher on Russia."

432 Donna Borak, "US Imposes Sanctions against Russian Oligarchs and Government Officials," CNN, April 6, 2018, https://www.cnn.com/2018/04/06/politics/russia-sanctions-oligarchs/index.html.

433 Alex Ward, "Trump Adds More Russians Who Interfered in the 2016 Election to a Sanctions List," *Vox*, September 20, 2018, https://www.vox.com/world/2018/9/20/17883552/trump-russia-sanctions-mueller-caatsa.

434 Josh Lederman, "U.S. Shutters Russia's San Francisco Consulate in Retaliation," *Chicago Tribune*, September 1, 2017, accessed

September 23, 2018, http://www.chicagotribune.com/news/nationworld/ct-russia-san-francisco-consulate-20170831-story.html.

[435] Evan Bush et al., "Russians Turned Away at Seattle Consulate after Trump Administration Announces Closure," *The Seattle Times*, March 28, 2018, accessed September 23, 2018, https://www.seattletimes.com/seattle-news/russians-turned-away-at-seattle-consulate-after-trump-administration-announces-closure/.

[436] James Ball, "Obama Issues Syria a 'Red Line' Warning on Chemical Weapons," *The Washington Post*, August 20, 2012, accessed September 25, 2018, https://www.washingtonpost.com/world/national-security/obama-issues-syria-red-line-warning-on-chemical-weapons/2012/08/20/ba5d26ec-eaf7-11e1-b811-09036bcb182b_story.html.

[437] Joby Warrick, "More than 1,400 Killed in Syrian Chemical Weapons Attack, U.S. Says," *The Washington Post*, August 30, 2013, accessed September 25, 2018, https://www.washingtonpost.com/world/national-security/nearly-1500-killed-in-syrian-chemical-weapons-attack-us-says/2013/08/30/b2864662-1196-11e3-85b6-d27422650fd5_story.html.

[438] Robert Farley, "Obama's Blurry Red Line," FactCheck.org, October 25, 2013, accessed September 25, 2018, https://www.factcheck.org/2013/09/obamas-blurry-red-line/.

[439] Ibid.

[440] Colum Lynch, "To Assuage Russia, Obama Administration Backed Off Syria Chemical Weapons Plan," *Foreign Policy*, May 19, 2017, accessed September 25, 2018, https://foreignpolicy.com/2017/05/19/to-assuage-russia-obama-administration-backed-off-syria-chemical-weapons-plan/.

[441] James Kirchick, "Why It's Hard to Take Democrats Seriously on Russia," *Politico*, July 24, 2017, accessed September 25, 2018, https://www.politico.com/magazine/story/2017/07/24/why-its-hard-to-take-democrats-seriously-on-russia-215415.

[442] Lauren Fish, "Operational-Level Strikes Finally Enforce Obama's Red Line," *National Review*, April 16, 2018, accessed

September 25, 2018, https://www.nationalreview.com/2018/04/trump-syria-strikes-obama-red-line-enforced/.

443 Kathryn Watson, "What Happened to Russia's Agreement to Eradicate Syria's Chemical Weapons?" CBS, April 10, 2017, accessed September 25, 2018, https://www.cbsnews.com/news/what-happened-to-russias-agreement-to-eliminate-syrias-chemical-weapons/.

444 Anne Barnard and Michael R. Gordon, "Worst Chemical Attack in Years in Syria; U.S. Blames Assad," *New York Times*, April 4, 2017, accessed September 25, 2018, https://www.nytimes.com/2017/04/04/world/middleeast/syria-gas-attack.html.

445 Barbara Starr and Jeremy Diamond, "Trump Launches Military Strike against Syria," CNN, April 7, 2017, accessed September 26, 2018, https://www.cnn.com/2017/04/06/politics/donald-trump-syria-military/index.html.

446 "John Kerry: US 'Paid a Price' for Not Enforcing Obama's 'Red Line' in Syria," Fox News, September 3, 2018, accessed September 26, 2018, http://insider.foxnews.com/2018/09/03/john-kerry-us-paid-price-not-enforcing-obamas-red-line-syria.

447 Daniel Victor, "Suspected Chemical Attack in Syria: What We Know and Don't Know," *New York Times*, April 11, 2018, accessed September 26, 2018, https://www.nytimes.com/2018/04/11/world/middleeast/syria-chemical-attack.html.

448 Veronica Stracqualursi, "Trump Declares 'Mission Accomplished' in Syria Strike," CNN, April 14, 2018, accessed September 26, 2018, https://www.cnn.com/2018/04/14/politics/trump-syria-strike/index.html.

449 David Filipov, "Russia Condemns U.S. Missile Strike on Syria, Suspends Key Air Agreement," *The Washington Post*, April 7, 2017, accessed September 28, 2018, https://www.washingtonpost.com/world/europe/russia-condemns-us-missile-strike-on-syria/2017/04/07/c81ea12a-1b4e-11e7-8003-f55b4c1cfae2_story.html.

450 Stepan Kravchenko, Henry Meyer, and Margaret Talev, "U.S. Strikes Killed Scores of Russia Fighters in Syria, Sources Say,"

Bloomberg, accessed September 26, 2018, https://www.bloomberg.com/news/articles/2018-02-13/u-s-strikes-said-to-kill-scores-of-russian-fighters-in-syria.

451 Steven Lee Myers and Ellen Barry, "Putin Reclaims Crimea for Russia and Bitterly Denounces the West," *New York Times*, March 18, 2014, accessed September 28, 2018, https://www.nytimes.com/2014/03/19/world/europe/ukraine.html.

452 "World Leaders Condemn Russia's Annexation of Crimea," GMA News Online, accessed September 28, 2018, http://www.gmanetwork.com/news/news/world/353202/world-leaders-condemn-russia-s-annexation-of-crimea/story/.

453 "Jay Carney: Press Briefing by Press Secretary Jay Carney - March 18, 2014," The American Presidency Project, March 18, 2014, accessed September 28, 2018, http://www.presidency.ucsb.edu/ws/index.php?pid=104924.

454 Zeke J. Miller, "Barack Obama Orders Sanctions in Russia-Ukraine Crimea Conflict," *Time*, March 6, 2014, accessed September 28, 2018, http://time.com/13902/barack-obama-ukraine-russia/.

455 Annie Gowan, "Has Russia Invaded Ukraine? Americans Shy Away from the I-word," *The Washington Post*, August 28, 2014, accessed September 28, 2018, https://www.washingtonpost.com/world/russian-and-ukraine-troops-battle-in-south-prompting-fears-of-widescale-invasion/2014/08/28/04b614f4-9a6e-40f4-aa21-4f49104cf0e4_story.html.

456 "Transcript: President Obama's Aug. 28 Remarks on Ukraine, Syria and the Economy," *The Washington Post*, accessed September 28, 2018, https://www.washingtonpost.com/politics/transcript president-obamas-aug-28-remarks-on-ukraine-and-syria/2014/08/28/416f1336-2eec-11e4-bb9b-997ae96fad33_story.html.

457 Jennifer Steinhauer and David M. Herszenhorn, "Defying Obama, Many in Congress Press to Arm Ukraine," *New York Times*, December 11, 2015, accessed September 28, 2018, https://www.nytimes.com/2015/06/12/world/europe/defying-obama-many-in-congress-press-to-arm-ukraine.html.

458 Jeremy Herb, "Obama Pressed on Many Fronts to Arm Ukraine," *Politico*, March 11, 2015, accessed September 28, 2018, https://www.politico.com/story/2015/03/obama-pressed-on-many-fronts-to-arm-ukraine-115999.

459 Josh Rogin, "Trump Administration Approves Lethal Arms Sales to Ukraine," *The Washington Post*, December 20, 2017, accessed September 28, 2018, https://www.washingtonpost.com/news/josh-rogin/wp/2017/12/20/trump-administration-approves-lethal-arms-sales-to-ukraine/.

460 Ibid.

461 Nolan Peterson, "Trump Approves US Lethal Weapons Sales to Ukraine, Angering Moscow," *The Daily Signal*, December 21, 2017, accessed September 28, 2018, https://www.dailysignal.com/2017/12/21/trump-approves-us-lethal-weapons-sales-ukraine-angering-moscow/.

462 "Russia Condemns US Move to Sell Weapons to Ukraine," *Al Jazeera*, December 23, 2017, accessed September 28, 2018, https://www.aljazeera.com/news/2017/12/russia-condemns-move-sell-weapons-ukraine-171223105437273.html.

463 "Ukraine—Javelin Missiles and Command Launch Units," Defense Security Cooperation Agency, March 1, 2018, accessed September 28, 2018, http://www.dsca.mil/major-arms-sales/ukraine-javelin-missiles-and-command-launch-units.

464 Lucas Tomlinson, "Pentagon Sending $200 Million in Nonlethal Aid to Ukraine in Move Expected to Rile Moscow," Fox News, July 20, 2018, accessed September 28, 2018, http://www.foxnews.com/politics/2018/07/20/pentagon-sending-200-million-in-nonlethal-aid-to-ukraine-in-move-expected-to-rile-moscow.html.

465 Michael R. Gordon, "U.S. Says Russia Tested Missile, Despite Treaty," *New York Times*, January 30, 2014, accessed September 28, 2018, https://www.nytimes.com/2014/01/30/world/europe/us-says-russia-tested-missile-despite-treaty.html.

466 Gordon, "Russia Is Moving Ahead with Missile Program That Violates Treaty, U.S. Officials Say," *New York Times*, December

21, 2017, accessed September 28, 2018, https://www.nytimes.com/2016/10/20/world/europe/russia-missiles-inf-treaty.html.

[467] Gregory Hellman, "Trump Approves New Russia Sanctions for Violating Cold War Arms Pact," *Politico*, December 8, 2017, accessed September 28, 2018, https://www.politico.com/story/2017/12/08/trump-russia-sanctions-cold-war-arms-pact-215837.

[468] W.J Hennigan, "President Trump Is Developing a Missile That Would Break a Nuclear Arms Treaty With Russia," *Time*, January 3, 2018, accessed September 28, 2018, http://time.com/5085257/donald-trump-nuclear-missile-russia-treaty/

[469] Ibid.

[470] "10 Things You Need to Know about NATO," North Atlantic Treaty Organization, February 27, 2018, accessed September 30, 2018, https://www.nato.int/cps/ic/natohq/126169.htm.

[471] Alexander Smith, "Why NATO Is Criticized by Trump and Opposed by Russia," NBC, April 19, 2018, accessed September 30, 2018, https://www.nbcnews.com/storyline/smart-facts/what-nato-what-do-trump-russia-think-about-it-n860411.

[472] Ewen MacAskill, "Nato [sic] to Announce 4,000-strong Rapid Reaction Force to Counter Russian Threat," *The Guardian*, September 5, 2014, accessed September 30, 2018, https://www.theguardian.com/world/2014/sep/05/nato-4000-rapid-reaction-force-baltics-russia.

[473] Amanda Macias, "The US Spent $686 Billion on Defense Last Year—Here's How the Other NATO Countries Stack Up," CNBC, July 6, 2018, accessed September 30, 2018, https://www.cnbc.com/2018/07/03/nato-spending-2017.html.

[474] "Press Conference by NATO Secretary General Jens Stoltenberg Ahead of the Meeting of NATO Defence Ministers," North American Trade Organization, accessed September 30, 2018, https://www.nato.int/cps/en/natohq/opinions_145415.htm.

[475] Michael Birnbaum and Thomas Gibbons-Neff, "NATO Allies Boost Defense Spending in the Wake of Trump Criticism," *The Washington Post*, June 28, 2017, accessed September 30, 2018, https://www.washingtonpost.com/world/nato-allies-boost-defense-spending-in-

the-wake-of-trump-criticism/2017/06/28/153584de-5a8c-11e7-aa69-3964a7d55207_story.html.

476 Kristina Wong, "President Trump Says He'll Tell NATO: 'You Gotta Start Paying Your Bills,'" Breitbart, July 5, 2018, accessed September 30, 2018, https://www.breitbart.com/big-government/2018/07/05/president-trump-says-hell-tell-nato-you-gotta-start-paying-your-bills/.

477 Meg Wagner, James Masters, and Veronica Rocha, "Trump Attends NATO Summit," CNN, July 13, 2018, accessed January 17, 2019, https://www.cnn.com/politics/live-news/trump-nato-summit-2018/h_5579f8d955299b8ae215ac13e5451e84.

478 Jeremy Diamond and Kaitlan Collins, "Trump Suggested NATO Countries Double Their Defense Spending Goal," CNN, July 11, 2018, accessed September 30, 2018, https://www.cnn.com/2018/07/11/politics/trump-nato-defense-spending/index.html.

479 Henry Ridgwell, "US Signs Defense Pacts with Baltic States, but NATO Allies Wary of Trump Era," VOA, January 18, 2017, accessed September 30, 2018, https://www.voanews.com/a/united-states-defense-pacts-baltic-states/3681669.html.

480 Lidia Kelly, "Poland Signs $4.75 Billion Deal for U.S. Patriot Missile System Facing Russia," Reuters, March 28, 2018, accessed September 30, 2018, https://www.reuters.com/article/us-raytheon-poland-patriot/poland-signs-4-75-billion-deal-for-u-s-patriot-missile-system-facing-russia-idUSKBN1H417S.

481 Luke Harding and Ian Traynor, "Obama Abandons Missile Defence Shield in Europe," *The Guardian*, September 17, 2009, accessed September 30, 2018, https://www.theguardian.com/world/2009/sep/17/missile-defence-shield-barack-obama.

Chapter 8

482 "Read Transcript of Former President Obama's Speech, Blasting President Trump," *USA Today*, September 7, 2018, accessed October 3, 2018, https://www.usatoday.com/story/news/pol-

itics/elections/2018/09/07/president-barack-obamas-speech-transcript-slamming-trump/1225554002/.

483 Matt Margolis, *The Scandalous Presidency of Barack Obama* (New York: Bombardier Books, 2018).

484 Ibid.

485 Ibid.

486 "Slain Border Patrol Agent's Brother Pleads for Trump, Sessions to Reopen 'Fast and Furious' Case," Fox News, March 6, 2018, accessed October 3, 2018, http://insider.foxnews.com/2018/03/06/slain-border-patrol-agent-brian-terrys-family-wants-president-trump-reopen-fast-furious.

487 Brooke Singman, "Trump Administration to Turn over Documents Related to Obama-era Operation Fast and Furious," Fox News, accessed October 3, 2018, https://www.foxnews.com/politics/trump-administration-to-turn-over-documents-related-to-obama-era-operation-fast-and-furious.

488 Margot Cleveland, "Trump Administration Agrees to Hand Over Fast And Furious Docs," *The Federalist*, March 8, 2018, accessed October 3, 2018, http://thefederalist.com/2018/03/08/trump-administration-agrees-to-hand-over-fast-and-furious-docs/.

489 Paul Bond, "'2016: Obama's America' Filmmaker Indicted for Violating Campaign Finance Laws," *The Hollywood Reporter*, January 23, 2014, https://www.hollywoodreporter.com/news/2016-obamas-america-filmmaker-indicted-673670.

490 Jennifer G. Hickey and John Gizzi, "Dershowitz, Law Enforcement Experts Slam D'Souza Targeting," *Newsmax*, January 29, 2014, https://www.newsmax.com/newsfront/dsouza-dershowitz-targeting-selective/2014/01/29/id/549845/.

491 Maggie Haberman, "Obama 2008 Campaign Fined $375,000," *Politico*, January 4, 2013, https://www.politico.com/story/2013/01/obama-2008-campaign-fined-375000-085784.

492 Andrew C. McCarthy, "Amnesty, But Not for D'Souza," *National Review*, February 1, 2014, accessed October 2, 2018, http://www.nationalreview.com/2014/02/amnesty-not-dsouza-andrew-c-mccarthy.

493 Singman, "Trump Pardons Dinesh D'Souza," Fox News, accessed October 2, 2018, https://www.foxnews.com/politics/trump-pardons-dinesh-dsouza.

494 Associated Press, "US Navy Sailor Jailed for Taking Photos of Classified Areas of Nuclear Submarine," *The Guardian*, August 20, 2016, accessed October 2, 2018, https://www.theguardian.com/us-news/2016/aug/20/us-navy-sailor-jailed-for-taking-photos-of-classified-areas-of-nuclear-submarine.

495 Josh Gerstein and Daniel Strauss, "Feds Reject Clinton Comparison in Classified Sub Photos Case," *Politico*, August 16, 2016, accessed October 2, 2018, https://www.politico.com/blogs/under-the-radar/2016/08/kristian-saucier-sentencing-clinton-227052.

496 Steven Nelson and Evan Vucci, "Trump Pardons Kristian Saucier, Former Sailor Jailed for Submarine Pictures," *Washington Examiner*, March 10, 2018, accessed October 2, 2018, https://www.washingtonexaminer.com/trump-pardons-kristian-saucier-former-sailor-jailed-for-submarine-pictures.

497 "Did the FBI Cover Up Evidence That China Hacked Clinton's State Dept. Emails?" *Investor's Business Daily*, August 28, 2018, accessed October 2, 2018, https://www.investors.com/politics/editorials/china-reportedly-hacked-clintons-state-department-emails-did-the-fbi-cover-that-up-too/.

498 Steven Nelson, "Sailor Cited by Trump as Evidence of Hillary Clinton Double Standard Now Works as Garbage Man," *Washington Examiner*, January 2, 2018, accessed October 2, 2018, https://www.washingtonexaminer.com/sailor-cited-by-trump-as-evidence-of-hillary-clinton-double-standard-now-works-as-garbage-man.

499 Ibid.

500 Ali Vitali, "Trump Pardons Ex-Navy Sailor Who Cited Clinton in His Defense," NBC, March 9, 2018, accessed October 2, 2018, https://www.nbcnews.com/politics/white-house/trump-pardons-ex-navy-sailor-who-cited-clinton-his-defense-n855301.

501 Nick Carey, "Racial Predatory Loans Fueled U.S. Housing Crisis: Study," Reuters, October 4, 2010, accessed October 2,

2018, https://www.reuters.com/article/us-usa-foreclosures-race/racial-predatory-loans-fueled-u-s-housing-crisis-study-idUS-TRE6930K520101004.

502 Matt Margolis, *The Scandalous Presidency of Barack Obama* (New York: Bombardier Books, 2018).

503 George F. Will, "The Justice Department's Bank Settlement Slush Fund," *The Washington Post*, August 31, 2016, accessed October 3, 2018, https://www.washingtonpost.com/opinions/the-justice-departments-bank-settlement-slush-fund/2016/08/31/a3b4da7a-6eec-11e6-8365-b19e428a975e_story.html.

504 Byron York, "Justice Department Steers Money to Favored Groups," *Washington Examiner*, March 16, 2012, accessed October 3, 2018, https://www.washingtonexaminer.com/justice-department-steers-money-to-favored-groups.

505 Will, "The Justice Department's Bank Settlement Slush Fund."

506 "Attorney General Jeff Sessions Ends Third Party Settlement Practice," The United States Department of Justice, June 7, 2017, accessed October 3, 2018, https://www.justice.gov/opa/pr/attorney-general-jeff-sessions-ends-third-party-settlement-practice.

507 Ibid.

508 Wikipedia, s.v. "Hammond Arson Case," accessed October 3, 2018, https://en.wikipedia.org/wiki/Hammond_arson_case.

509 Emily Shapiro, "Oregon Ranchers Report to California Prison Amid Armed Standoff," ABC, January 4, 2016, accessed October 3, 2018, https://abcnews.go.com/US/oregon-ranchers-expected-report-california-prison-amid-armed/story?id=36079385.

510 Steven Nelson, "Trump Pardons Dwight and Steven Hammond, Ranchers Whose Case Inspired Armed Standoff," *Washington Examiner*, July 10, 2018, accessed October 3, 2018, https://www.washingtonexaminer.com/news/white-house/trump-pardons-dwight-and-steven-hammond-ranchers-whose-case-inspired-armed-standoff.

511 Jeremy Lott and Don Ryan, "Trump Urged to Pardon Oregon Ranchers Who Sparked Armed Standoff," *Washington Examiner*,

November 20, 2016, accessed October 3, 2018, https://www.washingtonexaminer.com/trump-urged-to-pardon-oregon-ranchers-who-sparked-armed-standoff.

512 "Statement from the Press Secretary Regarding Executive Clemency for Dwight and Steven Hammond," The White House, accessed October 3, 2018, https://www.whitehouse.gov/briefings-statements/statement-press-secretary-regarding-executive-clemency-dwight-steven-hammond/.

513 John Gramlich and Kristen Bialik, "Obama Granted Clemency to the Most People Since Truman," Pew Research Center, January 20, 2017, accessed October 3, 2018, http://www.pewresearch.org/fact-tank/2017/01/20/obama-used-more-clemency-power/.

514 "Statement from the Press Secretary Regarding Executive Clemency for Dwight and Steven Hammond," The White House, accessed October 3, 2018, https://www.whitehouse.gov/briefings-statements/statement-press-secretary-regarding-executive-clemency-dwight-steven-hammond/.

515 Matt Margolis and Mark Noonan, *The Worst President in History: The Legacy of Barack Obama* (New York: Bombardier Books, 2018).

516 "Report: DOJ's Operation Choke Point Secretly Pressured Banks to Cut Ties with Legal Business," United States House Committee on Oversight and Government Reform, May 29, 2014, accessed October 4, 2018, https://oversight.house.gov/release/report-dojs-operation-choke-point-secretly-pressured-banks-cut-ties-legal-business/.

517 Frank Miniter, "FDIC Admits to Strangling Legal Gun Stores Banking Relationships," *Forbes*, January 30, 2015, accessed October 5, 2018, https://www.forbes.com/sites/frankminiter/2015/01/30/fdic-admits-to-strangling-legal-gun-stores-banking-relationships.

518 "Trump Administration Ends Another Obama-era Anti-Gun Policy," NRA-ILA, August 18, 2017, accessed October 4, 2018, https://www.nraila.org/articles/20170818/trump-administration-ends-another-obama-era-anti-gun-policy.

519 Binyamin Appelbaum and Michael D. Shear, "Once Skeptical of Executive Power, Obama Has Come to Embrace It," *New York*

Times, August 13, 2016, accessed October 6, 2018, https://www.nytimes.com/2016/08/14/us/politics/obama-era-legacy-regulation.html.

520 "Attorney General Jeff Sessions Ends the Department's Practice of Regulation by Guidance," The United States Department of Justice, November 17, 2017, accessed October 6, 2018, https://www.justice.gov/opa/pr/attorney-general-jeff-sessions-ends-department-s-practice-regulation-guidance.

521 John-Michael Seibler, "Court Ruling Rebukes Obama-Era Practice That Flouted Rule of Law," The Heritage Foundation, February 27, 2018, accessed October 6, 2018, https://www.heritage.org/courts/commentary/court-ruling-rebukes-obama-era-practice-flouted-rule-law.

522 "Attorney General Jeff Sessions Rescinds 24 Guidance Documents," The United States Department of Justice, July 4, 2018, accessed October 6, 2018, https://www.justice.gov/opa/pr/attorney-general-jeff-sessions-rescinds-24-guidance-documents.

523 Adam Serwer, "Obama Leaves His Mark on the Federal Bench," MSNBC, June 11, 2014, accessed October 12, 2018, http://www.msnbc.com/msnbc/obama-leaves-his-mark-the-federal-bench.

524 Philip Rucker and Robert Barnes, "Trump to Inherit More than 100 Court Vacancies, Plans to Reshape Judiciary," *The Washington Post*, December 25, 2016, accessed October 12, 2018, https://www.washingtonpost.com/politics/trump-to-inherit-more-than-100-court-vacancies-plans-to-reshape-judiciary/2016/12/25/d190dd18-c928-11e6-85b5-76616a33048d_story.html.

525 Guy Benson, "Whoa: Mitch McConnell Just Nuked Dems on Trump's Judicial Picks, and Schumer Is Fuming," Townhall, October 11, 2017, accessed October 12, 2018, https://townhall.com/tipsheet/guybenson/2017/10/11/mcdonnell-blue-slips-n2393579.

526 Jordain Carney, "Republicans Confirming Trump's Court Nominees at Record Pace," *The Hill*, May 1, 2018, accessed October 12, 2018, https://thehill.com/homenews/senate/385728-republicans-confirming-trumps-court-nominees-at-record-pace.

527 Calvin Freiburger, "Trump Judicial Picks Flip Two Federal Circuit Courts from Left to Right," LifeSiteNews, September 4, 2018, accessed October 12, 2018, https://www.lifesitenews.com/news/trump-judicial-picks-flip-two-federal-circuit-courts-from-left-to-right.

528 Kevin Schaul, "How Trump Is Shifting the Most Important Courts in the Country," *The Washington Post*, accessed October 12, 2018, https://www.washingtonpost.com/graphics/2018/politics/trump-federal-judges/.

529 "Garland's Judicial Philosophy Is Not Moderate," Senate Republican Policy Committee, accessed October 7, 2018, https://www.rpc.senate.gov/policy-papers/garlands-judicial-philosophy-is-not-moderate.

530 David G. Savage et al., "Supreme Court Nominee Merrick Garland Has a Record of Restraint, Not Activism," *Los Angeles Times*, March 18, 2016, accessed October 7, 2018, http://www.latimes.com/nation/la-na-garland-legal-analysis-20160318-story.html.

531 The Editorial Board, "Merrick Garland for the Supreme Court," *New York Times*, March 16, 2016, accessed October 7, 2018, https://www.nytimes.com/2016/03/17/opinion/merrick-garland-for-the-supreme-court.html.

532 Sarah Almukhtar, "Why Obama Nominated Merrick Garland for the Supreme Court," *New York Times*, March 16, 2016, accessed October 7, 2018, https://www.nytimes.com/interactive/2016/03/16/us/politics/garland-supreme-court-nomination.html.

533 Adam Bonica et al., "New Data Show How Liberal Merrick Garland Really Is," *The Washington Post*, March 30, 2016, accessed October 7, 2018, https://www.washingtonpost.com/news/monkey-cage/wp/2016/03/30/new-data-show-how-liberal-merrick-garland-really-is/.

534 Ben Shapiro, "No, Trump Isn't Going to Save The Supreme Court," *Daily Wire*, August 10, 2016, accessed

October 7, 2018, https://www.dailywire.com/news/8266/no-trump-isnt-going-save-supreme-court-ben-shapiro.

535 Jeremy Diamond, "Trump Unveils His Potential Supreme Court Nominees," CNN, May 19, 2016, accessed October 7, 2018, https://www.cnn.com/2016/05/18/politics/donald-trump-supreme-court-nominees/index.html.

536 Jane Coaston, "Polling Data Shows Republicans Turned Out for Trump in 2016 Because of the Supreme Court," *Vox*, June 29, 2018, accessed October 12, 2018, https://www.vox.com/2018/6/29/17511088/scotus-2016-election-poll-trump-republicans-kennedy-retire.

537 Ariane de Vogue and Dan Berman, "Neil Gorsuch Confirmed to the Supreme Court," CNN, April 7, 2017, accessed October 7, 2018, https://www.cnn.com/2017/04/07/politics/neil-gorsuch-senate-vote/index.html.

538 Thomas Jipping, "Senate Democrats' Document Complaints over Brett Kavanaugh Are Absurd," *Washington Examiner*, September 5, 2018, accessed October 7, 2018, https://www.washingtonexaminer.com/opinion/senate-democrats-document-complaints-over-brett-kavanaugh-are-absurd.

539 Deroy Murdock, "Feinstein v. Kavanaugh: Anatomy of a Character Assassination," Fox News, October 5, 2018, accessed October 7, 2018, https://www.foxnews.com/opinion/feinstein-v-kavanaugh-anatomy-of-a-character-assassination.

540 Matt Margolis, "Four Reasons the New Accusations Against Kavanaugh Are Weaker Than Ford's," PJ Media, September 23, 2018, accessed October 7, 2018, https://pjmedia.com/trending/four-reasons-the-new-accusations-against-kavanaugh-are-weaker-than-fords/.

541 Gabriella Muñoz, "Kellyanne Conway: The *New York Times* Contradicts New Yorker Allegations Against Kavanaugh," *The Washington Times*, September 24, 2018, accessed October 7, 2018, https://www.washingtontimes.com/news/2018/sep/24/kellyanne-conway-the-new-york-times-contradicts-ne/.

542 Natalie Andrews, Rebecca Ballhaus, and Sadie Gurman, "Friend of Dr. Ford Felt Pressure to Revisit Statement," *Wall Street Journal*, October 5, 2018, accessed October 7, 2018, https://www.wsj.com/articles/friend-of-dr-ford-felt-pressure-to-revisit-statement-1538715152.

543 Fox News (@FoxNews), ".@mercedesschlapp: 'President Trump stood by Brett Kavanaugh throughout this whole process, I don't know if any other Republican president would have done so,' Twitter, October 6, 2018, 5:14 AM, accessed October 7, 2018, https://twitter.com/FoxNews/status/1048547042564493312.

Conclusion

544 Jennifer Epstein, "Obama Defiant After GOP Wave," *Politico*, November 6, 2014, accessed October 25, 2018, https://www.politico.com/story/2014/11/obama-2014-midterms-response-112601.

545 "Trump's Deregulation Project," *Wall Street Journal*, April 17, 2017, accessed October 9, 2018, https://www.wsj.com/articles/trumps-deregulation-project-1492470927.

546 Paul Bedard, "Trump's List: 289 Accomplishments in Just 20 Months, 'Relentless' Promise-Keeping," *Washington Examiner*, October 12, 2018, accessed October 16, 2018, https://www.washingtonexaminer.com/washington-secrets/trumps-list-289-accomplishments-in-just-20-months-relentless-promise-keeping.

547 Ibid.

548 Andrea Riquier, "Manufacturing Jobs Growing at Fastest Rate in 23 Years," MarketWatch, August 3, 2018, accessed October 9, 2018, https://www.marketwatch.com/story/heres-why-manu-facturing-jobs-growth-has-been-so-strong-2018-08-03.

549 Ryan Saavedra, "U.S. Returns to #1 In Economic Category for First Time Since 2008," *Daily Wire*, October 17, 2018, accessed October 27, 2018, https://www.dailywire.com/news/37221/us-returns-1-economic-category-first-time-2008-ryan-saavedra.

550 Bedard, "Trump's List: 289 Accomplishments in Just 20 Months."

551 Kevin Mooney, "Carbon Dioxide Emissions Dip in Trump's First Year, EPA Says," *The Daily Signal*, October 22, 2018, accessed

October 28, 2018, https://www.dailysignal.com/2018/10/17/carbon-dioxide-emissions-dip-slightly-in-trumps-first-year-epa-says/.

552 Jessie Hellmann, "Trump Signs 'Right to Try' Drug Bill," *The Hill*, May 30, 2018, accessed October 16, 2018, https://thehill.com/policy/healthcare/389908-trump-signs-right-to-try-bill-for-terminally-ill-patients.

553 Bedard, "Trump's List: 289 Accomplishments in Just 20 Months."

554 Ibid.

ACKNOWLEDGMENTS

Every time I finish writing a book, I find myself thinking, "That's it, I'm done! I'm never writing another book again." Inevitably, something forces me out of retirement, compelling me to start the next one. Certainly, after writing *The Scandalous Presidency of Barack Obama* and *The Worst President in History: The Legacy of Barack Obama,* I never wanted to write about Obama again. I also never expected to write a book about Donald Trump, yet, I've managed to do both at the same time with this one. It took a lot of encouragement and support to not only get me to start writing again, but to get me to keep it up. This book certainly wouldn't have been possible with the support and enthusiasm of David Bernstein and the entire team at Bombardier Books. I'd also like to thank John Cox for the amazing cover art he created for this book and Matthew Souders for his incredible efforts cleaning up the manuscript. And another special thanks goes to everyone who has supported me over the years and read my books.

As always, this book could not have been written without the confidence and encouragement of my wife Beth and my son Isaac.

ABOUT THE AUTHOR

Matt Margolis is the author of *The Scandalous Presidency of Barack Obama* and the bestselling *The Worst President in History: The Legacy of Barack Obama*. He is also a contributor for PJ Media. He lives with his family on a vineyard near Buffalo, New York.